FAITH, CULTURE, and the WORSHIPING COMMUNITY

FAITH, CULTURE, and the WORSHIPING COMMUNITY

Shaping the Practice
of the Local Church

Revised Edition

Michael Warren

The Pastoral Press

Washington, DC

ACKNOWLEDGEMENTS

The material reprinted in *Faith, Culture, and the Worshiping Community* first appeared in the following publications and is reprinted with permission: J.A. Burns, C.S.C., *The Catholic School System in the United States: Its Principles, Origins, and Establishment*, New York, Benziger Brothers, 1908; Darrell J. Fasching, "Theologian of Culture," *Cross Currents* 35:1; *Of Singular Benefit: The Story of Catholic Education in The United States*, by Harold A. Buetow, copyright 1970, MacMillan Publishing Co.; Peggy Rosenthal, *Words and Values: Some Leading Words and Where They Lead Us*, Oxford University Press, 1984, p. 8; *The Seasons of a Man's Life*, by Daniel Levinson, New York: Alfred A. Knopf, 1978, pp. 41-42; *The Fall of the Public Man*, by Richard Sennett, New York: Alfred A. Knopf, 1977, p. 259; *Where Faith Begins*, by C. Ellis Nelson, Richmond, John Knox Press, 1967, pp. 184-185; *The Subversion of Christianity*, by Jacques Ellul, Grand Rapids, MI, Eerdmans, 1986, p. 4; "The Religion of the Privileged Ones," by Robert Coles and George Abbot White, *Cross Currents* 31:1, 1981, pp. 1-14 and p. 7; "The Amen Corner," by Robert Hovda, Worship 58:3, 1984, 251; *The Sacred Canopy: Elements of a Sociological Theory of Religion*, by Peter Berger, New York, Doubleday Anchor Books, 1969, pp. 16-17; *Journey of a Soul*, by Pope John XXIII, McGraw-Hill, 1964, pp. 41-42; "Have We Not Made Them a Heaven of Earth? Rich and Poor in the Early Church," by Rainer Kampling, in Leonardo Boff and Virgil Elizondo, eds., *Option for the Poor: Challenge to the Rich Countries* (*Concilium* 187), 1983.

ISBN: 1-56929-002-4

The Pastoral Press
225 Sheridan Street, N.W.
Washington, D.C. 20011
(202) 723-1254

The Pastoral Press is the publications division of the National Association of Pastoral Musicians, a membership organization of musicians and clergy devoted to fostering the art of musical liturgy.

Printed in the United States of America

This book is for

Tom Hoar, C.M. (1934-1988).

We first knew him as
> a scholar committed to justice
> an enlightened administrator
> a priest centered in the Gospel.

At the end, we came to know him
> as a man of remarkable patience and wisdom
> in the face of great suffering.

Contents

Foreword

"It should come as no surprise that young people bring with them into the classroom what they see and hear in the world around them, along with the impressions gained from the 'world' of mass media."[1] This quotation is from a document published by Rome's Congregation on Catholic Education, but the words might well be those of Michael Warren. *Faith, Culture, and the Worshiping Community* describes, analyzes, and critiques the mass media that shape the world of young people (and the not-so-young). It also exposes how these impressions are reinforced, unconsciously, by family, school, church, and society as a whole. Warren is concerned that, despite laments over the state of education in general and religious education in particular, parents, teachers, and church leaders are indifferent or insensitive to the impressions created by popular culture.

It is not a question of *fuga mundi,* as if one could escape the influence of culture. Christianity accepts the incarnation both as a premise and as a challenge. The word of God became enfleshed at a particular time and in a particular place. In the year that Caesar Augustus "published a decree ordering a census of the whole world" (Lk 2:1), Jesus was born. His immediate world was a Jewish household, and an extended family. His larger world was that of the towns and countryside of Galilee, a region of crossroads radiating in all directions. He found an "oral culture" that spoke with many voices: the religious voice of late Judaism, the political voice of Rome, the philosophical voice of Hellenism, and the economic voice of an agrarian society. Much of Jesus' preaching later in life attempted to sort out religious tradition from human ethos, Mosaic Law from human customs, all the while being culturally conditioned himself.

The disciples of Jesus, like Jesus himself, walk a narrow road. They are in the world but not of the world (Jn 17:14-16); they find themselves in the flesh, but they do not live according to the flesh (2 Cor 10:3; Rom 8:12). As the ancient letter to Diognetus put it:

> Christians are not distinguished from the rest of mankind by
> either country, speech, or customs; the fact is, they nowhere
> settle in cities of their own; they use no peculiar language; they
> cultivate no eccentric mode of life ... Yet while they dwell in both
> Greek and non-Greek cities, as each one's lot was cast, and conform
> to the customs of the country in dress, food, and mode of life in
> general, the whole tenor of their way of living stamps it as worthy
> of admiration and extraordinary. They reside in their respective
> countries, but only as aliens. They take part in everything as citizens
> and put up with everything as foreigners. Every foreign land is
> their home, and every home a foreign land ... (ch. 5).

> In a word: what the soul is in the body, that Christians are in
> the world. The soul is spread through all the members of the
> body, and the Christians throughout the cities of the world.
> The soul dwells in the body, but is not part and parcel of the
> body; so Christians dwell in the world, but are not part and
> parcel of the world ... (ch. 6).[2]

The Congregation on Catholic Education makes the same point
in more prosaic language: "We must always remember that, while
faith is not to be identified with any one culture and is independent
of all cultures, it must inspire every culture." To which it added a
statement of Pope John Paul II: "Faith which does not become
culture is faith which is not received fully, not assimilated entirely,
not lived faithfully" (n. 53).

It is precisely the interaction of faith and culture that provides the
framework of this work by Michael Warren. Like Welsh scholar
Raymond Williams, and George Gerbner of the Annenberg School
of Communications at the University of Pennsylvania, Warren is
less interested in culture as an abstract reality and static system
than in process and change. *Faith, Culture, and the Worshiping Community* focuses on how ideals and values are produced, communicated, experienced, and modified. The author alerts the reader to
the way societal, institutional, and economic factors influence (not
to say, compromise) church life and the communication of the
gospel message in subtle and not-so-subtle ways.

All the chapters, in one way or another, raise catechetical issues—the initiation and nurture of individuals in the Christian
community and their formation as disciples. Christian faith, like
hope and love, does not exist in books or in a scientific laboratory
like a genetic strain. It has no life, no meaning apart from believers.
Faith can only be expressed and communicated in symbols that

speak to people. The church—the Christian community—is the studio where the Christmas crib, the crucifix, the empty tomb, and other traditional symbols of the paschal mystery are placed in juxtaposition with symbols of modern culture. Warren calls on religious educators and catechists to carry on the dialogue between tradition and contemporary culture without compromising the former or being irrelevant to the latter.

Christians today face the same challenge that Jesus and the early disciples did. Their prophetic ministry demands that they stand outside contemporary culture, exposing whatever is false, dehumanizing and contrary to gospel values, while at the same time being unable (and unwilling) to detach themselves from the modern world. *Faith, Culture, and the Worshiping Community* holds up a mirror so that Christians in general and Christian educators in particular can see themselves against the background of contemporary culture. Through a series of stories, anecdotes, and analyses, Michael Warren presents a self-portrait of today's Christian and today's church confronting the limitations and inconsistencies of contemporary culture. He recognizes the opportunities that education, the media, and technology present for communicating the Christian message, and at the same time he warns individuals and the community against the temptation to baptize contemporary culture as if today's image makers were the authentic interpreters of gospel ideals and values.

Berard L. Marthaler, O.F.M.Cap.

Notes

1. "The Religious Dimension of Education in a Catholic School," *Origins* 18:14 (15 September 1988) n. 71.

2. J.A. Kleist, Ed., *The Ancient Christian Writers*, vol. 6 (Newman Press, 1948) 138-140.

Introduction

This book is the result of pastoral work and study that goes back almost twenty years. Over those years, I kept files on pastoral problems that seemed important but under-addressed. As I came across pertinent material about an issue, I would add it to the particular file. In my effort to share various themes with parish or diocesan groups or classes at St. John's University, most of the material grew in the light of the probing questions put back to me. The themes readers find here are the ones that were in the forefront of my mind many times when I was addressing issues about youth and youth ministry, and in fact provided the wider context of those writings, something readers who know my other writings will recognize.

As time went on and as I sought to understand the dilemmas catechesis faced in the local church, I saw more and more clearly that catechesis is not so much concerned with the condition of the understanding of the gospel message as with *the condition of the practice of that understanding.* I also came to see that the local church could not be a zone of the practice of the Gospel unless at the same time it boldly embraced Jesus' good news about justice. Finally, my recent study of the writings of Welsh thinker, Raymond Williams, showed me how a society's system of communication, especially in its modern form of electronic communications, tends to shape all its people, including those who claim to be religious, in habits of the heart that belie a religious commitment. These problems, of the life style of the local church, of catechesis as a vital ministry to that practice, and of the wider culture's pressures to subvert that practice, provide a unifying concern in this book. Here my earlier study of pastoral issues begun years ago comes together around an examination of the possibilities of the local church as a zone of cultural contestation. I presume those possibilities are weak without the power of worship as a counter-cultural act. Since the church (or synagogue) is one of the few public points of contestation left in our society, realizing these possibilities is important for secular society itself.

In this book I invite pastoral people at all levels in the church to dwell on the problem of theopraxis and to attend to its ramifications in local churches. Asian theologian, Aloysius Pieris, distinguishes between theology and theopraxis. Theopraxis is not a mechanical skill learned by applying all the right rules but an art of doing a thing in such a way that the art *is* the thing done. Theopraxis, as a way of living out our understandings, is already the formulation of a theology.[1] Whenever the church's theology was distorted, the distortion registered immediately in catechesis: the content of catechesis became distorted. On the other hand, whenever theopraxis or the way of living was distorted, the distortion registered just as surely in catechesis. And so if the theopraxis of local church communities became a living out of the social, economic and political assumptions of the wider society, catechesis always reflected that fact. Reformation and counter-reformation catechisms and their built-in methodology of exact wording formulated to oppose another position are perhaps an example.

The theopraxis plaguing catechesis today is the very lack of a gospel-based way of life in communities. Thus, because Christianity has ceased for many to be a particular way that affects the actual patterns of one's life, catechesis has become an activity exercised in classes, but not in homes or in interaction among those in a community who embrace it. Ironically, catechesis in the United States remains a church practice, at least for children, though the practice of the church, as a way of life, no longer remains behind catechesis as its indispensable support. In highlighting the problem of relating catechesis and the life structure of local communities, this book seeks to reclaim catechesis as a ministry to the life structure which will in turn enrich the community's message.

In this book I myself find a certain intentness on themes of commitment, fidelity, true discipleship, and so forth. These themes are indispensable in consumerist cultures, where the churches' proper role is one of resistance. As a zone of ultimacy, religion views and tends to question social and cultural arrangements through the lens of its ultimate concerns. Yet, I fear a "heresy of intentness," which makes fidelity a grim matter lacking in festivity. If discipleship pursued to the point of risk is sound and necessary, the test of its soundness will lie in its single-mindedness being balanced by festivity. As a sign of a light grasp on life, festivity characterizes those who can name the preciousness of God's gifts in the smallest, most ordinary events. Festivity is also a sign of a struggled-for hope that evil will not have the last word. What I mean by festivity one can find in the writings of Dorothy Day and also in the tough-minded Catholic Worker communities so ready to celebrate small achievements. These are people who have worked so hard at the Christian thing that they know both the limits of their own good efforts and the limitless goodness of God.

Readers will find throughout this book references to the writings of liberation theologians. Originally, I thought I would subtitle this book: "Toward a Catechesis of Liberation." So much catechesis done among the comfortable is so far from a catechesis of liberation that such a subtitle seemed appropriate in a book seeking to connect catechesis and justice. However, I decided that the "toward" in such a subtitle might seem to suggest a catechesis of liberation as a new development, whereas it is the oldest form of catechesis, found in the Gospels themselves and already reclaimed by Latin American liberation theologians, whose methodology is based in a catechesis of liberation. In a sense, the terms, "*catechesis* of *liberation*," are redundant, since any true catechesis is toward liberation. I realize that putting the matter this way puts much of the catechesis done in North America under intense suspicion, even to the point of denying that it is catechesis at all.

Liberation theology's own recent history shows the connection between a theology of liberation and a catechesis of liberation, since the concerns of liberation theology were first set forth in a catechetical study week. Too few persons are aware that the agenda of the now-famous 1968 Second General Conference of Latin American Bishops (26 August—6 September, 1968),[2] was actually set in the Medellin Catechetical Week (11-17 August, 1968)[3] held a week earlier. When the term, Medellin, is used, most people, even generally knowledgeable ones, think of the bishops' meeting, having forgotten the earlier catechetical week, which in fact set the tone and much of the agenda for the famous later meeting of bishops.

I have already explained how the ideas in this book evolved through pastoral work over time and with the help of astute questioners. In the end however, an important group of persons offered decisive help by reading the various chapters, making suggestions for revisions and even for the sequence of chapters: Donald Kraus, of Oxford University Press; Dr. Catherine Dooley of Catholic University; Fr. Jim Briglia of Our Lady Help of Christians Parish,

Melbourne, Australia; Sr. Rosemary Crumlin, former Director of the National Pastoral Institute for Religious Education, also in Melbourne; Martin Kennedy and Breda Brady Kennedy of Tullamore, Ireland; Philip Marinelli of New York's Youth Focus; and, above all, Connie Loos who read everything as it was written and with unerring pastoral sense always pointed out what I had missed. Also I must mention those at St. John's University in New York City, who were instrumental in granting me a semester's research reduction for doing my revisions. Finally, of course there is Berard Marthaler, who agreed to enrich the book itself with his Foreword. To all these I give my simple thanks. If this book succeeds in questioning taken-for-granted procedures of catechesis and in suggesting a more central role for catechesis in church renewal, all who have had a part in this book will be amply rewarded.

This book has had an interesting history in its brief life. At first it seemed to me to sink like a stone to the bottom of a lake. Almost no reviews appeared in the U.S., though a few appeared in other countries. Some, like Dr. Maurice Monette, told me of using it themselves or knowing of its use in a course on Christian education or catechesis; but otherwise its initial publication was met with, what seemed to me, intent silence.

Almost all the critique or even feedback I got came from individuals I met at various events. One woman on Long Island astonished me by telling me the book changed her life and then explained how and why. As time went on, the book became known mostly through word-of-mouth, from being used in discussion circles in parishes working toward renewal.

On being notified by the original publisher it was being allowed to go out of print, I at first shrugged. It was only after several parish ministers took the trouble, during a convocation on the catechumenate, to tell me how helpful it had been to them, that I began looking for another publisher to make this work available once more.

The quick decision of Pastoral Press to adopt my homeless waif of a book pleases me greatly. I hope in its revised form it will help those who care passionately for the possibilities of our churches as zones of liberation.

Jamaica, New York, January 1993

Notes

1. On this point, see Aloysius Pieris, "Towards An Asian Theology of Liberation: Some Religio-Cultural Guidelines," *East Asian Pastoral Institute* 16:4 (1979) 206-230, esp. 225-227. Another helpful essay by Pieris is: "A Theology of Liberation in Asian Churches?" *East Asian Pastoral Institute* 23:2 (1986) 117-137.

2. See, Second General Conference of Latin American Bishops, *The Church in the Present-Day Transformation of Latin American in the Light of the Council,* Vol 1: Position Papers; Vol 2: General Conclusions, ed. Louis Michael Colonnese (Washington, D.C.: United States Catholic Conference, 1970).

3. See Johannes Hofinger and Terence Sheridan, eds., *The Medellin Papers: A Selection from the Proceedings of the Sixth International Study Week on Catechetics, Medellin, Colombia, 11-17 August 1968* (Manila: East Asian Pastoral Institute, 1969).

1

Schools, Education, and Catechesis

The issues I am going to raise in this chapter may at first seem obscure and far removed from the concerns of those in the local churches working to help members understand and grow in faith. Yet the explanations here are important and even crucial to clarify issues arising throughout this book that must be approached, at least at the beginning, from a historical and theoretical angle. In my judgment many of the problems of parish catechesis are rooted in faulty theory and inadequate historical knowledge. My overall purpose at this point in my examination of catechesis in the local church is to clarify what we mean when we use the terms "education," "Catholic education," and "catechsis." The confusion regarding these words, especially as they have been and are being used by U.S. Catholics, should become clear in the following pages. These clarifications and the re-thinking they imply should have concrete, practical implications for what goes on in some of our parishes and even for what some of us do with our lives. With some adjustments, they may also have significance for what happens in the local church of other Christian denominations as well.

Schools and Education

One place to begin our clarification of these terms is with the reexamination of the history of American education that has been going on for some years, thanks, partly at least, to the historical research of Dr. Lawrence Cremin of Columbia University.[1] Cremin, who himself has undertaken an exhaustive history of American education,[2] has done considerable research on other, earlier histories of education in the United States. While conducting his research he discovered that the histories of American education have tended to be histories of American schools, that is, histories of but a single stratum of education.

Cremin's book exploring this problem, published in 1965, is entitled *The Wonderful World of Ellwood Patterson Cubberley*.[3] Ellwood Cubberley, professor of education at Stanford from 1898 until the 1930s, published in 1919 a work that for almost forty years was viewed as one of the monumental and definitive histories of American education. Cubberley's classic was entitled *Public Education in the United States*.[4] Although Cubberley's work was to influence more than two generations of American educators, it was not actually a history of public education; it was rather a history of public schooling in the United States. By tending to identify education and schooling, Cubberley's history unfortunately put education into a frame of reference that could not take into serious consideration the major problems that have faced education since 1920.[5]

Ironically, even as Cubberley was busy preparing his book for publication, events were taking place that would eventually demand that education be viewed in the broadest possible way, rather than in the narrow categories of schooling.

> At the very time he [Cubberley] wrote, a revolution was in the making, in the rise of mass media of communication and in the organization of a growing number of private, quasi-public, and public agencies committed to education but not organized as schools. The revolution has since occasioned a complete contemporary revision, one that clearly suggests the need for a more inclusive account of our educational history.[6]

Cremin points out that whatever the centrality of the public school in American educational history, it must be seen as one component of a variety of other educational agencies that have functioned throughout our history and which have helped shape American thought, character, and sensibility over the years. In addition to schools, educational history must also be aware of the educational influence of "families, churches, libraries, museums, publishers, benevolent societies, youth groups, agricultural fairs, radio networks, military organizations, and research institutes."[7] All these groups and institutions had a place in the formation of our people over generations. An adequate history of education would have to explore the role of newspapers in the eighteenth century, of social settlements in the nineteenth, and of mass television in the twentieth. Within the context of such varied educational influences as these, one might better understand the shifting influence of schools and colleges.

Although Cremin wrote *The Wonderful World of Ellwood Patterson Cubberley* for students of American educational historiography, his thesis about the need to view education on a much wider scale than that of schooling can be important to all concerned about the matter of education, including Catholic education. In recent years more and more persons have become alarmed at the non-school educative force of various forms of media, which right there in the home are shaping the consciousness and values of children, without the full awareness of many parents. This is a matter I will deal with in more detail in one of the final chapters of this book. At this point, however, I want to stress the fact of powerful "educative" forces, such as the advertising industry, that influence us daily, long after we have terminated our formal schooling.[8]

Catholic School and Catholic Education

One might expect in the wake of Cremin's little book that some historian would examine the histories of American Catholic education to see if the Cubberlian bias existed in these histories too. Such a historian appears to be Vincent Lannie, former professor of education at Notre Dame.[9] Not surprisingly, Lannie has discovered our very own Ellwood P. Cubberley among our historians of Catholic education. His name is Rev. James A. Burns. Burns received an M.A. from the Department of Education at Catholic University in 1907, after having written his thesis on "Catholic Education in the United States."[10]

During the six years following his degree at Catholic University, Burns produced two works dealing with the Catholic school system. The first was entitled *The Catholic School System in the United States: Its Principles, Origin and Establishment;*[11] the second, *The Growth and Development of the Catholic School System in the United States.*[12] Burns explained the reason for his focus on the schools thus:

> A direct relation existed between the development of the Church and the development of Catholic schools . . . The main factors in the Church's development—immigration and migration,

the hierarchy, parish and diocesan organization, the religious
Orders, the Councils—have constituted also the main factors
in the growth of the schools. And the influences that were at
work to retard the Church's progress have had a corres-
pondingly hampering effect upon the schools. The relation
between Church and school has been, in fact, so close that it is
impossible to disassociate the history of the one from the other.
The parish school has been from the very beginning an agency
of the Church.[13]

In other words, Burns claims one can trace the development of
the United States Catholic *Church* in an examination of the development of the *Catholic school system* in the U.S. In viewing matters this
way, Burns was a man of his times. According to Lannie, his thesis
about the progress of the church and of Catholic schools can be also
found in the bulk of Catholic educational histories written in the
nineteenth and early in the first decade of the twentieth century. In
addition, Burns's point of view was not entirely without logic. The
largest part of the church's commitment to education in his day was
bound up in schools. Since Burns and Cubberley were both influenced by the type of educational history written before their time
and with which they were familiar, it is not surprising that Lannie
finds a parallel between their histories on every major point, except
that Burns "baptized" Cubberley's secular victories for schools into
Catholic triumphs.[14]

Whereas Cubberley saw the rise of the public school as inextricably tied to the progress of America [sic], Burns saw the rise
of the Catholic school as inextricably tied to the progress of the
Church in America . . . Just as Cubberley's public school seed
evolved from colonial times and engaged in a series of major
battles before it became an integral part of American society,
so Burns' Catholic school system existed "in embryo" in colonial times, fought a host of battles against Protestantism and
secularism during the nineteenth century and became an integral part of Catholic life in the opening decade of the twentieth
century.[15]

If Cubberley's approach to educational history influenced the
perspective of his successors for decades, one might expect and
indeed does find Burns's preoccupation with Catholic schools as a
dominant theme of Catholic educational historiography for the
next fifty years. In fact one finds what might be called the Burns
bias at the heart of a more recent general history of Catholic educa-

tion. Written by Dr. Harold Buetow of Catholic University and entitled *Of Singular Benefit: The Story of U.S. Catholic Education*, this history appeared in 1970.[16] Defining education from an encouragingly broad point of view at the outset of his work, Buetow in short order uses the term as a synonym of schooling. Thus on the second page of his introduction, he writes:

> Education . . . is very frequently confused with such other terms as "teaching", "instruction", "training", "discipline", "schooling", and "formation". Etymologically, "education" comes from two cognate Latin words, "educere" and "educare", meaning to lead forth or draw out. A real definition in modern times adds nothing to Pythagoras, who spoke of education as that which enables a person to become what he is . . . Other disciplines refer to it also as acculturation and socialization.[17]

However, later in the same introduction he refers to Roman Catholic education in the restrictive sense of schooling, a use that characterizes the whole of his book.

> All of this brings us to the question of why we [sic] wrote this book. First, the subject is both relevant and important—not only because it shares in the advantages of history in general and in the history of education, but inherently. True scholarship recognizes that there has always been more than one pattern of education in this country, and at the present time the largest sector of American private education is the Roman Catholic. This establishment—tens of thousands of schools, hundreds of thousands of religious and lay teachers and staff, and many billions of dollars—is responsible for educating about one out of nine children in the United States, a sizeable proportion of the future of our country.[18]

In general, although Buetow, like his predecessor Burns, purports to discuss Catholic education, he focuses his attention almost exclusively upon schooling. Vincent Lannie judges that in so doing, Buetow missed an opportunity to break new historical ground in understanding the total educational history of the U.S. Catholic Church.[19]

Obviously, in a book about the role of the local church in catechesis, my concern in reporting of Cremin/Cubberley and Lannie/Burns/Buetow is not of itself a concern for historiography, as important as that matter may be, but rather for the practical results these ways of viewing our history have for our pastoral efforts at the local level. We have just seen the importance of recognizing from a secular point of view that education is broader than schooling. To ignore this long-neglected fact is to forget the contribution to human life made by countless ingenious systems, programs, and procedures by which people have communicated and influenced one another. On the one hand, the library system in the U.S., newspapers, ethnic-oriented societies of various sorts, and political rallies have all made important, if little-examined, contributions to the fabric of life in the U.S., while on the other, media have come to have more and more influence.[20] To pretend that schooling has been the sole source of education does a disservice to the facts.

It is also clear that Catholic education is a much broader reality than Catholic schools. One can make the assertion boldly, without any implication of a slight to the impressive contribution of Catholic schools. In any history of the Catholic Church in the U.S., the Catholic schools must have a place of honor. The fact remains however that they have not done the whole job. Not more than 50 percent of Roman Catholic children have been enrolled in Catholic schools at any time in our history.[21] The genius of the Catholic Church in the United States is that it buttressed the influence of the schools with a variety of other educational initiatives.[22] In a fine summary of the question, Lannie puts the matter thus:

> . . . Roman Catholicism had long operated under the doctrine that it is the sole agency of salvation. The laity needed instruction in the sacramental system of grace and guidance in the Church's assessment of cultural values. Catholics thus had to be socialized to accept the Church's rendition of the earthly city in order to gain entry into the heavenly kingdom. American Catholicism escalated the Church's commitment to this task. Interpreting American culture as antithetical to Catholic values, the immigrant hierarchy of the nineteenth century seemed overwhelmed by its religious and cultural responsibility. The growing number of Catholic immigrants and their ignorance of the faith confronted a fledgling Church with a seemingly impossible task. Thus, all available means had to be enlisted in the work of socialization: sermons to instruct those who could find seats in over-crowded churches; periodic religious revivals to reach beyond the Sunday congregations; catechism and Sunday school classes to prepare the young for active participation in the sacramental system; a network of sodalities dividing the parish by age, sex, marital status and

providing moral instruction and social intercourse for specific "stations in life," a system of educational and social agencies including parochial schools, private academies and colleges, asylums and protectories and hospital and prison apostolates. The written word was not forgotten. Priests and laymen edited diocesan newspapers and religious periodicals; and Catholic publishing houses printed European and American devotional, catechetical and fictional works under episcopal imprimatur.[23]

This passage gives some inkling of the ground that would have to be covered to survey adequately the true scope of Catholic education. Catholic education may have been used as a synonym for Catholic schools, but the actual, lived scope of Catholic education went, as Lannie point out so well here, far beyond the single educational work of the school. Many of these efforts could be properly classified, as we shall see, as catechetical, that is, as attempts to foster mature faith within the church. As usual, where truth is concerned the whole story is much more impressive than a part of the story, even when that part is the impressive story of Catholic schools.

There is however more to be said about the consequences of the error of equating Catholic education with Catholic schools. That error was accompanied by a tendency to consider the Church's task of influencing the faith of the rising generation largely fulfilled through the schools, especially through parish elementary schools. Though fewer than half of all Catholic children nationwide ever attended Catholic schools, the massive character of the effort to school them well tended to mean that the pastoral care of the others was neglected. In addition there was a tendency among parents to consider they had done their duty when they either sent their children to these church school or insisted they attend what were called CCD sessions. As historian Neil McCluskey puts it,

> Catholic leadership came to hope that the parish school would play surrogate for the agencies which during the age of devotion have kept men and women loyal and obedient to the Church. For the first time in history, the school was asked to become what it had never been: the primary guardian and tutor of the Catholic faith. The schools were established, accordingly, in response to the Church's pastoral concern. If a single theme characterizes the collective pronouncements of the American hierarchy over the past hundred years, it has been the insistence that education was primarily moral train-

ing and religious formation to be achieved through the separate confessional schools. So true is this that the question must
be asked: Was the school expected to replace the priest and the
parish in fulfilling Christ's commission to teach or, even more
fundamental, was the school to assume the natural obligation
of parents to prepare their young for admission to the Christian community?[24]

As for adults—though there were many innovative efforts to
help them grow in their faith—the financial and personnel energy
given to their growth was very limited. A review of church-related
literature after Vatican II will disclose intense concern for "adult
education" among those aware that many adults were still relying
on concepts memorized from their childhood catechisms and that
those concepts could not stand up in the re-thinking of doctrine that
was taking hold.[25] However, the worst effects of the schooling-as-
education error was that the chief ministry of some parishes became the school, so much so that when school diminished or closed
during the financial and personnel crises that occurred after Vatican
II, some parishes nearly died. In 1971, when 57 percent of Roman
Catholic parishes ran parish schools consuming between 40 and 65
percent of parish income, educational researcher, George Elford's
studies concluded that "it would be possible to establish the hy-
pothesis that `in the typical Catholic parish, the parish school is the
only major program in operation'." Elford asked to what extent
such parishes are dependent on their schools, which legitimize and
sustain the parish. He wrote:

> Considering the parish as a Christian community of service,
> one might . . . suspect that, apart from the national programs
> related to Catholic Relief Services, there is little going on. Most
> parishes deal exclusively with the internal problems and needs
> of their own parishes . . . At times, the parish school is cited as
> an instance of community service. While it surely serves a
> public purpose, one must admit that it is not operated with
> that in mind. The self-interest motive which accounts for the
> existence of the parish school prevents it from being taken as a
> sign (witness) of the parish's concern for the community at
> large.[26]

With the start of Vatican Council II's theological and pastoral renewal, the confusion caused by the conflation of education and schooling has to a certain extent been corrected through reclaiming the
ancient tradition of catechesis.

Education and Catechesis

Using the above controversy about schooling and education as background, I seek in the rest of this chapter to clarify the way we think about catechesis and about Catholic schooling. The more thoroughly the U.S. bias about schooling has influenced the way we have tended to think about the process of nurturing faith, the more crucial these clarifications for a sound understanding of catechesis.[27] The purpose of this book is to re-examine the local church as the zone that makes growth in discipleship a reality.

Catechesis in the
General Catechetical Directory

The most sound recent guidance about the role of catechesis is that offered by the 1971 General Catechetical Directory,[28] issued as one of early signs of the depth of the pastoral renewal begun in Vatican II. Even when not cited explicitly, the Directory's broad principles have been influencing pastoral thinking worldwide. According to this set of pastoral guidelines, catechesis is an aspect of the pastoral ministry of the church. Though the Directory would never deny that catechesis is educational, it chooses to view it within the framework of ministry, as one of the forms of the church's ministry of the word. Other forms are missionary preaching or evangelization, liturgical proclamation, and the systematic investigation of the tradition called theology.

To repeat: by viewing catechesis this way, the Directory has made a significant choice, placing catechesis within the church and pastoral concerns, not within the frame of education. Such a way of viewing catechesis has the value of encouraging close links between catechesis and not just the ministry of the word but all the ministries of the church: those of healing, of festivity and worship, of guidance and education. These ministries are meant to be mutually enhancing, working together to foster the ecclesial mission, but always with the understanding that "the Church, the community of believers, is constituted precisely by the proclamation of the Word" and "once constituted, lives and is nourished by the Word of God as much as by the Eucharistic Bread."[29]

Perhaps the best illustration of these thrusts can be found in the most succinct description of catechesis offered by the Directory.

> Within the scope of pastoral activity, catechesis is the term to
> be used for that form of ecclesial action which leads both

communities and individual members of the faithful to maturi-
ty of faith. (Par. 21)

The phrase "ecclesial action" locates the context of catechesis in the
community and names the chief agent of catechesis as the same
community. Within this principle lie the seeds of a revolution in
how local churches think of the process of fostering a maturing
faith and in how they actually do it.[30] If its insight is followed, the
misplaced emphases of the past, described in previous pages of this
chapter, will be corrected. Properly understood, catechesis is a kind
of therapy for fostering the corporate health of the *ekklesia*, with
adult catechesis as its chief form (Par. 20). Seen this way, it is not to
be a peripheral endeavor largely affecting those too young to resist.
It is rather a multiform activity, the chief agent of which is the
community itself.[31] With particular emphasis the document continues:

> With the aid of catechesis, communities of Christians acquire
> for themselves a more profound living knowledge of God and
> of his plan of salvation, which has its center in Christ, the
> incarnate Word of God. They build themselves up by striving
> to make their faith mature and enlightened, and to share this
> mature faith with those who desire to possess it.

In other words, the community's life "forms" its people, according
to its own religiously centered understanding of reality. We will see
in the next chapter that maintaining this formation is no easy
matter.

If the corporate faith of the local church is the goal of catechesis,
these local embodiments of the Gospel themselves have great catechetical power as signs. Proclamation of the word is more than a
verbal matter, as the Synod of Bishops that met weeks after the
promulgation of the General Catechetical Directory made clear.

> Action on behalf of justice and participation in the transforma-
> tion of the world fully appear to us as a constitutive dimension
> of the preaching of the Gospel, or, in other words, of the
> Church's mission for the redemption of the human race and its
> liberation from every oppression.[32]

The Directory likewise affirms the proclamatory power of deeds, in
this case the corporate stance of the community:

> The Church is in Christ like a sacrament or sign and an in-
> strument of the salvation and of the unity of the whole human

race. It will be more noted as such, however the more mature in faith the individual communities of the faithful become. (Par 28)

The message proclaimed by the assembly claiming to be Jesus' followers cannot be demonstrated rationally. Its most convincing proof is the witness of the actual living which either verifies or belies the claims of the assembly. In the early church the word for witness was *martyrion*, signifying the special credibility of those whose fidelity was, like Jesus' own, unto death. An Asian theologian comments:

> ... Liberation is the only proof of liberation. Saying that Jesus is the medium of salvation requires that the ones who say it display the fruits of liberation . . . A christology receives its authenticity from a transforming praxis which proves that in the story of Jesus, which continues in his followers, the medium of salvation is operative . . . In the Christian theological vocabulary, this medium is designated by the traditional titles applied to Jesus, since liberation is believed to take place through Jesus the man (therefore through every woman and man *in* Jesus).[33]

From a catechetical angle, the community's life of fidelity *is* the message, its prime, but not its sole, expression. Without catechesis that corporate fidelity is easily in jeopardy, as Amalorpavadass reminds us so graphically.

> Without the ministry of the Word everything degenerates: liturgy into magic and ritualism, the law into legalism and juridicism, institutions into institutionalism, and pastors into administrative bosses. A constant prophetic effort is called for to set right this deviation and degeneration.[34]

A correctly focused catechesis is at the service of the corporate discipleship of the worshiping assembly.

Grounded in this primal sign, catechesis searches out widely varied, indeed unlimited, forms.

> Because of varied circumstances and multiple needs, catechetical activity necessarily takes various forms . . . In a word, catechetical activity can take on forms and structures that are quite varied, that is to say, it can be systematic or occasional, for individuals or for communities, organized or spontaneous, and so on. (Par. 19)

Seen here the forms of catechesis are limited only by the human imaginations of those seeking to help their fellows grow in the faith that binds us together in the Christian community.

Additional Features of Catechesis

For the purposes of this chapter, two other features of catechesis need to be highlighted. One is its celebrative character. Catechesis most properly fits into the context of worship, as can be seen in its place in the early church's catechumenate: the ritual step-by-step walking into the center of the community's life. The focus of catechesis, in its most perfect moments, was not the classroom but the chapel, where its instructions either anticipated or were in the context of ritual.[35] In the catechumenate, the goal of catechesis was not so much understandings as it was activity directed by those understandings, especially the activities of prayerful worship and care for the outcasts.

Although the ritual, celebrative aspect of catechesis had been suppressed for centuries, it was never totally lost.[36] Josef Jungmann reminded us of this fact when he wrote, "The most effective form of preaching the faith is the celebration of a feast."[37] Today that celebrative aspect needs to be recovered, a matter I will treat in a later chapter. Those engaged in ministry to young people are coming to see that it is almost impossible for churches to succeed with out-of-school initiatives unless they have a strong celebrative dimension. It is the celebrative component that allows all participants to be human together on an equal footing because celebration—like play—functions most properly out of statuslessness and out of what humans have in common rather than out of higher-and-lower roles. As educational theorist, Dwayne Huebner, once put it, emphasizing the potential power of church educational efforts, "In the chapel all are meant to be equal."[38] Indeed, the chapel is a key locus where catechesis finds its fulfillment in the ritual acts of worship. The other key "place" where catechesis is fulfilled, though not so easily localized, is in the pursuit of justice in the world.

A final and key feature of catechesis is its occasional but lifelong character. Clearly, as practiced in many places, catechesis functions in a way quite the opposite of this character. The usual formula for catechesis is one that makes it continuous and terminal. It begins about age seven and continues, fall semester and spring semester, with possible vacation schools thrown in, until these captive audiences reach an age when they can shout, "Enough." At that point, often immediately after confirmation, catechesis is terminated.

Catechesis, however, is meant to be occasional, with the prime occasion being the early intense period of preparation for Easter and its accompanying baptism of a new group of initiates.[39] Naming catechesis as occasional does not deny that it *may* function continuously and programatically; it rather emphasizes "occasion" as an important traditional feature of catechesis, one needing to be reclaimed. Catechesis is occasional in other senses as well. Faith-questions erupt in the lives of individuals and communities in unplanned ways, especially during periods of transition, and those questions must be dealt with as they arise. This occasional character of catechesis makes most sense when tied to its lifelong character. In any person's biography, transitions are lifelong, and crises that call for systematic kinds of learning erupt more or less regularly. The same could be said for any group's biography. Through catechesis the community attends to these seasons of a person's life throughout his or her lifetime but also to such seasons in its own communal life. Indeed it is the lifelong character of catechesis that allows us not to try to do too much on any single occasion, not to try each time to recapitulate every understanding.[40]

In the following chapters, I seek to shed light on these features of catechesis, while highlighting their importance for the corporate life of local churches. Behind what I write is a conviction that the great crisis facing the churches in our day is not so much one of creed as of credibility, that is, of so embodying belief that one's corporate life is believable. In the face of the great power of the wider, secular culture, a credible corporate life may be the only way of maintaining an alternative way of looking at reality. To this matter I now turn.

Notes

1. I wish to acknowledge here that the person who first put me onto many of the historical sources used in the following pages and especially onto the unpublished work of Vincent Lannie was Dr. Robert O'Gorman, now professor of religious education at Loyola University of Chicago.

For useful background on the scope of recent educational revisionism, see Marvin Lazerson, "Revisionism and American Educational History," *Harvard Educational Review* 43 (1973) 269-283.

2. Cremin"s chronological studies of various periods in the history of American education are not yet complete. See Lawrence A. Cremin, *American Educational History: The Colonial Experience, 1607-1783* (New York: Harper and Row, 1970).

3. Lawrence A. Cremin, *The Wonderful World of Ellwood Patterson Cubberley* (New York: Teacher's College Press, 1965).

4. Ellwood P. Cubberley, *Public Education in the United States* (Boston: Houghton Mifflin Co., 1919).

5. See Cremin, *Wonderful World* 46-48.

6. Ibid. 46-47.

7. Ibid. 48.

8. I have dealt with this problem in many places in *Youth, Gospel, Liberation* (New York: Harper and Row, 1987) esp. 41-53, 118-123.

9. Vincent P. Lannie, "Church and School Triumphant: The Sources of American Catholic Historiography." Talk given at a meeting of the History of Education Society, Chicago, 24-27 October, 1973. See also Vincent Lannie, "The Teaching of Values in Public, Sunday and Catholic Schools: An Historical Perspective," *Religious Education* 70:2 (March-April, 1975) 115-137.

10. See Lannie, "Sources," p. 2, note 4, for an account of the problem of Burns's doctorate.

11. J.A. Burns, *The Catholic School System in the United States: Its Principles, Origins, and Establishment* (New York: Benziger Brothers, 1908).

12. J.A. Burns, *The Growth and Development of the Catholic School System in the United States* (New York: Benziger Brothers, 1912).

13. Burns, *Catholic School System: Principles* 14-15.

14. See Lannie, "Sources" 29-42.

15. Ibid. 10-11.

16. Harold A. Buetow, *Of Singular Benefit: The Story of Catholic Education in the United States* (New York: The Macmillan Co., 1970).

17. Ibid. xii.

18. Ibid. xv.

19. Lannie, "Sources" 23.

20. The churches are more and more looking into this zone of influence, as evidenced by the Study Commission on Theology, Education, and the Electronic Media, set up by the National Council of Churches in 1985, and whose report and study papers can be found in *Religious Education* 82:2 (1987). It is worth noting that the first page of the Report acknowledges its debt to Cremin's insistence that education is broader than schooling (p. 163).

21. See Vincent Lannie, "Catholic Educational Historiography in the Twentieth Century." Unpublished address given before the History of Education Society, Atlanta, November 1974, pp. 27 and 31.

22. Two helpful descriptions of some of these initiatives are: Jay P. Dolan, *Catholic Revivalism: The American Experience, 1830-1900* (Notre Dame: University of Notre Dame Press, 1978); and Mary Charles Bryce, *Pride of Place: The Role of the Bishops in the Development of Catechesis in the United States* (Washington, D.C.: Catholic University of America Press, 1984).

23. Lannie, "Catholic Educational Historiography" 26-27.

24. Neil McCluskey, "Catholic Americans and the Future of the Public School," in Robert F. Drinan, ed., *The Right to Be Educated* (Washington, D.C.: Corpus Books, 1968) 120.

It is worth noting that this tendency was not limited to the churches; other parents looked in a similar way to the public schools. See the very interesting essay by Henry Steele Commanger, "The School as Surrogate Conscience," *Saturday Review* (11 January 1975) 54-57, and notice that Commanger uses in his title the same word that appears in McCluskey's first sentence: "surrogate."

25. An example of this literature is Kevin Coughlin, "Motivating Adults for Religious Education," *The Living Light* 13:2 (1976) 264-298.

26. George Elford, "School Crisis—or Parish Crisis?" *Commonweal* (29 January 1971) 418-420.

27. An examination of catechetical literature of other countries shows that this bias is not exclusively American. The writer's hunch is that where a nation has a well-developed Catholic school system or allows for religious instruction in state schools, catechesis tends to be cast in the categories of schooling. Such countries include England, Ireland, Australia, and to a lesser extent, Germany; however, France and Italy seem, especially in recent years, to have resisted viewing catechesis within the perspective of schooling. Catechists in so-called missionary countries and third-world countries see catechesis as a pastoral function with its own principles and procedures, one reason why valuable catechetical theory is emerging in these countries. See Joseph Colomb, *Le Service de l'évangile* (Paris: Desclée et Cie, 1968), vol. 1 and vol. 2; R.M. Rummery, *Catechesis and Religious Education in a Pluralist Society* (Sydney: E.J. Dwyer, 1975); Joseph Pathrapankal, ed., *Service and Salvation: Nagpur Theological Conference on Evangelization* (Bangalore: Theological Publications in India, 1973).

28. Congregation for the Clergy, *General Catechetical Directory* (Washington, D.C.: United States Catholic Conference, 1971). The best text of the General Catechetical Directory for study purposes is Berard L. Marthaler, *Catechetics in Context: Notes and Commentary on the General Catechetical Directory* (Huntington, IN: Our Sunday Visitor Press, 1973).

29. D.S. Amalorpavadass, "Catechesis as a Pastoral Task of the Church," in M. Warren, ed., *The Sourcebook for Modern Catechetics* (Winona, MN: St. Mary's Press, 1983) 340. Amalorpavadass' classic statement about cate-

chesis was given at the International Catechetical Congress held in Rome in 1971, the event at which the General Catechetical Directory was introduced.

30. C. Ellis Nelson's *Where Faith Begins* (Atlanta: John Knox Press, 1971) and John H. Westerhoff's *Will Our Children Have Faith?* (New York: Seabury Press, 1976) are examples of a search for a community-based revolution in fostering faith.

31. Secular education has also been struggling with the relationship of the community to the educational environments and institutions meant to serve the community. See, for example, Lawrence A. Cremin, *Public Education* (New York: Basic Books, 1976) esp. 21-29.

Over the past twenty years a number of critiques have appeared of the way the educational needs of adolescents are met in U.S. society and of their eventual impact on the relationship between young people and local communities. See James J. Coleman, ed., *Youth: Transition to Adulthood* (Chicago: University of Chicago Press, 1974); John H. Martin, ed., *The Education of Adolescents* (Washington, D.C.: U.S. Government Printing Office, 1976); Joseph F. Kett, *Rites of Passage* (New York: Basic Books, 1977) esp. chaps. 7-9, pp. 173-272; Gisela Konopka, *Young Girls: A Portrait of Adolescence* (Englewood Cliffs, NJ: Prentice-Hall, 1976) esp. chaps. 6-7, pp. 112-136. See also the important essays by Michael Apple and Dwayne Huebner in *Curriculum Theorizing*, ed. Wm. Pinar (San Francisco: McCutchan, 1975).

32. *Justice in the World*, par. 6, in Michael Walsh and Brian Davies, eds., *Proclaiming Justice and Peace: Documents from John XXIII—John Paul II* (Mystic, CT: Twenty-Third Publications, 1984) 188-203.

33. Aloysius Pieris, "Christianity and Buddhism in Core-to-Core Dialogue," *Cross Currents* 37:1 (Spring 1987) 47-75, at 73.

34. Amalorpavadass, "Catechesis" 340-341.

35. For source material see Hugh M. Riley, *Christian Initiation* (Washington, D.C.: Consortium Press, 1974).

36. See, for example, the emphasis on worship, prayer, the singing of hymns, and other forms of celebration found throughout Dupanloup's classic *The Ministry of Catechizing*, written in 1868. The final section of personal recollections of childhood catechesis is quite instructive about the celebrative character of catechesis. See Bishop Felix Dupanloup, *The Ministry of Catechizing* (London: Griffith Farran Okeden and Welsh, 1890) esp. 539-612. However, there are many other examples in the history of catechesis.

37. Joseph Jungmann, "The Kerygma in the History of the Pastoral Activity of the Church," in M. Warren, ed., *Sourcebook for Modern Catechetics* (Winona, MN: St. Mary's Press, 1983) 200. This essay of Jungmann was written in the early 1950s.

38. These remarks by Dwayne Huebner were made in private conversation. His point was that when compared with secular education he expected church education, especially when it is done in the chapel, to be informed by the oneness in the Spirit proclaimed by the church and thus to be more readily characterized by mutuality. Obviously, among Roman Catholics at least, not all are in fact equal in the chapel; men are given greater status than women. In this sense the church apes the hierarchical thinking fostered by dominant elites down through history, and for many the fact is a scandal.

39. Here I do not deny the already-quoted par. 19 of the Directory which explicitly holds systematic catechesis as one of its varied forms. My point here is that, based on the tradition of the early church but also on catechetical forms most true to the natural rhythms of life, *occasional catechesis* should be its prevalent form.

40. For concrete application of these ideas to young people, see M. Warren, "Youth Catechesis in the 80's," in *Youth and the Future of the Church* (New York: Harper and Row, 1982).

2

Religious Formation in the Context of Social Formation

Tertullian once wrote, "Christians are made, not born." For the Englished form of this quote, I would prefer to say, "*fashioned*, not born," to highlight the gradual, deliberate, and artistic process of guiding persons to discipleship. Catechesis is one part of that fashioning process. In this chapter, however, I will not have much to say directly about catechesis. Instead, I will deal with a matter that is fundamental to catechesis in the sense that it must be understood well before we can grasp the deeper issues of catechesis. That matter is the question of formation, taken from a broad social angle. A better understanding of the overall matter of formation should shed light on why catechesis is so crucial an activity that all in the local church need to engage in it.

The underlying thesis I am following here is that formation, far from being a process used mainly by religious groups to reproduce among adherents beliefs and lifestyle considered appropriate, is a central and inevitable process in all of human life. Understanding how "formative" all aspects of social and cultural life are will lay a groundwork for understanding the importance and even urgency of formation within religious groups. Actually, as we shall see, formation assumes its inevitable importance in religious groups precisely in the face of the powerful formative structures found in wider social and cultural life. Overlooking the relationship between formation as a social and cultural fact of life and religious formation leaves one open to misconstruing religious formation as a kind of structure of manipulative control, which brings about compliance without full awareness or consent. Though distortions are possible in religious formation and they need examination and critique, categorical dismissals of religious formation's value and importance will not stand up under critical scrutiny. Here I wish to give three examples of "formations" that affect us all but of which we tend to be marginally aware and then examine religious formation, using formation in the Christian Churches as my main example.

Formation of Perception

At the beginning of *The Long Revolution*, Raymond Williams explores the ways in which all persons from their earliest moments must learn how to see. Though many assume their senses provide them with an accurate means of understanding the world, our senses alone cannot teach us unless the data the senses offer us are interpreted for us within some system. Williams reminds us that the information received through the senses has to be interpreted according to certain schemas before what we call "reality" forms.

> One's version of the world one inhabits has a central biological function: it is a form of interaction with one's environment which allows a person to maintain life and to achieve greater control over the environment . . . We "see" in certain ways— that is, we interpret sensory information according to certain rules—as a way of living. But these ways—these rules and interpretations—are, as a whole, neither fixed nor constant. We can learn new rules and new interpretations, as a result of which we shall literally see in new ways.[1]

These rules of interpretation, then, according to which we "see" and name reality are handed on to us from others. At least in the beginning, these rules are "givens" we are not capable of questioning. We are formed to see in the way we do. Those familiar with Berger and Luckmann's *The Social Construction of Reality* or with the thought of philosophers of science such as Abraham Kaplan and Michael Polanyi may find little new in my account of Williams' point. However, Williams moves into and strives to map the territory from a somewhat different angle, namely, that of the production of culture.

Culture is human formation at it widest angle.

> . . . the particular interpretations carried by particular cultures give us certain "rules" or "models," without which no human

being can "see" in the ordinary sense, at all. In each individual, the learning of these rules, through inheritance and culture, is kind of creation, in that the distinctively human world, the ordinary "reality" that culture defines, forms only as the rules are learned. Particular cultures carry particular versions of reality, which can be said to create, in the sense that cultures carrying different rules ... create their own worlds which their bearers ordinarily experience.[2]

In helping us see how our own seeing is shaped by culture's ultimate sort of formation, Williams' interest is toward being able to critique and question culture as a human product. Understanding culture and its rules of interpretation as human products is a first step in questioning and talking back to these human constructs. We shall see later the significance of this matter for religious formation.

Language and the Formation of Thought

Another person who helps us understand how thoroughly "formed" our lives are is Peggy Rosenthal, in *Words and Values*, her study of the patterns that exist in language.[3] As the subtitle of her book, "Some Leading Words and Where They Lead Us," suggests, her interest is not so much with the syntactical patterns of language, even though these are themselves a kind of mold into which our thought is poured and by which it is formed. She explores another dimension of the formative power of language: the way in which the meanings of words shift over time and take on colorations and nuance that predate our thought and form it as a kind of mold within a mold. "Words . . . act as receptacles into which different disciplines and ideologies and traditions of thought pour their particular meanings, their favorite value-laden concepts."[4] Rosenthal conceives of her "leading words" as those which assume positions of power in a particular language and which then direct us to think and act in particular ways. Admitting that her view of our relation to these words might be alarming, she further admits that in her approach:

We aren't seen as leading our own language anywhere at all, but as being led by it. Our words, even our common everyday ones, are seen as an active force in our lives; our own position with respect to them is seen as passive. This is indeed a disturbing position to find ourselves in, but . . . the normal operations of language do put us in this passive position:

language works to give us much less control over "what we mean" than we generally assume we have. Even when we think we're choosing our words with care and giving them precise meanings, they can mean much more (or less) than we think; and when we use them carelessly, without thinking, they can still carry thoughts. These thoughts we're not aware of, these meanings we don't intend, can then carry us into certain beliefs and behavior—whether or not we notice where we're going.[5]

Rosenthal's position is similar to Williams',[6] since she is pointing out how thoroughly "formed" is the linguistic world we come to inhabit. We like to think of our choice of language as under our conscious control so that we say what we mean, while in fact "words say what *they* mean more than what *we* mean."[7] Certain words attract us and so we select them, but dimensions of that attraction and selection lie outside our conscious intentions. Rosenthal examines our culturally-conditioned predilection for the word "self" and for word clusters like "growth," "development," and "potential"; our preference for these words has a history, which can be examined and interpreted. Like Williams, Rosenthal's interest is in helping us become conscious of the connotative meaning already structured into words and word clusters, so we can expand our awareness and control of our own meaning. As she puts it:

We can indeed increase the extent of our consciousness of [language's] operations, as we're doing here, and thereby give ourselves more control over our language than we usually have. But unless we make this deliberate effort to watch how our words are working, we'll be worked on by them and manipulated by their meanings unawares.[8]

Basically her book is an exercise in cultural analysis, bringing into close examination the way culture puts forth "leading words" which are formative of meaning apart from ordinary consciousness.

This matter is of central importance in modern thought, so much so that I do not even attempt to compile a bibliography of related works.[9] Instead, I cite briefly a single book providing important question for religious persons in the U.S.: *The Habits of the Heart*. If Rosenthal's book extends Williams' *Keywords*, then Bellah's *Habits of the Heart* extends hers, by examining how moral confusion is masked by, at the same time it is helped along by, one's use of language, including some of the same leading words she ana-lyzes.[10] In many ways, *Habits* is an examination of language, scruti-nizing the choice of words and word patterns used by the persons under study. As examples, the following passages:

> . . . We are not saying that the people to whom we talked have empty selves. Most of them are serious, engaged, deeply in-volved in the world. But insofar as they are limited to a language of radical individual autonomy, as many of them are, they cannot think about themselves or others except as ar-bitrary centers of volition. They cannot express the fullness of being that is actually theirs.

> We found . . . people often on the defensive, struggling for the biblical and republican language that could express their aspi-rations, often expressing themselves in the very therapeutic rhetoric that they consciously reject. *It is a rhetoric that educated middle-class Americans, and through the medium of television and other mass communications, increasingly all Americans, cannot avoid.* [Italics mine.] And yet even those most trapped in the language of the isolated self are troubled by the nihilism they sense there and eager to find a way of overcoming the empti-ness of purely arbitrary "values."[11]

Bellah and his associates here seem to suggest not only that we are formed by the language available to us but also that we can be trapped within that language, locked into a mindset that an alterna-tive language must unlock. To extend Rosenthal's metaphor, the formative mold is an iron one.

Hegemony and the Formation of Consciousness

Pierre Bourdieu, in his social critique of the production of taste, notes that every economic system produces among the people in it the dispositions needed for that economy to succeed.[12] If we ac-cepted that the production of religious dispositions and frames of reference is religious formation, then, at least in part, we must also accept that the production of dispositions by an economic system is also a kind of formation, though perhaps far less conscious. This second kind of formation needs more attention if we are to under-stand the efficiency with which it "forms."

The Italian thinker, Antonio Gramsci, in his theory of hegemony, has provided a helpful theoretical base for understanding how this social process of formation can succeed outside of our awareness.

Basically hegemony is a process by which the consent of the dominated classes is obtained for programs not in their best interests.
The dominant classes shape the issues in such a way that these
issues seem to embrace the needs and interests of the subordinate
groups, at the same time that they mask and hide the deeper,
controlling and directing interests of the dominant.[13] For those who
insist on ignoring the significance of class structures, hegemony is
irreversible. Hegemony then is not raw coercion; it is one group's
orchestration of compliance in another group through structuring
the consciousness of the second group. Hegemony is by its nature
covert, and because it shapes consciousness and action, religious
persons need to understand how it works. An effective translator of
Gramsci's idea for English-speakers is Raymond Williams.

Williams explains that hegemony makes use of a total way of
looking at reality that saturates society to such an extent and is
lived at such a depth that it becomes for those immersed in it,
simple commonsense.[14] Perhaps the best current example of hegemony is the network of commonsense, accepted "truths" that emerge
from an economic order of consumption. Persons are defined as
consumers, and readily accept that definition as an appropriate *self-
definition*, which as it is lived out takes on an even more stubborn
taken-for-grantedness. The endless rush to the malls has this self-
definition embedded in it. As Williams put it:

> ... [hegemony] is the central, effective and dominant system of
> meanings and values, which are not merely abstract but which
> are organized and lived. That is why hegemony is not to be
> understood at the level of mere opinion or mere manipulation.
> It is a whole body of practices and expectations; our assign-
> ments of energy, our ordinary understanding of the nature of
> man and of his world. It is a set of meanings and values which
> as [because] they are experienced as practices appear as recipro-
> cally confirming. It thus constitutes a sense of reality for most
> people in the society, a sense of absolute, because experienced,
> reality beyond which it is very difficult for most members of
> the society to move, in most areas of their lives.[15]

If hegemony is more than consciousness but an entire "way" of
being in the world, it is not a static system but is actively being
reproduced in the rising generations, especially by what Williams
calls "the systems of incorporation into a society." He names the
modes of incorporation into a society as having "great social significance," citing educational institutions as key agencies for the transmission of hegemony.[16]

Not only is hegemony an active process in the sense it is lived; it is also highly adaptive, ever ready to co-opt even critiques within its wider definitions of reality.

> . . . [hegemony] isn't just the past, the dry husks of ideology which we can more easily discard . . . It is something more substantial and more flexible than any abstract imposed ideology. *Thus we have to recognize the alternative meanings and values, the alternative opinions and attitudes, even some alternative senses of the world, which can be accommodated and tolerated within a particular effective and dominant culture.* [Italics mine here and below.] This has been much under-emphasized in our notions . . . of hegemony. And the under-emphasis opens the way for retreat to an indifferent complexity. In the practice of politics, for example, there are certain truly incorporated modes of what are nevertheless, within those terms, real opposition, that are felt and fought out . . . Whatever the degree of internal conflict or internal variation, *they do not in practice go beyond the limits of the central effective and dominant definitions.* This is true, for example, of the practice of parliamentary politics, though its internal oppositions are real. It is true about a whole range of practices and arguments . . . Whatever the degree of internal controversy and variation, they do not exceed the limits of the central corporate definitions.[17]

Williams' description of hegemony is so laid out that he seems to be saying almost that there is no hope of countering it. Yet Williams' life-work, if I be permitted to interpret it, has been to point out the stubborn-because-unseen structures that tend to determine our lives, so they can be contested and, if need be, shifted. As a cultural critic, he brings out of hiding procedures and processes that have a human face and a human form, which he then fingerprints.

Williams explicitly states that in religious groups he find what he calls residual cultural forms, that is, experiences, meanings, and values, that do not fit and are not able to be expressed in terms of the dominant culture but which continue to be lived and practiced. These experiences and meanings are of course in contrast to the majority of religious meanings which are subsumed under the umbrella of the dominant system,[18] and they provide an important wedge in the seemingly impenetrable facade of hegemony. Religious people dare not forget the importance of this wedge.

At this point, I have noted that the proper avenue for approaching religious formation is by the route of understanding how "formative" social and cultural systems are for all persons. I illustrated my point with somewhat brief descriptions of how culture forms our perceptive system, how language molds our thought, and finally, how hegemony, a notion that embraces entire social and cultural systems, permits us to think and act only within limits set by dominant elites. These examples were selected from a number of possible ones because they are of personal interest to me, having been of help in my own study of "how things work." Now there remains the task of showing the significance of religious formation precisely in the face of the power of the wider social and cultural forces.

I hope that the above descriptions, especially of hegemony, clarify that the question is not one of whether or not there will be "formation" in human life. The question is rather: How does formation work in the wider culture and how must religious persons undertake a "counter-formation" in order to insure the viability of their communal religious meaning systems. This question appears to be easily overlooked by many persons today. I met a woman recently, a former Roman Catholic, who told me of the pains she had endured at the hands of functionaries in the church and of her decision, long-held at this point, not to give any religious formation to her children but let them "decide for themselves" the entire question of their religious orientation. I told her that while she would be silent about her faith, the marketeers and panderers to consumer lust would not be silent or inactive. They are not going to let her children "decide for themselves." They would be at her children, selling them a very clear vision of the world and a vision that is fact functions as a religion, meaning, it proposes its values as the ultimate ones worth living one's life for and even worth dying for. A religion imagines the possibilities of human life for us; and the marketeers imagine existence, so I told her, at its least. As I reflected on the matter later, I saw that the question was not whether or not the children would receive formation; formation was inevitable. The question was which kind of formation would help them imagine a human life.

Behind my words to this woman was a conviction that both religion and the wider culture claim the meanings they propose are the ultimate ones. The wider culture, as Williams hints in describing hegemony, makes its claims to ultimacy *covertly*; a religious system makes its claims overtly. The problem is that the covert claims can be more powerful because, never explicitly made, they are harder to identify and resist. When cast in the hegemonic form, the wider culture forms us, creates in us "habits of the heart" and dispositions needed by the economic system, and we tend, not just to overlook what is happening, but to be unable to notice.

Religious Formation

Religious educators understand the importance of the processes by which religious groups help new members participate in their understandings and way of life. Among religions, these processes vary widely, with some relying on carefully structured steps of initiation and subsequent reality maintenance, while others expect ordinary life lived with the believing group to be the most usual and sufficient means of taking on their religious way. Within religions, these processes have varied over time, as can be seen in the development of the catechumenate in the early Christian churches, a lengthy period of preparation that gradually fell into disuse starting about the year 300 A.D. only to be revived in the last twenty-five years. The importance of these processes, either informal or carefully structured, has been highlighted by modern sociology,[19] particularly by the theoretical framework offered by Berger and Luckmann in *The Social Construction of Reality*.[20]

Religious formation today is an issue of special significance among religious groups in areas of the world where electronic communications technology has been made widely available at the local level. My reasons for making this claim are as follows. Any particular religious tradition is itself a culture, that is, a "signifying system through which a social order is communicated, reproduced, experienced and explored."[21] It is a zone of signification, and one, as pointed out above, that explicitly claims its meanings to be the ultimate ones. But a religious zone of signification exists within a wider culture, which, especially in pluralistic societies, does not espouse a particular religious vision. Even if it did, its vision would not be identical to or as focused as the explicit religious culture. In either case, the religious tradition has to maintain its own meanings in the face of the wider culture.

In modern industrial and post-industrial societies, however, the wider culture is based on understandings and values that run counter to a religious vision. These values run toward unfettered capitalism, strategies of domination to protect financial privilege, and an ethic of consumerism. Taken together such values represent a zone of ultimacy, which becomes a kind of secular religion. As I have already explained, these claims to ultimacy are covert, possessing the special power of the non-explicit: that it is more difficult to name and resist. However in a world that has developed the technology for electronic communications media and made that technology widely available, the communication of meaning has taken on a new power unprecedented in the history of the race. Not the technology and its accessibility only, but the techniques of communication within the various forms of communication empower the consumer culture in a decisive way, to convince, to "reproduce the dispositions needed by the economy," and to enforce its covert claims to ultimacy.

The force and plausibility of the electronic imagination of the self as consumer works to undercut, decisively I would say, a person's commitment to a religious vision and a local group's commitment to a religious way.[22] Stating that the electronically imagined world tends to subvert religious sensitivities might alarm some as an attack on modernity and a nostalgic yearning for simpler times. Though the statement certainly questions culture from the point of the Christian sacred writings, it is not *against* what is current but insists that cultural developments should not be allowed to hide behind a label of modernity. Rather it is an affirmation of *the particularity and uniqueness of a religious vision*, which quite properly can be used as a norm by which to measure and judge the influences in our lives.

What I have described here is more than a crisis of conflicting claims; it is rather a crisis of conflicting imaginations of the nature of human life. Claims are verbal and, regardless of commitments, one can spar over verbal claims. However an imagination of life has gone beyond the verbal, deep into the psyche. When a person *lives* one imagination, which is a consumerist one, but continues to *talk* another but religious one, the illusion of the spoken commitment tends to mask the fact of the lived commitment. According to U.S. philosopher Charles Peirce, the definition of a belief is that it orients the behavior of those who hold it.

> Belief consists mainly in being deliberately prepared to adopt the formula believed in as the guide to action; the essence of belief is the establishment of a habit; and different beliefs are distinguished by the different modes of action to which they give rise.[23]

The lived commitment is the one that is actually formative. Jacques Ellul reminds us of this fact in a telling comparison.

> In one respect there is . . . an obvious point of similarity
> between what takes place in Marxism and in Christianity. Both
> have made practice the touchstone of truth or authenticity. In
> other words, it is by practice that we have to appreciate or not
> the intentions or purity of the doctrine, of the truth of the
> origin or source.[24]

If practice defines doctrine, Ellul also notes that false practice inevitably engenders false doctrine and false theory, and, I would add, a false life among the community. Dorothee Soelle points out that even prayer becomes subverted and it becomes impossible to pray words like, Create a pure heart in me, O God, and give me a new and steadfast spirit (Ps 51:10). "A prayer like this presupposed certain needs for renewal and change that have been destroyed. In the time of hedonism . . . all the needs that once had reference to being have now been exchanged for new ones which have reference to more having."[25] Her view is echoed by the claims of another religious thinker that "religion is tending to degenerate into a decent formula wherewith to embellish a comfortable life."[26]

A good model of how a religious tradition in its local communities can deal with the rival imaginations of the human can be found in the catechumenal process of the early church and its emphasis on the way one lived one's life. Here I do not intend to lay out the catechumenal process, so readily accessible now in multiple sources,[27] but rather to emphasize how the restructuring of lived commitments was central to the whole ethos of the catechumenate.

The catechumenate was a method of formation, not just in doctrinal purity, but in the re-imagined self, with a re-directed affect and re-structured patterns of life. This theme of shifts in primary commitments comes up again and again in the writings of early Christian writers. Origin writes:

> When it becomes evident that the disciples are purified by the
> word and have begun, as far as possible, to live better, only
> then are they invited to know our mysteries (C. Cels. 3,59),

adding in another place,

> The profound and secret mysteries must not be given, at first,
> to disciples, but they must be first instructed in the correction
> of their life style (Hom. V,6 in Iud).[28]

For Origin, re-structuring of life was prior to being given the secrets of the Christian way. Tertullian makes the same point:

> It [penitence and change of one's ways] presses most urgently
> ... upon those recruits who have just begun to give ear to the
> flow of divine discourse, and who, like puppies newly born,
> creep about uncertainly, with eyes as yet unopened ... We are
> not baptized so that we may cease committing sin but because
> we have ceased ...[29]

Regis Duffy maintains that the early communities demanded re-
oriented commitments and life styles as prior conditions for admitting to full membership those who would join their fellowship. He
points out that the reason the usual length of the catechumenate
was three years was that it took that long for the re-direction of
one's life structure.[30]

Conclusion

I am aware that I have not laid out here any specific proposal for
religious formation, such as "developmental steps" that could be
followed. In a sense the ancient catechumenate provides a fine
model. What I have done has been rather to lay out the problem,
one not that cannot be solved by strategies designed for children
alone. As I will explain in greater detail in later chapters, when not
integral to the lived life of actual communities, religious education,
Christian education and catechesis are puny endeavors. The main
formative agent is the believing community,[31] and, its verbal decla-
rations not withstanding, its communal or corporate commitments
and way of viewing reality are, for better or worse, the key formative factors. The reason John Westerhoff's tract, *Will Our Children
Have Faith?*[32] has had such an influence in the Christian Churches is
that he brought to new awareness this very truth.

Communities are formative in the stances they take. I believe
that certain stances are so out of tune with the dominant culture
that once they are taken, they seriously disrupt the hegemonic
meaning patterns as well as the hegemonic living patterns. In the
face of a consumerist culture, one such stance is solidarity with
victims, especially with those judged to be non-productive and
useless. In a culture like ours, no community will espouse solidarity with victims without going through a struggle with conflicting
ideas and values, but the dialogue such a struggle would involve
could be important, even salvific.[33]

The assembly of believers is one of the few places in current U.S.
society where a group of persons publicly gathers in the name of a
vision that counters so many of the assumptions of the consumer

culture, a fact that gives such an assembly a special political potential. In such assemblies, the process of maintaining within a community a reality that contradicts the wider hegemonic culture always involves intense dialogue, as sociologist Peter Berger reminds
us.

> It is possible to sum up the dialectic formation of identify by
> saying that the individual becomes that which he [sic] is ad-
> dressed as by others. One may add that the individual appro-
> priates the world in conversation with others and, further-
> more, that both identity and world remain real to himself only
> as long as he can continue the conversation.
>
> The last point is very important, for it implies that socialization
> can never be completed, that it must be an ongoing process
> throughout the lifetime of the individual . . . The difficulty of
> keeping a world going expresses itself psychologically in the
> difficulty of keeping this world subjectively plausible. The
> world is built up in the consciousness of the individual by
> conversation with significant others (such as parents, teachers,
> "peers"). The world is maintained as subjective reality by the
> same sort of conversation, be it with the same or with new
> significant others (such as spouses, friends, or associates). If
> such conversation is disrupted (the spouse dies, the friends
> disappear, or one comes to leave one's original social milieu),
> the world begins to totter, to lose its subjective plausibility. In
> other words, the subjective reality of the world hangs on the
> thin thread of conversation . . . The maintenance of such
> continuity is one of the most important imperatives of the
> social order.[34]

To Berger's analysis of the *conversational* aspect of reality maintaine-
nce, I would add an emphasis on the key role that patterns of
behavior, i.e., life structure, have in keeping a counter-cultural
vision plausible.

Most of the issues I have touched on in the preceding several
paragraphs will be treated in greater detail in later chapters of this
book. But even so, I myself do not believe that commitment is
chartable in a blueprint sense, and those who seek such a blueprint
here will be disappointed. There is a process that must be engaged
in by the local church, though that process is not a technology like a
computerized mailing list; it is more like the process of parenting,
which is an art and a delicate one. My hope in this book is to offer
clues, suggestions for engaging in that human process, and some
models, such as the one I describe in Chapter 6.

Notes

1. Raymond Williams, *The Long Revolution* (New York: Columbia University Press, 1961) 18.

2. Ibid.

3. Peggy Rosenthal, *Words and Values: Some Leading Words and Where They Lead Us* (New York: Oxford University Press, 1984).

4. Ibid. 42.

5. Ibid. viii.

6. One of the first books Rosenthal cites in grounding her own study is Williams' *Keywords* (New York: Oxford University Press, 1976); her own book is in some senses an extension of Williams'.

7. Ibid. 42.

8. Ibid. 42.

9. One I have found very helpful and used recently—*Youth, Gospel, Liberation* (New York: Harper and Row, 1987)—is George Steiner, *Language and Silence* (New York: Atheneum, 1967).

10. Though I find correlations between the two books, such as in their examination of the use of the word "self," Bellah and others do not refer to Rosenthal's work. See Robert N. Bellah, Richard Madsen, William M. Sullivan, Ann Swidler, and Steven M. Tipton, *Habits of the Heart: Individualism and Commitment in American Life* (Berkeley: University of California Press, 1985).

11. Ibid. 81, 83; see also 306 and 336, though the entire book is, I claim, an examination of language.

12. Pierre Bourdieu, *Distinction: A Social Critique of the Judgement of Taste* (Cambridge: Harvard University Press) 100-101. I find a very graphic working out of Bourdieu's thesis in Raymond Williams' earlier book, *The Country and the City* (New York: Oxford University Press, 1973). See especially his survey and analysis of how vagrancy came to be redefined in England, so as to serve the labor needs of the new industrialism, Chapter 8, "Nature's Threads," pp. 68-86. Also, Bourdieu's notion of the creation of disposition is similar to Williams' own notion, repeated often in his writings, of the creation of "a structure of feeling." See *Country and City*, [where the idea is not indexed], pp. 73, 79, 87, 96, 112, 178, 195, 209, 236, 252, 270, 297.

13. In his analysis of sexuality, Eric Fuchs provides a telling example of how even revolt against middle-class values can *reinforce* the presuppositions of a society's economic system.

> . . . the ideology of bourgeois marriage expressed the needs of a society that was based on the values of real estate, and the requirement of fidelity was motivated by the comparable economic necessity not to sell off the land. Challenging this concept of bourgeois ideology could signify that liberal capitalism no longer needs this

ideology of property in order to function. Isn't the utopia of sexual desire—freedom to go wherever and do whatever it pleases really the ideology of a society where capital is also free to go and be wherever it pleases? A certain kind of contemporary discussion on fidelity, which in interpreted as faithfulness to self, to one's duty, to one's own expansion, to one's pleasure—doesn't that correspond to an economic discussion about investment which should how some profit or else be pulled out? To be faithful means to invest desire wherever it can get the expected returns . . . This whole approach to sexuality and sexual desire reproduces, while desiring to fight against, a model of liberal capitalism founded on the free circulation of money (i.e., desire) and free trade.

Eric Fuchs, *Sexual Desire and Love* (New York: Seabury, 1983) 17. The writings of educational analyst, Michael Apple, abound with similar examples from the world of schooling.

14. Raymond Williams, "Base and Superstructure in Marxist Cultural Theory," in *Problems in Materialism and Culture* (New York: Schocken Books, 1980) 31-49. Also in Roger Dale and others, *Schooling and Capitalism: A Sociological Reader* (London: Routledge and Kegan Paul, 1976) 202-210.

15. Ibid. 38.

16. I have found a helpful survey of some Marxist critiques of education, including some valuable material on hegemony from an educational perspective, to be Henry Giroux, "Theories of Reproduction and Resistance in the New Sociology of Education: A Critical Analysis," *Harvard Educational Review* 53:3 (August 1983) 257-293.

17. Williams, "Base and Superstructure" 39-40.

18. Ibid. 40-42.

19. Here I would call attention to studies of the ways the Jewish people maintained their identity in the face of cultural forces that might have fully undermined it. For example, Norman K. Gottwald, *The Tribes of Yahweh* (New York: Orbis, 1979).

20. Peter L. Berger and Thomas Luckmann, *The Social Construction of Reality: A Treatise in the Sociology of Knowledge* (New York: Doubleday Anchor Books, 1967).

21. Raymond Williams, *The Sociology of Culture* (New York: Schocken Books, 1982) 13.

22. For an overview of some efforts to face this problem, see Paul Giurlanda, "The Challenge of Post-liberal Theology," *Commonweal* (30 January 1987) 40-42. Giurlanda pays special attention to the work of Stanley Hauerwas. For a current, Jewish example of a religous group resisting the wider culture, see Lis Harris' three-part essay on the Lubovitch Hasidim, written from the point of view of a secular Jew in searching out her religious roots but who came to write her account in relation to the

key liturgical celebrations of this sect. Lis Harris, "The Holy Days: Parts I, II, III," *The New Yorker* (September 16, 33, 30, 1985).

23. Cited in Thomas McCarthy, *The Critical Theory of Jurgen Habermas* (Cambridge, MA: MIT Press, 1978) 63. The source of the quote is Pierce's essay, "How to Make Our Ideas Clear," in *Writings of Charles Sanders Pierce: A Chronological Edition*, vol. 3 [1872-78] (Bloomington: Indiana University Press, 1986) 257-275, at 263-264.

24. Jacques Ellul, *The Subversion of Christianity* (Grand Rapids, MI: Eerdmans, 1986) 4.

25. Dorothee Soelle, "'Thou Shalt Have No Other Jeans Before Me,': The Need for Liberation in a Consumerist Society," in Mahan and Richesin, eds., *The Challenge of Liberation Theology* (New York: Orbis, 1981) 4-16, at 6.

26. Matthew Fox, *Original Blessing* (California: Bear and Company, 1980) 10.

27. An especially helpful catechumenal "manual" is Julia Upton, *Journey into Mystery: A Companion to the R.C.I.A.* (Mahwah, NJ: Paulist Press, 1986); revised under the title *Becoming a Catholic Christian: A Pilgrim's Guide to the Rite of Christian Initiation of Adults* (Washington, D.C.: The Pastoral Press, 1993).

28. Both quotes appear in D. Capelle, "L'Introduction du catéchumenat à Rome," *Recherches de théologie ancienne et médiévale* 5 (1933) 151, notes 38 and 39.

29. Tertullian, "On Penitence," *Treatises on Penance*, trans. W. Le Saint (Westminster: Newman, 1959) 24, 25-26.

30. Regis Duffy, "Liturgical Catechesis: Catechumenal Models," unpublished paper given as The Mary Charles Bryce Lecture, Catholic University, Washington, D.C., April 1983.

31. Here I agree with C. Ellis Nelson's assertion in *Where Faith Begins* that the family is a necessary formative element in Christian faith but not sufficient. Two key quotes from Nelson on this matter:

> . . . What is the natural agency for communicating that reality [faith]? . . . the natural agency of communication is the community of believers (p. 30).

> A family is not a society, although it has some of the qualities of a society, such as different work assignments to the individuals in the family and rewards and punishments given to individuals according to the way they behave. A family is not a society because as a unity it does not have continuity: new families are formed, but particular families die out. Also, the relationship within families is highly personal, whereas in a society relationships are impersonal. If a political leader is killed he is replaced, for that role in a society must be played; but if an individual in a family is killed, he as a person cannot be relaced. This distinction is an important one. On

the one hand, the family is one of the most important units for communicating faith and the meaning of faith. On the other hand, we cannot work out a system of Christian nurture based on the family alone because the family is more an agent of culture and society than it is an independent unit. We cannot assume that society can be "family-like, only bigger." The difference between the family and society is a difference in kind rather than in degree or size. We must watch this point carefully. There is always a tendency to assume that the problems of society would be solved if we could just expand the virtues of the family to the society (pp. 37-37).

See C. Ellis Nelson, *Where Faith Begins* (Atlanta: John Knox Press, 1971).

32. John H. Westerhoff III, *Will Our Children Have Faith?* (New York: Seabury-Crossroad, 1976). Those who examine Westerhoff's career to date will find that his life-long preoccupation has been with contexts, with culture, and with the possibilities of the local church.

33. C. Ellis Nelson brings out the inescapablilty and importance of conflict at various places in *Where Faith Begins*; see pp. 87-94 and 182-211, passim.

34. Peter Berger, *The Sacred Canopy: Elements of a Sociological Theory of Religion* (New York: Doubleday Anchor Books, 1969) 16-17.

3

Catechesis and the Captive Audiences

The goal of catechesis is right living. As suggested in the previous chapter, we find this goal's clearest illustration in the early catechumenate, with its gradual correction of lifestyle, completed only when the candidate was able to walk as a follower of Jesus among the followers of Jesus. Correct doctrinal understanding was an aspect of that slow process but only as directed to right living. Even in the catechumenate, doctrine cut off from living would have distorted catechesis, as it did later through many centuries of catechetical deterioration.

The fact of the decline of catechesis—along with the distortions that marked that decline—should give pause to any person concerned with the progress of catechesis today. What had been a matter of delicate but insistent attention—initiation into the meanings that bound the community together—became a taken-for-granted routine fostering not insight but ignorance. The enduring threat to catechesis is that as a process it can reproduce certain counter-gospel thrusts of modern culture, thus betraying both its original genius and its original commitments. This essay, written to expose a possible distortion of catechesis and to propose ways of avoiding it, begins with the story of how I first came to see this problem in sharp focus.

At an international meeting of religious educators several years ago, I attended a session on adult religious education run by publishers, at which the specific topic was the problem of producing

quality materials for adults. In the course of the meeting, a representative of a U.S. publisher of religious materials mentioned that
her company produced materials for adults only through the profits made on what she called the "captive audiences."

Whatever it was she said next I cannot recall, probably because
my imagination leaped up and romped as I began to work out the
complex significance of her statement. A captive is one who is
caught and held, most usually in a prison or some other kind of
confinement. Of course history has known an entire category of
captives not always held in walled-in confinement. These were the
slaves, taken into captivity, which was to be not temporary as in
some instances of imprisonment but permanent, a lifelong condition.

I thought also about the positive meanings of captive. We say a
performer or a speaker is captivating when the quality of the
person's ability to communicate holds us rapt. To be captivated is
the exact opposite of being a captive. One is caught, but not by
force. Instead one is held rapt, by sharing in another's feelings,
thought, performance, or entire persona. The captivated person has
entered a quasi-ecstatic state that is a peak of release and freedom.
The captivated spirit soars; the captive spirit sours.

And what of the captive audiences? The reference by the publishing representative was to a very particular audience—the young. In
whose interests was their captivity, I asked myself. Clearly it was in
the interest of religious education, religious understanding, "knowing one's faith." Ironically, none of the activities toward faith can
proceed properly unless it faces the fact that faith is an option. It
cannot be forced. Faith-seeking is an activity of open hands, in the
double sense that the seeker looks for the favor of God, but also in
the sense that the community offers the faith-seeker an open hand
as a welcoming sign of its willingness to enter and walk on the
same ground as the seekers. This open hand is toward helping the
spirit soar, not toward making it sour.

My meditation did not stop when I left that room in a mood of
numb agitation over the idea that publishing funds for the liberation of adults are being generated on the backs of children. I
realized I needed to ponder long and well the problem of the
captive audiences. I also realized that in the context of the woman's
statement, the anonymous captives were clearly not adults, who
are old enough to break quite simply the bonds of their religious
captivity and walk away. No, the captives referred to were the

children and those older youth who are still not old enough to be allowed to choose for themselves. If there were actually a kind of captivity going on in the name of religious growth, did that fact need the attention of those concerned for catechesis or religious education? How would one go about raising that question?

I began to make notes on the problem of the captives and to search out writing that shed light on the problem. One of the best pieces I found was an essay by Dwayne Huebner,[1] then of Columbia Teachers College, that dealt with the problem from a secular schooling point of view, and in what follows I have freely adapted his analysis to a catechetical frame of reference. This essay is the result of that meditation years ago and many others in the years since. I have been slow to make public these thoughts because they seemed too abstract and not grounded enough in applying its analysis to concrete instances. Now, however, after being encouraged by several catechetical leaders with whom I have shared my ideas, I offer the following analysis in hopes that it may, abstract as it may be, help my fellow catechists face up to a key problem in our pastoral work.

Communities and Traditions

In examining the way communities seek to hand on their traditions to the next generation, we can find two distinct, even divergent, approaches. Some communities have traditions of care for one another and for their communal possessions and memories. These memories are stored in their poetry, songs, rituals, and in their artifacts. Such a community hands on these traditions in an embodied mode, that is, hands on their full complex richness. Other communities, however, might have a rich tradition but make the mistake of trying to hand it on in an abstracted, disembodied mode. Communities in this second category develop a program abstracted from the prayer, poetry, ritual, and song of their full tradition and instead seek to hand on their treasures in categories of logical thought only, which when cut off from the tradition's full richness, distort the tradition rather than disclose it.

When some people say they are concerned that children "know their faith," they themselves may in fact be so insufficiently aware of the richness of the community's memory stored in song, ritual and other expressions of that memory that as a result the only way they can conceive of a child's religiousness is in the disembodied categories of their own abstracted understanding. Perhaps they do not concern themselves with passing on the community's collective wealth, its rich embodied tradition, because they themselves do not understand it, do not "care" about it, and do not see handing it on as a way of caring. Too bad, for the child may not be able to be delighted by the tradition in any other form, and short of that delight, may not be able to cherish it.[2]

Edward Schillebeeckx points out in his book, *Ministry*,[3] how in the early Christian communities the leaders were those recognized as possessing the ability to keep the community in lively touch with its traditions and with the meanings embedded in those traditions. In other words, the enliveners of the community functioned by standing as "cherished menials" squarely within the community's life, pointing out the community's significance as a kind of living text, and urging its members to greater fidelity to the tradition.[4] Such enliveners of communities may have been replaced in many modern churches by an entirely different kind of person, who functions as a bureaucratic functionary, a manager of doctrinal inputs.

There is no doubt that the disembodied mode can communicate the logical ideas abstracted out of the tradition. There is, however, a large question whether the living tradition can be communicated in that mode. The living tradition must be passed on at least in part— and I would say, in large part—through festivity, that is, through the live interaction of the community engaged in celebrating its own life. When religious understandings are so vital they go beyond words, they must be danced, sung, shouted, pondered in silence around symbols that whisper.

It is important to understand how festivity functions in a community. Festivity abolishes rank, and to the degree that rank is maintained, festivity is diminished. In festive enactments of the community's understanding, all are equal, with each participating on his/her own level, each entering the understandings at his/her own level as a unique subjectivity. Where one enters and celebrates the community's tradition at the level of festivity, the twin laws governing that activity are equality and gradualness. In festivity, adult and child walk on the same earth, have assumed a temporary equality life-giving for each. Festivity suspends imperious demands for progress and delights in what is. The community's life, as viewed through festivity, is so rich and so vital that the community can tolerate and even encourage both equality and gradualness, because both treasure the subjectivity of all within the community.

Although there is a definite role for the person who would function as the catechist helping members understand the tradition in a more abstract and systematic way, such a person must realize that abstractions both connect to the lived life of the community and artificially give distance from it. A special danger arises should the catechist ever cease to or forget to care for the fullness of the community of which he or she is part and for the memories, tales, poetry, prayers, and rituals of that community. The catechist to be effective must cherish the tradition as alive in the community. To mediate to the child the tradition-as-abstraction and to omit any of the festive re-telling and re-living of the tradition is effectively to separate the whole enterprise of catechizing from the community. The catechist who forgets the lived tradition has ceased to be part of the pilgrimage of the community and no longer dwells in its memories and celebrations. Once the catechist has moved from anamnesis, the memories remembered because they are cherished, to memorization, the facts that are drilled in but will never be cherished, the catechist has moved from being an enlivener to being a doctrinal manager.

Obviously there is another side to this problem. When the community itself gets out of touch with its own tradition and the festivity needed to embody it, when it enacts its rituals out of habit but ceases to take life from the power of its own understandings, then it loses its religious center. Further, when the community's native genius for embodying its tradition in its present life erodes, then it can easily tend to push its responsibility entirely onto the shoulders of single persons, the catechists, who come to bear the whole task of imparting the tradition, now sadly fragmented. Cut off from its own story and living ritual, the community finds the only resources left to itself in its fragmented condition are the resources of abstraction and logical thought, enforced by the catechist. At such a juncture there is a danger that the community is actually disguising its loss of its inner life by continuing to impose on the powerless, especially on the children, an account of that life, but not now in the mode of festivity but of its opposite, the mode of compulsion. A related danger here is that the community, with the catechist as its proxy, can move entirely from celebrative, festive renderings of its tradition to textual ones.

At that point, religious faith is not given to the child as part of the living genius of the community but as part of texts on printed pages. The child's religious encounter is textual learning presided over by a textual overseer, demanding attention to the text and insisting on the prior significance of textual renderings of the faith. Is the textual rendering a faithful one? Can it, apart from the embodied community, be a faith-filled one? Can the compelled gathering of those bound to the significance of the textual renderings ever in fact have access, in that isolated activity, to the genius of the lived tradition, which is in fact the most convincing text? I claim not. When the text on printed pages is cut off from the text of the community's life, the printed text is dead.

When the catechist has ceased to be a mystagogue, a wise and loving guide to the mysteries that engulf the community,[5] and has moved to being a manager of doctrinal inputs, catechesis itself has become dead. The catechized need persons of wisdom, able to crack open the shell of the community's formulas to reveal the tasty and nourishing meat inside. A person of little understanding will demand they swallow the shell unopened, apparently unaware they might choke on it. The master catechist, Augustine, was concerned about such doctrinal choking when he suggested the catechist be like a mother who carefully chews a morsel of meat in her own mouth before she puts it into the mouth of her little one.[6] Augustine would understand why I call the catechist the "cherished menial."

An apt example here of how understandings that have shifted in the larger community continue to be imposed on the child might be the current practice of confession in the United States. It is no secret that since Vatican II's liturgical and sacramental renewal with its firmer understanding of the nature of penance, many bishops have ceased in their own devotional lives, to use the confession form of penance, as have many nuns and brothers, and very large numbers of "lay" persons. However, it appears that almost *because* these groups of persons have opted to move away from the confession-mode of the sacrament of penance, that children must submit to confession, and at very early ages, and even in some places, prior to first communion. As a theorem, the situation might be stated: "Because these others in fact don't, the children must." We have here a double standard so often visited upon children and older young people in the church.

Reimagining the Place of the Child

Another example of the same theorem in practice might be the way children are expected to submit to regular renditions of the tradition, at the same time that adults engage in little or no adult catechesis, or even that priests engage so reluctantly in continuing education. What once was the ritual and joyfully celebrative way of journeying to full incorporation in the community—the catechumenate—has somehow shifted in many places to lessons on a once-a-week basis. These sessions, I am claiming, can easily tend to feel non-celebrative to the child, though I am certain many adults running them will vigorously deny my claim.

These sessions feel like so many areas of a child's life—a zone of compulsion, one more zone of no-say, no-power, one more zone where one must knuckle under, patiently awaiting a time of freedom. Within the zone of compulsion, the child is affected from the outside in, not from the inside out. The child is not encouraged to search out his/her own place in the community's understanding of its traditions. The child's role is to accommodate him/herself to a rigidly ordered set of formulations, falsely believing that these are the tradition.[7]

Here, some readers may recognize in my description the contours of situations and policies they themselves support, however reluctantly. Their tendency may be either to deny the problem by claiming the situation is part of the inevitable condition of children in society or to look quickly for immediate solutions. However, before solutions are worked out, the scope of the problem needs more analysis. Let us look now more closely to the child involved in the captive audience.

For the unfortunate child, an important emerging quality is being smothered in the process I have described above. Even very young children are developing the activities of negation and negotiation, which are so central to human agency. They are coming to the point of owning their personal no's and of expecting others to take these negations seriously. The child's "no" and subsequent demand for negotiation in resolving conflicts is an important moment in a person's political and religious development. The child can learn either that these negations are important ways of questioning the world of power or that the public world is so little open to question that all one can do is to adapt to it. Similarly the child can learn that openness to God comes from within—with the assistance of the community—or is another of those area of life pressed on one from without. Educator Dwayne Huebner has examined this problem in relation to secular education and, addressing the situation of very young children, puts it this way:

> The young child . . . has too frequently been overpowered by
> the already existing world and the power of the adult. He has
> had the incipient political activity of negation and negotiation
> associated with two-and four-year-old children knocked out of
> him by adults who see negation as bad. They do not see these
> negative periods as the establishment of political schemas at a
> sensory-motor and preoperational level. Hence, the child . . . is
> left with the awareness that the public world is made and that
> he is a misfit, rather than with the awareness that the public
> world is always in the process of being re-worked and that he
> has a right to rework it.[8]

Notice that I am not claiming here that every whim of a child is to
be indulged or that every choice a child makes is wise and to be
allowed.[9] I am instead claiming that policies of compulsion are ones
of non-negotiation and of non-dialogue. At the very least, the
ekklesia should not be one more place that refuses to take seriously
the child's no's and calls for negotiation.[10] In the ekklesia the child
must be taken with loving seriousness and so, come to expect that it
is one zone where his or her compliance will not be taken for
granted.[11]

On the other hand, where festivity and celebration characterize
catechesis, it moves from the zone of compulsion to the zone of
choice. Festivity is the cousin of freedom and cannot co-exist with
compulsion. Compulsion always tends to subvert festivity by means
of sullenness. Perhaps the only ones who can produce festivity on
command are actors and actresses whose artistic skills allow them
to imitate reality. The point at issue here is not that catechesis
should be festivity only, but that it should be marked with some
character of festivity.

We can mistakenly think that somehow the gospel tradition can
be sedimented among children in a definitive way—one that is
sedimented for a lifetime—without a constant effort and a lifelong
one, at keeping alive in the understandings of the adult community
that same tradition.[12] However, the tradition cannot be maintained
without inquiry, without working through misunderstanding, without an ongoing search made possible by the support of the living
body of believers. The fuller one's confidence in depositing the
tradition in some final and definitive way in children, the more one
can ignore or at least treat as entirely secondary or less important
the work of preaching and teaching and group inquiry at later life
stages.

Applying the Analysis

As noted earlier, I realize that this account of how and why the catechesis of the captive audiences functions is itself abstracted and not fully faithful to the various embodiments of parish life, which are not as black-and-white as my analysis might imply. This account will have value only as it sheds light on the catechetical programs of particular groups. I wish to apply briefly the above line of thought about the catechesis of children to two older catechetical groups: twelve-year-olds and those preparing for confirmation.

Catechetical programs for twelve-year-olds, who are often designated by their year in school as "seventh graders," can be set up for the convenience and according to the interests of those in power. These persons may not take the time to explore either the convenience or the interests of those expected to submit to the program. Consequently, these catechetical programs can be marginal to the interests of these young people at the same time they are claimed to be in their very "best interests." However, if the young have no say in the program, the term "best interest" can become a code-word legitimating the imposition of the agenda of the dominant group onto the dominated group.[13]

At the age of twelve, however, some young people are arriving at the time when those with no-say are able to decide to say no, that is, when their compliance can no longer be forced. Without such force or compulsion, a poorly conceived program will tend to collapse. When programs collapse or are somewhat successfully resisted by young people, the dominant group tend not to blame themselves. The cause is usually blamed on the recalcitrance of the dominated group. The seventh graders are "impossible"; "they don't care." They are "unteachable," "uncooperative," and "ungrateful." In such thinking the dominant group may never face themselves, their own lack of wisdom, lack of caring, patience, their inadequate strategies, or their own backward understanding of the processes by which one group influences another. At this point catechesis for the captives has reached its limits. If it were to continue, it could only do so on a different footing, more dialogal, more integral to the life of the community, grounded in greater hospitality and festivity.

The problem of confirmation—as most commonly practiced [14]— is more complex, partly because of the family pressures on the young persons to be confirmed. These problems have to be, and can be, worked out for those making confirmation in their late teens, though the difficulty to do so will be in direct ratio to how thoroughly the young people had been treated as captives when they were younger. My special concern here, however, is with confirmation for pre- and early adolescents, those between 12 and 14 or 15 years of age.

Current thinking about the Rite of Christian Initiation of Adults generally acknowledges that the end of the pre-catechumenate is reached only when an adult knows enough about the Lord, his word, and his church to make an intelligent decision to seek admission.[15] In many parishes, however, preparation for confirmation among young people actually reverses this process. The date has been pre-set according to the needs of a particular bishop's calendar. Announcing a pre-scheduled date in effect says, "You be ready by May such and such, when the bishop will be here to confirm." The end of one's preparation is no longer the point at which one is able to make an intelligent decision to seek admission to the sacrament, but the pre-set date of the event. While it is true that the deadline does not of itself deny the possibility of an intelligent decision, it is also true that the deadline "crowds" the intelligent decision, puts it under a certain duress. Since schedules are aspects of intelligent planning, the problem does not lie in the schedule itself, but in the overlooking the potential problems caused by tying religious readiness to a pre-set schedule.

When the young person is told, "You may say either yes or no, but you have to say it by this particular date," a subtle note of coercion has come into play, especially for these younger persons. In a situation where family and peer pressures against a "no" are already in place, those helping the confirmands need to be wary of orchestrating, however, subtly, a "yes," that never becomes an intelligent decision. After being told the decision was their own, that they could say yes or no, some young people I have met confided that in the privacy of their own lobes, they thought, "Yeah, just try saying no and see what happens." Those who come from the tradition of the captive audiences may have difficulty recogizing the importance of choice in this matter. Actually, it is the heart of the matter.

If a marriage shown to have been entered into under some duress can easily be annulled, the reason is that once one has reached the age of consciousness and reflectiveness, a sacrament has to be freely entered into. Sacraments not freely entered into are null, and that nullity is sometimes publicly declared, as when a non-marriage is declared. The full inadequacy of the catechesis of the captives is disclosed in confirmation, where, if choice has not been properly treasured, a person could go through the rite but not receive the sacrament, just as a couple could go through a wedding rite but not marry. In formulating future pastoral strategy for this sacrament, the question of how many people have gone through the rite of confirmation without receiving the sacrament will need close attention.

Confirmation has about it a special irony when viewed from the perspective of the captive audiences. We all know now, thanks to the revised rite for the baptism of infants, that at the moment of baptism the parents and the entire community commit themselves to the gradual nurture of the child's life-in-Christ. The commitment of the community taken on at that moment is not a perfunctory promise. It is a commitment to be worked out through the various ministries of the church and meant to last a lifetime. While the child's commitment to the community will never be under the full control of the community, the community's commitment to this child always remains under that community's intention and control.[16]

During the childhood years, the appropriate mode of the community's care is one of delicate attentiveness rather than of peremptory command, of the light touch of loving invitation rather than of heavy-handed obligation. If any group in the church understands and live out this mode, I would say, as a generalization, it is those doing youth ministry. When confirmation is finally put in its rightful place in the rite of baptism, the full complexity of the community's baptismal commitment to an emerging life in the Spirit will at last be clear. To state the point more baldly: confirmation is first *the community's commitment* to take seriously the faith-growth of this person, and only secondarily that person's eventual commitment. Confirmation as the sacrament of the community's commitment to be faithful to the Spirit present in its midst and to hand on that Spirit to all its members needs much more reflection than it has received so far. A fine New Testament passage to guide the catechesis of children might be 1 Thessalonians 2:7-9 where the writer expresses a delicate catechetical attitude:

> While we were among you we were as gentle as any nursing mother fondling her little ones. So well-disposed were we to you, in fact, that we wanted to share with you *not only God's tidings, but our very lives,* so dear had you become to us. You

> must recall, friends, our efforts and our toil: how we worked
> day and night all the time we preached God's good tidings to
> you in order not to impose on you in any way.

What a fitting motto for every parish catechetical program: "Not
Only God's Tidings But Our Very Lives!"

Conclusion

In an essay on ecclesiology, Joseph Komonchak notes that "an
ecclesiology . . . [is] a theory about practice."[17] Komonchak would
also accept a corollary: Actual church practice shows us its lived
theories rather than its stated theories. In some of the catechetical
practices I have described in this chapter, we find that the church
can ape the domination-subordination procedures so prevalent in
society.[18] Similarly some catechetical "programs," which are actually sets of printed materials, make substantial claims about fostering the liberation, including the critical thinking of those who use
them. Yet these same programs rarely deal with the basic problem
of the freedom of those who will use these materials.

Those who author such materials might claim that freedom is
taken for granted as a given, but we know it cannot be. The fact
remains that few such programs, even those with impressive sound-
ing sub-titles, raise the question of negotiating with children their
participation in catechesis. There is no true catechesis without their
consent. Though they may have been baptized without their consent, they cannot become disciples without it. Beware of anyone
who talks catechesis and ignores freedom. In a church that follows
Jesus' life and teachings, a child's acquiescence can never be taken
for granted. To do so places the child in the captive audiences.

I cannot conclude this chapter without coming back to the comments of the woman who first sparked my awareness of catechesis
as captivity. Her point was that significant financial profits were
being made from the captives. We now know that not only text-
book authors and publishers make significant profits from the
captive audiences, but sometimes parishes and dioceses selling
these texts get a percentage of the profits.

In a capitalist economy profit is not a dirty word, though in
fostering the freedoms of the daughters and sons of God, the
system of producing and selling textbooks has so many benefits for
those in positions of power that the system may be not questioned
when it should be. For instance the catechetical materials used by

the poor in Latin America appear to be produced cheaply and meant to be easily revised.[19] Even more importantly, these materials tend to come more directly from the community than do more sophisticated and polished materials. Such materials do not certainly give the text writer and publisher the margin of profit common in the U.S., but they might be better suited to the heart of catechesis.[20] Whatever direction the production of catechetical materials in North America, this chapter was written to suggest that the freedom of the captives be a starting point in our catechetical thinking and practice.

Notes

1. Dwayne Huebner, "Toward a Remaking of Curricular Language," in William J. Pinar, ed., *Heightened Consciousness: Culture, Revolution and Curriculum Theory* (Berkeley: McCutcheon, 1974) 36-53.

2. Some have asked me to include in this analysis a treatment of the role of the embodied and disembodied traditions in families. I have omitted that significant aspect of the question because my effort here is to focus on the *ekklesia,* while recognizing that the embodied tradition at the family level is a true sign of the wider *ekklesia.* There are close analogies between the two contexts. There is abundant research that what is not embodied in the family is not taught by the family to the child.

On the other hand it is possible, as historical examples show, for institutions to decide they are more effective than parents in handing on traditions to children, as when in the nineteenth century those running asylums for children came to believe that their regimens were actually better for children than living in families with their own parents. In turn, persons from these institutions wrote books on parenting that tended to cast the parent as a manager, effectively redefining parent in line with their own institutional duties. See David Rothman, *The Discovery of the Asylum* (Boston: Little, Brown and Company, 1971) 206-236.

3. Edward Schillebeeckx, *Ministry: Leadership in the Community of Jesus Christ* (New York: Crossroad, 1981).

4. To appreciate fully the position I am taking in this chapter, readers should re-read the history of authority in the church, such as the well-documented one by Yves Congar over twenty years ago: Yves Congar, "The Historical Development of Authority in the Church: Points for Christian Reflection," in John M. Todd, ed., *Problems in Authority* (Baltimore: Helicon Press, 1964) 119-156. I believe that the high and low points of church catechesis correspond with similar points in the church's understanding and use of authority. Hierarchical imperialism coincides with

catechetical decadence. It is significant that so many of the great cate-
chists have been from among the lowliest in the church—and among them
I would include the seminarians who led the catechetical programs at the
Church of St. Sulpice in Paris, so well described in the writings of Bishop
Dupanloup.

Also helpful in rounding out my own position here would be Leonardo
Boff, "Theological Characteristics of a Grassroots Church," in Sergio
Torres and Thomas Eagleson, eds., *The Challenge of Basic Christian Com-
munities* (New York: Orbis, 1981) 124-144.

5. For a fine, succinct description of mystagogy, see Hugh Riley,
Christian Initiation, Studies in Christian Antiquity, vol. 17 (Washington,
D.C.: The Catholic University of America Press, 1974) 1-10.

6. St. Augustine, *The First Catechetical Instruction: De Catechizandis
Rudibus*, trans. Joseph P. Christopher (Chicago: Henry Regnery Company, 1966) 37-38.

7. For an approach to the catechesis of children along the lines I am
trying to describe, see Jerome Berryman, *Godly Play: A Way of Religious
Education* (San Francisco: Harper and Row, 1990).

8. Huebner, "Toward a Remaking" 50.

9. Admittedly, the question I raise here is a complex one needing
extended treatment on its own. Somewhere in such a treatment, Janet
Baker Miller's distinction between temporary and permanent inequality
will deserve special notice; see Janet Baker Miller, *Toward a New Psychology of Women* (Boston: Beacon Press, 1976).

10. My use of the term *ekklesia* is much influenced by the important
treatment of the term in Congar's essay cited above (note 4), "The Historical Development" 124-126 and 136-138.

11. Again and again in catechetical and religious education literature,
but most especially in the latter, the child's participation in various
strategies and programs is quite taken-for-granted. It is a non-question.
And yet, the question of the motives and interests under which any group
of persons assembles is of the first importance, never to be taken for
granted. Yet, even proponents of a so-called "critical" religious education
overlook this matter. For a recent example out of countless possible ones
of how this problem can be overlooked even in a piece about re-designing
religious education toward more dialogue and freedom, see James H.
Ebner, "Talk About God," *Religious Education* 81:3 (Summer 1986) 466-
484.

12. The term sedimentation might at first seem like an inflated bit of
jargon. Actually its use in this context is from the sociology of knowledge,
where it describes the process by which human experiences become
retained as recognizable and memorable entities; see Peter L. Berger and
Thomas Luckmann, *The Social Construction of Reality* (New York: Anchor
Books, 1967) 67-72.

13. Gregory Baum notes how domination rules out any true dialogue:

> The discovery of truth in its totality must take place in a dialogue in which the various sections of humanity—cultures, classes and races—listen to and learn from one another, and such a dialogue demands the equality of partners. True dialogue takes place only among equals. There is no dialogue across the boundary between masters and servants for the master will listen only as long as his power remains intact and the servant will limit his communication to utterances for which he cannot be punished. In fact, to recommend dialogue in a situation of inequality of power is a deceptive ideology of the powerful, who wish to persuade the powerless that harmony and mutual understanding are possible in society without any change in the status quo of power. The openness of truth to totality, then, implies a political elan that fosters significant social change in the distribution of power and the abolition of the master/servant relationships in the human family: a commitment to emancipation.

Gregory Baum, *Truth Beyond Relativism: Karl Mannheim's Sociology of Knowledge* (Milwaukee: Marquette University Press, 1977) 43-44.

14. I emphasize that here I am dealing with current practice and setting aside for the moment the question of whether it should be part of the rite of baptism.

15. Similar instructions are given for the period of the catechumenate itself. The introductory essay in the official rite of initiation allows for a great deal of adaptation in order to achieve this goal of readiness. In fact this essay itself is a study in applying the principal of adaptation to local needs. Thus:

> The period of time suitable to the catechumenate depends on the grace of God and on various circumstances, such as the plan of instruction to be given, the number of catechists, deacons, and priests, the cooperation of the individual catechists, the means necessary to reach the place of the catechumenate and to live there, and the help of the local community. *Nothing can be determined a priori.* [Italics mine.] The bishop has the responsibility of setting the period of time and directing the discipline of the catechumenate. After considering the conditions of their people and region, episcopal conferences should regulate this matter more specifically.

International Committee on English in the Liturgy, *Rite of Christian Initiation of Adults* (Washington, D.C.: United States Catholic Conference, 1974) 1-15. It is worth noting that 1974 was the year that another landmark document of liturgical and catechetical adaptation appeared: The Sacred Congregation for Divine Worship's *Directory for Masses with Children.*

16. The point I make here is similar to the main thrust of Gerard Fourez's thoughtful essay on confirmation, though I find his works/faith dichotomy overstated. Gerard Fourez, "Celebrating the Spirit with Adolescents: More on Confirmation," *The Living Light* 23:3 (1987) 199-206.

17. Joseph A. Komonchak, "Ecclesiology and Social Theory," *The Thomist* 45 (1981) 262-283, at 283.

18. While many catechetical materials, especially those from Latin America offer a critique of economic structures in the light of Jesus' teachings, very little has been written in any language about the economics of the catechetical enterprise itself. When these structures are hidden or ignored or presumed to be religiously sound, they are put beyond critique. Much more attention needs to be given this question, especially in industrialized countries.

19. See for example, *Vamos Caminando: A Peruvian Catechism* (New York: Orbis Books, 1985). The authors of this catechism are listed as the "Pastoral Team of Bambamarca," a most significant way of stating authorship, since it chooses to identify the group, and a clearly stated, "pastoral" group, as its authors. Most important here is how simple the materials are and how open to constant revision they appear to be.

20. For an analysis of some of the issues involved in the writing of textbooks, see David R. Olson, "On the Language and Authority of Textbooks," *Journal of Communication* (Winter, 1980) 186-196. Educational theorist, Michael Apple, raises similar issues in an important essay on the way economic elites successfully dictate curriculum priorities to educators. Written from a secular standpoint, his essay invites correlation with curriculum material used by the churches; see Michael Apple, "Curriculum in the Year 2000: Tensions and Possibilities," *Phi Delta Kappan* (January 1983) 321-326.

4

Liturgy and Catechesis as Counter-Cultural

I have already stated more than once my convictions about the celebrative character of catechesis and its relationship to the ministry of worship. If I am to examine how the local community actually embodies the Gospel, I must look at how it worships and the possible inconsistencies between its celebration of its understandings and its other ways of living out those understandings. The question, I find, is not such an easy one to get at, and so I intend to use two examples—I dare not call them stories, since they are more about stories than actual stories—to help illustrate the problems and opportunities of the conjunction of catechesis and liturgy. Worship and catechesis are liable to become embedded in patterns of practice unshakable without the power of a jolting illustration. The first is a modern-day parable of the Good Samaritan; the second is more of an cautionary tale. The first has to do with the Nazi-era exploits of one Oskar Schindler, a German mechanical engineer born into a Roman Catholic family in a corner of what was formerly East Germany, quite near the Czech and Polish borders. Much to the distress of his devout mother, Schindler, even as a youth, was a negligent Catholic.

Though we actually know few specifics of Schindler's early religious life, evidence from his later life shows it had no hold on him. As his biographer, Thomas Keneally, writes, "If he spends a part of some June morning at Mass, he does not bring back to the villa [his home] much of a sense of sin."[1] Schindler, whatever his earliest catechetical or liturgical experiences, became a notorious

53

womanizer, a drinker of almost legendary capacity, a lover of fast cars and motorcycles, a wheeler-dealer. At one time, he had, in addition to his prayerful Roman Catholic wife, a German mistress, a Polish secretary with whom he had a long affair, and so many more casual liaisons that nobody has tried to number them. He drank only the best and he drank a lot of it, though it proved important he was able to keep his wits through frequent late-night carousings.

What is significant for us, however, is that Schindler, the fallen-away Catholic and sexual profligate, risked his life many times over to protect the lives of Polish and Central European Jews who worked in the munitions factories he managed as part of the Nazi war effort. He had told so many lies and pulled so many strings to save the thousand or so Jews who worked in his factories that he was three times jailed by the Gestapo and could easily have been killed for using his factories as "cover" for a sort of Noah's ark in which to save Jewish lives. Each time arrested he escaped death, but only by bribing his way with large sums of money, jewels, and goods.

Near the end of the war, in a last desperate and ultimately successful effort to preserve his workers' lives for a few more months, he moved his factory from Cracow to a somewhat remote area in the village of Brinnlitz, not far from where the Czech, German, and Polish borders meet. Since it was an area near where Schindler himself was born and since a Roman Catholic church was a prominent structure in the town, we know that some or even many Roman Catholics lived there, certainly many Christians. And yet, some of these villagers—the exact number is unknown to us— tried what political power they had to keep out these Jews. In fact when the first group of Jewish workers arrived, they met graffiti signs exhorting, "Keep the Jews out of Brinnlitz!"

As a Roman Catholic, I could not read Keneally's book and especially this part of the book without wondering about the worship life of these people—Christians whose inhospitality denied not just place to these condemned Jewish workers but would also have denied them the slender threads of life they had managed to preserve. What gospel did these "believers" follow? Were some of these haters-of-Jews considered devout? Did any of them have a devotion, piously saying their daily rosary? Did any often spend hours in prayer before the Blessed Sacrament? Did some of them attend daily Mass in the village church at Brinnlitz? But then, why all these questions?

For me they arise from the irony that the one in this tale closest to Jesus' way is the womanizing, non-worshiping, Oskar Schindler, who risked his life to stand in solidarity with victims, the man for whom every single life of these victims was precious and priceless. Keneally's story, masterfully told from a literary point of view, faces us all with basic questions about what being religious means in our day and what following Jesus means. Like the parables of the New Testament, Schindler's story gives us pause, calls for us to stop, scratch our heads, and mutter aloud, "Wait, I don't understand." Over-exposed to the Good Samaritan, dulled to the ironies of his goodness, we need to find him again in the face of Oskar Schindler, the liturgical and doctrinal illiterate. The one who chose to absent himself from the worshiping assembly was more a disciple than those who named God as loving creator in that assembly and ate the bread of unity.

The second story—and one to which I will return in the following chapter—was begun for me in a chance conversation with a Maryknoll missioner hounded out of Guatemala by death threats. Chatting over coffee at a conference we both were attending, he told how he had worked training catechists in a remote area of Guatemala near the Mexican border. Before he finally left the country, three hundred of the peasant catechists he had trained had been murdered by government death squads.[2] Told in a matter of fact way by a man my own age intimately involved in what he described, this man's account, together with the numbers killed and the fact that he knew each one personally, shocked me and kept recurring to mind in the following weeks, until one day during our Peace through Justice Week at St. John's University, a woman from Nicaragua showed slides of camps in her country for refugees from Guatemala. She casually remarked that in one camp there were only women and children because their husbands who were catechists had been murdered. Only then did I see the catechetical significance of what I had heard.

Here we have the catechist as subversive, the catechist as a dangerous person. The phrase for catechist in Latin America is "delegado de la palabra," representative of the word. Obviously, to some in Guatemala that word is a dangerous word because it is a transforming word, an upsetting word, one that calls for the replacing of everyday injustice and unjust systems with ways in keeping with the kingdom of God. And so a simple man translating the word of God into ordinary speech is such a threat to the status quo that he must be eliminated, murdered. What struck me forcefully in that moment of insight was that in many United States parishes—I would say in most—the catechist is the most predictable and the safest of persons. There is little to fear from the catechist's ministry or message. Aimed predominately at children and rarely dealing with questions of justice, the catechist's word tends to foster predictable and correct behavior.

I choose to start with these two examples because they potentially harbor some of the questions liturgists and catechists must face now and for the future. The fact of liturgical assemblies in itself guarantees nothing at all about fidelity to Jesus' way; nor does the fact of catechesis, which can in one case electrify with its message and in another impose a kind of social blindness. In exploring the implications of each example, we face ironies about communities of persons who name themselves as disciples of Jesus and who seemingly celebrate that fact in worship, but on whom the Gospel has little hold. In one we have a man who was almost killed doing what I judge to be the word of God; in the other we have many men who were murdered for announcing that word in a way that challenged social structures. Both tales raise questions about the possibilities of trivializing our liturgical and catechetical concerns: of liturgists becoming preoccupied with the worship act or event and of forgetting that its context is the life of a group of persons who do or do not embody gospel values in deeds, not just in words; of catechists being satisfied with renditions of the Gospel that induce a kind of religious slumber.

We could be aesthetically astute in our latter-day village churches of Brinnlitz, while ignoring the matters of greater moment. On the other hand, parish catechetical leaders can become the technicians of sacramental preparation and ritualization, focused behaviorally if not theoretically on programs for children and in effect avoiding the deeper questions of the lived faith of the community. Such a catechesis has little relationship with the dangerous message of the Guatemalan martyrs. In hopes of probing more deeply into questions hidden in my two illustrations, I wish to highlight an important recurrent theme found in contemporary liturgical writing.

Worship as Communal Embodiment

The theme is this: liturgical action is an embodiment of the community's life. I have been interested in this theme since being asked several years ago to address the question of whether the liturgy can speak to teens?[3] I quickly decided that the question was wrongheaded. The liturgy is not some sort of message; nor is it a communiqué system. It does not speak to; it speaks out of. Liturgy is expressive human activity and acts as a symbolic expression of the life of a particular group of people. It is like what eating is for married couples. Watch a couple engage in the familiar activity of eating together and you may get insight into their relationship, since eating together embodies more than personal nourishment. It tends to embody a way of being together. Like such a common meal, liturgy is expressive activity.

Several liturgical scholars have worked on this matter. Geoffrey Wainwright's book, *Doxology* has helped us see that liturgical practice embodies an entire stance toward God.[4] Worship is as much a key theological source as are doctrinal statements, and if one wishes to find out the lived belief of a particular church, examine the prayers, hymns, and rituals they use. Jungmann and others had traversed and charted that terrain before him, but Wainwright, also a cartographer, produced a new conceptual map.[5] Liberation theologians are carrying on and extending this work, emphasizing the social context of worship. They recognize the possibility of a group sacramentalizing their own kinship, ethnic, and socio-economic bonds and privileges, blessing these with religious symbols that should radically question them. To gather around the altar to celebrate Jesus' victory over evil, while tolerating or even colluding in the victimization of one's sisters and brothers, is to be at least incoherent, if not actually to participate in a lie.

Problem of the Dominant Culture

Another person writing about this matter, but at a more popular level, was the late Robert Hovda. In his "Amen Corner" pieces for *Worship*,[6] Hovda examined the relationship between culture and worship, alerting us to the danger that worship could embody a dominant culture when it should be confronting it. A community's consciousness could be so dominated by cultural presuppositions that even in worship those presuppositions have more meaning and power for us than our commitment to Jesus' way. Hovda warned us of being locked into particular cultural horizons. He wrote, for example:

> Cultural adaptation is a two-edged sword in the liturgical life of the churches. If it means that liturgy is the work of a concrete

faith community in a particular time and place, and therefore, that it cannot be celebrated except in the context and out of the stuff of that church's life and experience, it is simply a requisite of true public worship. If, however, it should become, by some jaded process in the corporate psyche of the local church, an excuse for capitulating to inimical aspects of the culture of the time and place, then it is devilish indeed. Then it becomes an excuse for avoiding the gospel call to reconcile, to liberate and unify the human family, to witness to and work for the reign of God.[7]

Hovda's point is that liturgy embodies the life of a group of people. Where such a group seeks to espouse Jesus' way, they must resist the negative aspects of the dominant culture, lest it find its way in just as sand on a windy day at the beach gets into everything, including your sandwich.

I find somewhat more attention to this problem in liturgical studies than I do in catechetical writing. For example, for twenty years the youth retreat movement, a catechetical effort, has been presenting to youth, pretty much unchallenged, a middle-class Jesus, a Jesus of comfort representing God's personal love for the individual youth, the assuager of adolescent anxieties, the giver of the Jesus hug. What is missing is the Jesus who confronted social, including political structures, and paid for it with his life. The catechetical message in such an approach is that the Jesus who exposed injustice in his day and who was dangerous like the Guatemalan catechists is dismissible, while the Jesus of the personal hug is indispensable. Thus, in this catechesis and the worship which confirms it on these weekends, the man for others has been transformed into the man for us, who accepts and cherishes our cultural values. The question of how catechetical or liturgical programs embody cultural presuppositions is one around which catechists and liturgists can unite in common effort.[8]

Worship and Class

For a glimpse of how cultural presuppositions operate in the worshiping assembly, Robert Coles' description of worship among the middle and upper classes is helpful. In the churches of the privileged classes, he writes:

> There is more order [than in the churches of the poor], but order of a different kind, more self-regard in the way in which

one worships. Attention is paid, and in a certain way: to what one sees and what one hears and what one reads, yes, but also, significantly, to oneself. You enter the churches of the privileged full of yourself. You are well-dressed, pleased to be in a place where you are treated well, with great respect and personal attention, and where there will be—and this is important—no surprises. The format is fixed and the words and music are modulated, no extremes either from church or from those who are at worship. Without having been told, you understand that if anything happens to you of a spiritual nature, you are to keep it to yourself. Just as there are certain words used in certain ways in rural services, these privileged places of worship have theirs and time moves along here in a measured (but pleasant) fashion. By contrast [with the worship of the poor] there are no unplanned stops at this word, no responses or outbreaks to that moment of sound; in these places of worship there are no abrupt moves forward or doubling back, either in response to the minister or those at worship. As I said, the privileged ones do not like to be surprised; they have not come to be confronted or to be put into situations where they are not in control.[9]

The problem Coles describes here is a fundamental one affecting worship.

The worship of the assembly actually does truly embody and express the *lived* commitments of the group, whatever these are.[10] The fact that worship is expressive human activity has its negative side. When the life of the community is in some fundamental way unfaithful to the Gospel, then worship somehow expresses that fact *also*, becoming a counter sign. I have already raised this question about those Christians of Brinnlitz, who sought to exclude the Jews, but it must also be raised about the elites of countries like Guatemala—almost all of whom consider themselves Christians—but who profit from a social system inflicting misery and death on victimized multitudes. Of course the same question must be raised about all in the nations of the Northern Hemisphere who profit from the exploitation of those in the South. "It remains a persistent challenge to the Gospel and culture debate that the first atomic bomb in human history, the bomb that destroyed Hiroshima, has been called the `Christian bomb'."[11]

Coles' depiction of the worship of the privileged ones suggests how thoroughly the life patterns built into groups of people by

their class and social situation enter and become part of the worshiping assembly. These patterns affect their habits of the heart,
their spirits. Behind the question of worship is that of spirituality,
understood not as the mode of one's prayer but as the shape of
one's human spirit. This is a matter I will deal with in greater detail
in the following chapter, but some comments about it are in order
here.

A special dilemma for both liturgists and catechists is that of
helping middle class and upper class Christians find a gospel-
centered spirituality that affects lifestyle.[12] Why should this task be
so difficult? The reason is that there are cultural forces so massive
affecting all of us today that these forces in effect over-ride whatever the outcome might come from an hour's dalliance before the
altar or of time spent in some catechetical program. Our society is
now dominated by hundreds of thousands of well-trained, highly
paid, clever, and technically proficient orchestrators of attention,
whose task is to make sure we pay attention to those matters to
which their employers want us to attend.[13]

We live in a world characterized by a wild proliferation of
images, printed images, both verbal and graphic, electronically
reproduced images and audio images. If it is true that those who
control the way the world is named control consciousness, it is also
true that those who control the images by which we interpret the
world also control consciousness.[14] In a world where there are so
many forces vying for our attention, the crisis of the human spirit
may very well be the crisis of knowing what matters are worth our
attention. Our spirits are defined by our attention.

Attention and Imagery

Pay attention—as an individual or as a group—to trivial matters
as a way of life and one's life becomes characterized by trivia. Pay
attention to commercial imagery concocted to bring endlessly before consciousness the next set of products to purchase, and one's
spirit becomes preoccupied with having and consuming, and even
one's ordinary speech becomes littered with commercial imagery.
One may eventually approach worship or catechesis as a commercial product, evaluated by whether it does or does not satisfy, that
is, enlarge the self or comfort the self. I am alluding to here a
problem for those of us wishing to direct attention to Jesus' own
imagery of compassion, of mutuality across culturally set barriers,
and his call to imagine a new day of justice and loving kindness
among persons.

It may be clear to all of us that worship involves a re-focused attention and that catechesis is a sort of attention therapy. Still, our volunteer catechists inhabit the land of commercially concocted imagery as do the chief celebrants presiding at our eucharists.[15] To compound the problem so do we ourselves dwell in that land, and we tend to dwell there not as if it were the place of our exile or of our wandering passage but as if it were the land of milk and honey. The positive side to this problem is that it joins us together, catechists and liturgists in a common task. Since the religious meanings in ritual can be easily overridden or dominated by cultural presuppositions, liturgists cannot counter the power of high-tech enculturation by themselves. Neither can catechists by themselves successfully counter this problem, as current attempts at a catechesis of peace are showing us.

The only decisive counterforce to the cultural pressures of our time may be the power of whole communities struggling together toward an appropriate spirituality characterized by a transformed way of paying attention. These communities will be formed with the collaboration of liturgists and catechists. We know that in our Christian origins, liturgy and catechesis were siblings, but like some other siblings they have tended to drift apart as they have gotten older. Now we need to re-establish their proper close bonds if we are to assist communities in becoming credible as measured by the Gospel.

Understanding Images

An important task in liturgical-catechetical collaboration in an image-dominated culture is that of becoming more aware of images and how they work. While it is true that in an image culture like ours we are all almost assailed by images, the deeper problem is not that we look at images ceaselessly. The deeper problem is that we look at reality through images.[16] In particular cultures, certain images provide the lenses through which we view reality. As with any kind of lens, we can easily forget that we are seeing through it. We do not see the lens exactly because we are so busy looking through it.

A good example of a lens image might be the image of woman in our society.[17] This "image" goes beyond any image of an particular woman and even beyond the specific knowledge we might have of anatomy, physiology, psychology, or even history. Actually the lens image of woman precedes such specific kinds of knowledge. Instead the image of woman we have selects the aspects of knowledge we choose to pay attention to but selects them according to certain values and arranges them into a pattern. In this sense, the image of woman has with it a whole train of associations and expectations that are pre-conscious and closely tied to feelings.

At the university where I teach I find two very different images of woman in the young men I meet. They in turn are continually evaluating the womanliness of the women they meet according to criteria latent in these lens images. For some a woman is a coy, dependent, not-overbright individual with a particular "look," usually a look corresponding to fashion and to anatomical calculations. Such a woman does not readily disagree with a man, is apt to smile a lot in his presence, and takes special pleasure in his sense of humor, that is, laughs at his jokes. Other men have a different image of woman. For them, a woman is a self-directed adult, compassionate, reflective, possibly witty, but in general able to meet other adults of either sex on an equal footing. She is not better than men but she is not less either. She does not hold that men and women are the same, but she does hold they are equal.

What we have here is more than simple personality preferences. We have lens images that select and arrange for us the significance of what we see and experience. To understand images more fully, we must recognize that underlying these lens images are even more basic images, which Gibson Winter calls comprehensive metaphors, functioning almost the way the eye does as the primal lens through which we see.[18] If the lens image is taken for granted because we are too busy seeing through it, the lens of the eye is taken for granted in a much more fundamental way. Comprehensive metaphors, then, furnish coherence to our world and impose a fundamental pattern on all our experience.

The comprehensive metaphor I wish to examine briefly is the domination-subordination metaphor, mainly because it is a metaphor that characterizes the consciousness of many in our society and because it is at odds with the message of Jesus.[19] This metaphor or mindset tends to break personal and social reality down into two groups: superior and inferior. Within this metaphor, the inferior need to be directed by the superior, need to be under their control or their domination. The domination-subordination metaphor, then, works out of dichotomies and a variety of them. There is the winners-losers dichotomy. In victory or winning we get proof of superiority and of how rightful it is to dominate the beaten, defeated, or simply unequal group. The winner-loser dichotomy splits the superior from the inferior but also the stronger from the weaker.

It may be difficult, for example, to convince a young man who unconsciously uses this metaphor that because women's physical strength is of a different sort than men's, it does not necessarily follow that women are poorer athletes. In the universe interpreted through the domination-subordination metaphor, stronger means superior and dominant. These dichotomies—superior-inferior, winner-loser, stronger-weaker—find their way into our everyday language, as when in popular speech certain individuals are named "losers" and other "winners." Winners are those who successfully dominate. They are the ones on top of things.

In domination-subordination thinking, we have the spatial imagery of those on top and those on the bottom, higher to lower, superior to inferior. Also in popular speech we have a range of expressions about being ahead or getting ahead or getting the advantage, as having an advantage in a race. Of course, we spoke of the arms "race" where the Soviets were ahead and where we must be ahead. Thus images from the playing field are transformed to address the political arena.[20] "Clout" might be another popular word that fits into domination-subordination thinking, combining imagery of the baseball bat with that of the pre-historic club.

If we examine the imagery that emerges from this comprehensive metaphor, we might decide it is at odds with the Gospel. Think for a moment of the use of the word "one" in various contexts in our society, especially in two very different celebrative contexts. In sports, the word "one" usually means number one, the victors, those who have dominated their inferiors. We have all often seen persons prancing around, shouting ecstatically, "We're number one." In the eucharistic liturgy, however, the word "one" is used over and over again, but here to signify the human unity of those joined together by the Spirit of Jesus. Here "one" means communion and unity.

Once one sees the metaphor or examines the lens as a lens, a fundamental shift takes place in one's consciousness. No amount of theological sleight-of-hand, for instance, about why women may not preside at the assembly will hide for those aware of this metaphor an understanding that hidden in our ritualization of unity is a cultural pattern of male domination. So there I am back to our problem. We ourselves can find ourselves operating out of the same culturally conditioned mindset as everyone else in our society.[21]

To use a catechetical example, the problem of confirmation today is not inadequate catechesis. Reams have been written about how to do such a catechesis. The problem is not our understanding of the history of the sacrament, which by now has been amply spelled out in easily accessible sources. The core problem is not even the question of pastoral strategy. The problem is that in the implementation of pastoral strategy for this sacrament, we have been replaying in a sacramental mode the basic domination-subordination metaphor, which is in such ascendency in our society.

The anger shown by the nineteen and twenty-year olds I meet about their own confirmations is that it was forced on them. They had no choice. They were told they had one, but that telling was all the more galling because they knew in fact that they had none. As I explained in the last chapter, because of their tender age they were coerced, dominated, and now they resent it. I usually tell them I want to set up new tribunals in every diocese to process confirmation annulments for all those who were forced through the ritual and who never received the sacrament.

To echo the argument of the previous chapter, could it be that the reason so many of our parish catechetical programs are still preoccupied with the sacramental catechesis of children rather than with adult catechesis as called for by the General Catechetical Directory is that children more easily come under adult domination?

The reason the three hundred peasant catechists were murdered in Guatemala, I presume, is that their very presentation of the word questioned and subverted the domination-subordination patterns operative in that nation. The reason catechetical leaders in our own country are no trouble is not that the metaphor is not operative here but that we do not question it. We could all ask ourselves how many times we have heard pastors praise their parishes and found underlying their euphoria, not joy in fidelity to Jesus' way but a subtle claim their parish had surpassed others and was better.

Shifting the Images

If I come to any conclusion from my own study of how images and metaphors function in our society and of how easily they can co-opt the network of meanings we call our tradition, it is that catechists and liturgists alike need to explore more consciously the power-laden metaphors proclaimed in our catechesis and dramatized in our worship.[22] We can too easily sidestep the radical, culture-questioning images and substitute slicker, more easily acceptable ones. For instance, an easily overlooked but a highly appropriate metaphor for Christians in our time may be that of the exile. How can we live in a nation that has a first-strike policy still not abjured after the 1993 SALT II nuclear weapons reductions, a policy that theoretically at least contemplates killing millions of our sisters and brothers in other lands, without feeling like an exile, at least in the sense that the psychological and spiritual landscape is quite foreign to us? And yet we can develop our catechesis of faith story and faith journey in ways that exclude any sense of exile while justifying individualistic progress toward greater religious self-actualization.[23]

To use another example, the potentially powerful imagery of the people of God, who in and out of exile communally embody the promise of God, can be reduced to family imagery with its concurrent metaphors of warmth and intimacy, an imagery of private relationships rather than of public witness.[24] These shifts reduce the ambience of catechesis and worship to middle-class ones and in doing so take the edge off the gospel message.

The re-examination of Christian imagery with an eye to posing it as a counter imagery to that of the dominant culture is being done by liberation theologians. Enrique Dussel reclaims from Latin American history the figure of Bartholome de las Casas, the first priest ordained in the New World. De las Cases had accompanied a conquistador in the conquest of Cuba and was given as a reward a band of Indian slaves to work his lands. But this priest and slave-owner was converted and came to see that the wheat for the eucharistic bread was harvested by his slaves beaten down by criminally oppressive exploitation. So clearly did he see the blasphemous connection between the bread harvested in oppression and the eucharistic bread that, after freeing his slaves, he declared himself unable to celebrate the eucharist and began denouncing on gospel grounds the oppression of the Indians. Refusing to celebrate the eucharist as a protest against injustice that had in a sense infected the very altar of the eucharist is a potentially powerful example that questions the social context of the eucharist and reclaims the counter-cultural power of shared bread and cup.[25]

I was reminded of de las Casas when I heard a speaker provoke and deeply disturb a group of committed adults with the following idea: Christians should have no church building so that they could be more prompt to worship in those places where the poor and outcasts are found. Her reasoning was that since we come from a long tradition of announcing the good news to captives we ought to assemble with them and recall the presence of the Lord in their, and our own, midst. The God named Father by Jesus should be worshiped, she maintained, only in the context of care for others, especially the poor. *They are the house of God.* She was using poetic speech, stretching the limits of language while also stretching human vision and breaking through neat categories.

She added another important corollary to her first insight: her conviction that no worship is possible except in the context of a community's sense of its own poverties and in the recognition of this poverty as it links with all other poverties in the world. Her point is borne out by the parable of the pharisee and tax collector, with its suggestion that true worship arises out of the conviction of one's own poverty and its connectedness to that of others.

Insights like hers and those of Enrique Dussel can aid middle class persons seeking to re-direct their own spirituality more toward liberation and resistance.[26] In our day, Christian spirituality involves moving away from patterns of compliance and toward patterns of resistance. If ever our communities come to adopt a public stance of solidarity with victims, then we will know we are moving again as a people in response to God's will. We will be in good company with others who similarly have established such solidarity with victims. Leading the way will be Jesus whom we call Lord and, among a horde of others, somewhere will be one Oskar Schindler, happy to find himself in the good company of the Guatemalan martyrs.

Notes

1. Thomas Keneally, *Schindler's List* (New York: Penguin Books, 1983) 33.

2. The missioner is Rev. Daniel Jensen, M.M. His catechists were from the Department of Huehuetenango, which comprises the diocese of the same name. Jensen left Guatemala in 1981, but the murders, which began in 1978, continue to the present. For background and corroboration, see note 1 of Chapter 7.

3. See "Can the Liturgy Speak to Today's Teenagers," in Michael Warren, ed., *Readings and Resources in Youth Ministry* (Winona, MN: St. Mary's Press, 1987) 30-40.

4.. Geoffrey Wainwright, *Doxology: The Praise of God in Worship, Doctrine, and Life* (New York: Oxford University Press, 1980).

5. Similarly, Mary Collins has helped us see the patriarchal presuppositions embodied in the very symbols and rubrics of our rituals, though I fear the importance of her study may have been overlooked. Her view is that

> Part of the task of liturgical theology will be always be descriptive: What is being set out in these texts and rites? I suggest that the

contemporary task of liturgical theology is preeminently critical: Is the faith vision being celebrated adequate? Is it congruent with human and ecclesial experience and expectations of the saving grace of Christ?

See Mary Collins, "Critical Questions for Liturgical Theology," *Worship* 53:4 (1979) 302-317, at 302.

6. I have in mind especially his columns for *Worship*, Volume 58 (1984), Numbers 1, 2, 3.

7. Robert W. Hovda, "The Amen Corner," *Worship* 58:3 (1984) 251.

8. A valuable contribution to the question I am raising here is David Power, "Liturgy and Culture," *East Asian Pastoral Review* 21:4 (1984) 348-360.

9. Robert Coles and George Abbott White, "The Religion of the Privileged Ones," *Cross Currents* 31:1 (1981) 1-14, at 7.

10. I realize the matter is somewhat more complicated than I have expressed it here. More is being expressed in worship than the community's activity would indicate. Worship, when it is authentic, expresses also the unfinished character, the "more," of the community's life. The Spirit of Jesus who gathers the community together is testimony that there is more to its life than can be fully worked out by its participants. But when this fact is part of what the community expresses in the worshipping assembly, the act of worship itself subverts the self-congratulatory atmosphere described by Robert Coles, above. Repentance must be an integral part of worship.

11. Brigitte Kahl, "Human Culture and the Integrity of Creation," *Ecumenical Review* 39:2 (1987) 129.

12. Much more work needs to be done along the lines of Matthew Lamb, "Christian Spirituality and Social Justice," *Horizons* 10:1 (1983) 32-49; Joe Holland, "The Spiritual Crisis of Modern Culture," Occasional Paper, Washington, D.C.: The Center of Concern, 1983. I find concern for lifestyle to be the underlying one in Regis Duffy, *Real Presence* (San Francisco: Harper and Row, 1982); Matthew Lamb, *Solidarity with Victims* (New York: Crossroad, 1982); John F. Kavanaugh, *Following Christ in a Consumer Society* (New York: Orbis, 1982). For even more sources on this concern, see Chapter 11.

13. For a useful overview of this problem, see Stuart Ewen and Elizabeth Ewen, *Channels of Desire: Mass Images and the Shaping of American Consciousness* (New York: McGraw-Hill Co., 1982).

14. See Barbara Goldsmith, "The Meaning of Celebrity," New York *Times Magazine* (4 December 1983) 75ff., and Kennedy Fraser, "The Fashionable Mind," *New Yorker* (13 March 1978) 87ff.

15. John H. McKenna shows that liturgy need not contravene popular culture in "Liturgy: Toward Liberation or Oppression," *Worship* 56:4 (1982) 291-308; see also A. Pieris, "Spirituality in a Liberative Perspective," in *An Asian Theology of Liberation* (New York: Orbis, 1988) 3-14, esp. 4-7.

16. A valuable work on this question is Gibson Winter, *Liberating Creation* (New York: Crossroads, 1981).

17. Here I am following Charles Davis, "Religion and the Sense of the Sacred," CTSA *Proceedings* 31 (1976) 87-105, esp. 87-91.

18. See Winter, *Liberating Creation* 1-28.

19. This metaphor is explored in Lamb, "Christian Spirituality." Of special help has been "Domination-Subordination," Chapter One of Jean Baker Miller, *Toward a New Psychology of Women* (Boston: Beacon Press, 1976) 3-12.

20. See George Orwell's treatment of this transformation in his brief essay "The Sporting Spirit," in George Orwell, *Selected Writings* (London, Heinemann, 1947) 159-162.

21. Those wishing to examine the matter of images and metaphors more deeply may find helpful Chapters 5 and 6 of my book on cultural analysis; see Michael Warren, *Communications and Cultural Analysis: A Religious View* (Bergin and Garvey, 1992).

22. A valuable treatment is Mark Searle, "Liturgy as Metaphor," *Worship* 55:2 (1981) 98-120.

23. See Gregory Baum's critique of the journey image as middle-class, in "Theology Questions Psychiatry," *The Ecumenist* 20:4 (May-June 1982) 55-59; and Gustavo Gutierrez' use of the exile metaphor in *We Drink from Our Own Wells* (New York: Orbis, 1984).

24. See Parker Palmer, *The Company of Strangers* (New York: Crossroad, 1983), and Robert N. Bellah, "Religion and Power in America Today," *Commonweal* (3 December 1982) 650-655.

25. Enrique Dussel, "The Bread of the Eucharist Celebration as a Sign of Justice in the Community," in Mary Collins and David Power, eds., *Can We Always Celebrate the Eucharist? Concilium* 152 (1982) 56-65. See also in the same volume, the important treatment of the problem of tablesharing in 1 Corinthinans: Elizabeth Schüssler Fiorenza, "Tablesharing and the Celebration of the Eucharist" 3-12.

26. Two useful sources for further reflection on resistance are: "Toward a Theology of Resistance," in Gordon Zahn, ed., *Thomas Merton: The Nonviolent Alternative* (New York: Farrar, Straus, Giroux, 1980) 186-192; and Dorothee Solle, "Resistance: Toward a First World Theology," *Christianity and Crisis* 39:12 (23 July 1979) 178-182.

5

Catechesis and Spirituality

The origins of this chapter lie in several years of undertaking what I used to call "ministry to spirituality." Actually the ministry was a catechetical ministry with adults who initially were seeking deeper theological understanding and a renewed prayer life. I came to see that they needed a way of thinking about spirituality that would help them connect and unify the various aspects of their lives. I assumed that a correct understanding of spirituality would give them insight into the broad scope of discipleship today and enable them to undertake the ultimate form of spiritual direction, the direction of one's own life. Thus my intention was to provide a language by which they might accurately name and discuss their search for an appropriate spirituality. Eventually I came to see how the very undertaking of a catechesis of spirituality involves an irony to be explained at the end of this chapter.

Apart from these origins, the central "interest" behind this chapter is a search for an approach to spirituality that would be congruent with a commitment to justice among Christians in the *ekklesia*. I am seeking a connection between spirituality and justice, especially for those struggling toward discipleship in a consumerist society. The obstacles to this discipleship assume a new character in a time when the promotion of products is tied to the amplification of images, which capture the imaginations of all and subtly shape their lifestyle. Thus I am seeking a spirituality appropriate to those living in industrialized societies and struggling against a consumerist ethos.

I begin with two convictions about a spirituality for Christians appropriate to our time and situation in the "first world." First, one cannot approach the question of a Christian spirituality, particularly in cultures tied to an economics of consumption, without careful attention to lifestyle. The challenge of finding an appropriate spirituality is partly the challenge of finding an appropriate lifestyle. Second, the crisis of the human spirit in our time is the crisis of knowing what things are worth paying attention to. For a follower of Jesus, the discipline of spirituality in our time must in large part be the discipline, not so much of praying effectively as of paying attention effectively to the proper matters. By binding attention and action, consciousness and commitment, these convictions admittedly serve the biases of an educator seeking to influence consciousness, ways of perceiving, and ultimately, ways of acting. Any sidestepping of the twin religious challenges of attention and behavior would betray the inner core of spirituality and lead to a false understanding.

Mistaken Approaches to Spirituality

There are two ways of approaching spirituality that lead us away from the sort of holistic understanding I wish to propose. Each approach makes an opposite sort of error: one a conjunctive error, in the sense that it equates two realities that are not quite the same; the second, a disjunctive error, separating two matters that need to be conjoined. Here I will deal with the first error and then with the definition of spirituality before getting to the second error. The "conjunctive" error equates spirituality with prayer. One might think that this wrongful equation was ended among Roman Catholics by the theological renewal ratified by Vatican II, but the error survives. Aloysius Pieris, in an analysis of the spirituality problematic, notes that "in . . . some recent pronouncements of the official Church, there is a tendency to take a narrow concept of contemplation as spirituality *par excellence*, if not also as spirituality *per se*."[1]

In identifying prayer and spirituality, the idea seems to be: get praying and one will become more spiritual. However, prayer is an aspect of spirituality, indeed a key aspect,[2] but one that emerges from a spirituality. If the wider dimensions of spirituality are ignored, then one's prayer will be inauthentic. Jon Sobrino's detailed analysis of the prayer of Jesus highlights the many times in the New Testament Jesus points out the dangers of inauthentic prayer.[3] To stress the non-identifiability of prayer and spirituality, one must be ready to lay out a definition of spirituality. Here, before examining my second, disjunctive error, I must turn to this matter.

Among Roman Catholics over the past quarter century there have been many attempts to heal the disjunction and recover a broader, more holistic understanding of spirituality than the one that puts spirituality and prayer into the same shoe.[4] For example, in *A Theology of Liberation*, Gustavo Gutierrez claims "a spirituality is *a concrete manner*, inspired by the Spirit, *of living the Gospel*; it is *a definite way of living* 'before the Lord,' in solidarity with all persons. . ."[5] [Italics mine.] Here Gutierrez sees spirituality as broader than prayer, though his elaboration of this matter was to wait almost fifteen years till publication. His book, *We Drink from Our Own Wells*, is an attempt to lay out in a nuanced detail the Christian spirituality of the oppressed. As the metaphor in its title implies, his book sees spirituality as a religious culture, that is, as an entire way of perceiving and of structuring one's commitments.[6] Prayer is authentic only in the context of the wider way of life called for by a particular religion.[7] In a similar, broad approach, Carolyn Osiek describes spirituality as "the experience, reflection and articulation of the assumptions and consequences of religious faith as it is lived in a concrete situation."[8] This description emphasizes the relation between the habits of the heart and the actual concrete way of living one's life.

For my own description of spirituality, I look for a approach that will allow us to recognize the crucial point that everyone has a spirituality. In a very real sense, one cannot *not* have a spirituality. Every human person as an embodied spirit is a being whose spirit has been shaped by commitments, choices, hopes, uses of time, and so forth. The question can never be: Will we have a spirituality but rather what kind of spirituality will we have. Hitler had a spirituality, as did Harry S. Truman. Their spirits stood for something. There is danger in consumerist societies that many persons who verbally name themselves as religious in fact have consumerist spiritualities, with their hearts ever intent on the next things they will buy.[9] Noting that such life-directing desires represent a root kind of spirituality should give pause to all seeking a Christian spirituality. We get this sense of spirituality when we stand at a person's coffin and find ourselves reflecting on what this individual stood for in his or her life. Perhaps we could refer to this kind of spirituality as "lower case" spirituality.

Upper-case spirituality involves an active, disciplined search for God, the result of a religious transformation seen as a gifted act of God. For a description of spirituality in this explicit religious sense, I have found most helpful the following one: Spirituality is a *systematic way* of attending to the presence of God.[10] Several features of this description are helpful. First, it is open to recognizing that every religious system has its own spirituality, because each is a system for paying attention to the presence of God. In spite of the impression sometimes given by Christian writings, spirituality is not an exclusively Christian term. Christians in no way diminish their special attention to the presence of God-in-Jesus by acknowledging that spirituality is something they have in common with all other faiths.[11]

Also valuable in this description is its stress on "way," modified by the sort of purposefulness implied by "systematic." In this sense spirituality can also be examined as a discipline, that is, the careful way of following worked out by those who wish to be disciples. Further, the way we follow provides us access to its consequent form of attention; our way of living determines our consciousness and the matters we can choose to attend to. I find this last feature especially important in our time, which could be called the time of fractured attention. Finally, if we accept this understanding of spirituality, the whole matter moves from abstraction to the level of concrete acts. Ways are specific and thus discernable. I will return to these aspects of spirituality after examining the second mistaken approach to spirituality.

The disjunctive error in spirituality is the one that separates spirituality from the world in which we live. As a disjunction, it splits things apart which are not meant to be cut off from each other. Though many writers warn against this error,[12] the approach to spirituality that pays attention to the things of God in such a way that attention is drawn away from pressing human issues persists.[13] Matthew Fox outlines three "spiritual cultures" that have influenced Roman Catholics in the U.S. and which he claims need to be unlearned: the Platonic, Jansenist, and Roman-Ecclesial. Fox rejects all three precisely because they tend to ignore the world in which we live, as if there is some spiritual world outside time and even cut off from the body.[14] The point will be obvious enough to most of those who read this essay, though it is not so clear to many adults seeking a sharper attentiveness to the presence of God. In clarifying this disjunction for adults, a helpful illustration of the problem can be found in a comparison between the early and later life of Pope John XXIII.

In earlier sections of Pope John's *Journal of a Soul*, his journals give insight into a spirituality that was a mix of the three "spiritual cultures" noted by Fox. For example, his entry of September 3, 1898, written while he was home on a visit from the seminary:

> I still need more invocations, especially while I am studying. They will help me out in the difficulties I often come up against because of my lack of brains—and they will give me more energy. I must take note also that I tend to linger too long in the kitchen after supper, talking things over with my family. They always talk about their worries and this depresses me. Indeed, it would not be surprising if at times they led me to forget the great law of charity. So as soon as the rosary is over, I will say a few words and then go to my room.
>
> They certainly have their worries, and many of them! *But my own worries are of a different kind. Theirs are about their bodies and material things; mine are about souls.*[15] [Italics mine.]

In his own words, the young Roncalli was expressing his difficulty with seeing and accepting the connection between his spiritual quest and the concrete circumstances of his life at that moment, living in a specific home with specific people coping with their concrete circumstances of life.

The previous year during a retreat, he set out for himself guiding principles of a rule of life. He called these the "Rules for Purity." Rules 2, 3, 4 give their overall flavor.

> 2. I will take pains to mortify my own feelings severely, keeping them within the bounds of Christian modesty; to this end I will set a special guard on my eyes, which St. Ambrose called "deceitful snares" and St. Anthony of Padua "thieves of the soul," avoiding, as far as possible, large gatherings of people for feasts, etc., and when I am obliged to be present on these occasions I will make quite sure that nothing that even suggests the sin against holy purity may offend my eyes; on such occasions they shall remain downcast.
>
> 3. I will also take care to behave with the greatest decorum when I am passing through towns or other places full of people, never looking at posters or illustrations, or shops which

might contain indecent objects, bearing in mind the words of
scripture, "Do not look around in the streets of a city; nor
wander about in its deserted sections."

And even in the churches, besides behaving with edifying
decorum during the sacred functions, I will never gaze at
beautiful things of any sort, such as pictures, carvings, statues
or other objects of art which, however slightly, offend against
propriety, and particularly where paintings are concerned.

4. With women of whatever station in life, even if they are
related to me or are holy women, I will be particularly cau-
tious, avoiding their familiarity, company or conversation,
especially if they are young women. Nor will I ever fix my eyes
on their faces, mindful of what the Holy Spirit teaches us: "Do
not look intently at a virgin, lest you stumble and incur penalties for her." [Eccles. 9:5] So I will never confide in them in any
way, but when I have to speak with them I will see that my
speech is "dry, brief, prudent, and correct."[16]

While we may appreciate the cautions a young seminarian seeking a celibate life might have over the "temptations" found in the
places and circumstances named here, they indicate, among other
things, a disjunctive spirituality. Of course, he did not carry this
spirituality to his grave but was able to replace it with a quite
different orientation, best illustrated perhaps by a small incident
that occurred near the end of his life. Presiding in St. Peter's amidst
the elaborate celebration of a beatification or canonization, he became totally distracted in communicating through signs with a
little girl in the assembly with whom he had established eye contact. Apparently for the later Roncalli, his special attention was
reserved for God's presence in persons, especially the little ones.
His life offers hope for spiritual transformation, though for many
others that transformation can be and needs to be aided through a
catechesis of spirituality. As extreme as some of the earlier Roncalli's statements might be, owing perhaps to youthful overstatement,
there are other, some more subtle, forms of this disjunctive approach to spirituality still abroad.

One who advocates a more holistic spirituality uniting concern
for the things of God and the things of humankind is Rabbi Abraham
Heschel. In explaining "prophetic spirituality," Heschel asks:

What is the essence of being a prophet? *A prophet is a person who
holds God and man in one thought at one time, at all times.* [Italics
mine.] Our tragedy begins with the segregation of God, with

the bifurcation of the secular and the sacred. We worry more about the purity of dogma than about the integrity of love. We think of God in the past tense and refuse to realize that God is always present and never, never past; that God may be more intimately present in slums than in mansions, with those who are smarting under the abuse of the callous.

For Heschel, the consequences of this unitive vision are more than notional but rather direct the prophet's compassionate attention to the sufferings of others.

The prophet is a person who suffers the harms done to others. Wherever a crime is committed, it is as if the prophet were the victim and the prey. The prophet's angry words cry. The wrath of God is a lamentation. All prophesy is one great exclamation: God is not indifferent to evil! He is always concerned. His is personally affected by what man does to man. He is a God of pathos.

If God is present in the suffering and victimized, then indifference to their pain is a denial of God, an active inattention to God's presence. Heschel clearly highlights the importance of a transformed religious attention: "The prophet's great contribution to humanity was the discovery of *the evil of indifference.* One may be decent and sinister, pious and sinful."[17]

Spirituality and Life Structure

In the first section of this chapter, I noted my conviction that spirituality always affects lifestyle. I used "lifestyle" at that point for clarity, because it was a term easily understood and not needing explanation. Now, however, I will use a term more accurate and requiring more explanation: life structure. Spirituality in its explicit religious sense should always—but in fact does not always—affect life structure, whereas life structure *always* affects spirituality, often as the most decisive factor. These claims need to be explained.

If upper case spirituality is the systematic approach to the presence of God, then it is a system, a way, and not just a way in the mind. A spirituality is a way of walking, a particular way of being in the world. It is entirely possible to have two conflicting spiritualities, a verbal or notional one, which we might claim guides our lives, and the lived one, which is the actual one. The first is an illusory spirituality, which is named and not lived, but which belies the actual spirituality, which is lived but not always named. Thus, it is possible to claim in verbal declaration that we have a Christian spirituality, whereas the actual way we structure our lives right down to our simplest decisions, is not based on the Gospel at all. Quite simply, a spirituality that does not affect life structure is not the actual spirituality; it is ghost of one. My own hunch is that the reason people so often fail in their attempts at "spiritual renewal" is that they never let the new program affect their life structure. Similar to dieting, if the program fails to change, not just the way we think but the way we act, then it has no effect.

Understanding Life Structure

What is life structure? Is it possible to clarify this concept in a way that will shed light on the life structure tied to spirituality? I have found helpful the brief treatment of life structure offered by Daniel Levinson in his attempt to plot shifts in the lives of middle age males. He writes:

> By "life structure," we mean the underlying pattern or design of a person's life at a given time. Here we are studying the lives of men. A man's life has many components: his occupation, his love relationships, his marriage and family, his relation to himself, his use of solitude, his roles in various social contexts—all the relationships with individuals, groups and institutions that have significance for him. His personality influences and is influenced by his involvement with each of them. . . The concept of life structure—the basic pattern or design of a person's life at a given time—gives us a way of looking at the engagement of the individual in society. It requires us to consider both self and world, and the relationships between them.[18]

Even this description, however, is somewhat vague, and Levinson's readers find themselves asking many questions about the relationships among various aspects of life structure and about how accessible it is to analysis. Levinson himself seems aware of this problem, to which he offers the following suggestion.

> How shall we go about describing and analyzing the life structure? The most useful starting point, I believe, is to consider the choices a person makes and how he deals with their consequences. The important choices in adult life have to do with work, family, friendships, and love relationships of various kinds, where to live, leisure, involvement in religious, political and community life, immediate and long-term goals.[19]

Here Levinson seems to be giving his readers permission to work out their own charting of life structure. The value of his comments on this matter, brief as they are, is to give access to a way of thinking about an important aspect of life that tends to be overlooked: the *ways* of a particular life. Life structure is bound up with what we pay attention to. One could do an in-depth analysis of life structure by examining a person's check book; phone bills, especially if the bills included the numbers actually phoned; a list of the books purchased over a year or of the magazines subscribed to; stubs of tickets that gave a person admission to various kinds of events; a time chart gauging the amount of television watched as well as the names of the programs. Out of an intuitive grasp of life structure's significance, a student from Ireland once suggested he could analyze the social situation of church leadership in his country if he knew where the various bishops of his country ate when they took meals outside their homes, with whom they ate, and who paid the bills. The context of his suggestion was his claim that Irish bishops are out of touch with the unemployed young people of his country.

Life structure is the vehicle in which spirituality moves. What is important to remember here is that life structure shapes perception and attention, just as the kind and size and shape of any vehicle determines in part one's view of the terrain. Travel is a different matter in a train, plane, automobile, space capsule, atop a camel, on a bicycle, or in a rickshaw. Some vehicles lend themselves to clearer outward attention than others. Some, such as a subway car, severely restrict outside attention. I choose this vehicle metaphor to emphasize how life structure shapes our perception and to suggest how certain life structures do not lend themselves to the sort of altered attention called for by the Gospel. As noted above, the crisis of the human spirit in our time is the crisis of knowing what things are worth our attention, and further, of insuring that we actually pay attention to them. Our spirits are shaped by what we pay attention to.[20] In the previous chapter, I noted that in every industrialized country there are many thousands of well-paid, well-trained "orchestrators of attention," whose every waking moment is directed to directing our attention in ways that suit those who pay their salaries. The influence of such persons cannot be overstated.

Concern for the connection between spirituality and life structure is not new and is not a side issue. In Chapter 2 I have already shown how preoccupied the early Christian communities were with proper life structure, and for the initiates seeking admission to their fellowship they set out a lengthy period called the cate-chumenate that could well be termed "life structure therapy." The previously quoted passage from Origen bears repetition: "The pro-found and sacred mysteries must not be given, at first, to disciples, but they must be first instructed in the correction of their life style." In another place, also previously cited, Origin is more explicit: "When it become evident that the disciples are purified and *have begun, as far as possible, to live better,* [Italics mine.] only then are they invited to know our mysteries."[21] Regis Duffy, who has examined the catechumenate as the shaper of life structure, emphasizes that the candidate had to have succeeded, beyond any merely stated desire, in transforming his or her way of life before being admitted to the community of worshipers.

> One major characteristic of the catechumenal process ... [was]: God's Word leads to commitments long before it leads to initiation . . . Three years "hearing the word" in the catechumenate of Hippolytus at Rome might seem long until we reflect on the quality of commitment that was expected of any Christian at the time. Hippolytus tells us that the first time inquirers came "in order to hear the word," the teachers ques-tioned them on their motivation, their life situation, and their willingness to change work that might hinder the practice of God's word.[22]

Unfortunately, the implications of the early communities' preoccupation with life structure has not been explored sufficiently. The fact that the way of worship is also the way of believing has come to be widely accepted, as in the formula, *lex orandi, lex credendi.* Just as true would be the formula: *lex vivendi, lex credendi* or even *lex vivendi, lex orandi.*[23] As life structure goes, so go the actual beliefs of the community; the quality of the community's worship is deter-mined by the quality of the community's life structure. For a cred-ible Christian life, the proper relationship among all three elements: life structure, worship, and belief, is crucial. In appreciating this relationship, the position of philosopher C.S. Peirce, already cited in Chapter 2, will be helpful.

> Belief consists mainly in being deliberately prepared to adopt the formula believed in as the guide to action; the essence of belief is the establishment of a habit; and different beliefs are

distinguished by the different modes of action to which they give rise.[24]

According to this understanding of belief, where the behavior consonant with the belief is lacking, one has grounds for doubting whether there is in fact a belief.

The centrality of life structure has been getting more and more detailed attention in recent years. Jacques Ellul, for example, points out that concern for the actual practice of truth is something Christians and Marxists have in common. Though part of Ellul's text has already been cited it bears repetition.

> In one respect there is . . . an obvious point of similarity between what takes place in Marxism and in Christianity. Both have made practice the touchstone of truth or authenticity. In other words, it is by practice that we have to appreciate or not the intentions or purity of the doctrine, of the truth of the origin or source.
>
> The link between praxis and theory in Marx is well known. One should not forget, however, that it is a circular link. This means finally that false practice inevitably engenders false theory, and one can see the falsity of practice not only from its effects . . . but also by the new theory to which it gives birth . . . Christianity too, judges itself by practice. We thus confront a constant challenge in this regard.[25]

In examining the parable of the house built on rock or sand [Mt 7:24-27], Ellul highlights the way the Christian Churches have tended to overlook the importance of practice. He finds most interpretations hold the key to the parable to be the fact that Jesus is the rock allowing the house to resist tempest and torrent, and so misunderstand the parable. According to Ellul:

> What Jesus says is that those who hear his words and do them are like the one who builds on the rock. In other words, the rock is hearing and doing. The second part, however, is more retrictive. Those who hear the words he speaks and do not do them are like the one who builds on the sand. Here undoubtedly practice alone is at issue. We can thus say that it is the decisive criterion of life and truth.[26]

Here Ellul is getting at the issue of deeds and way of life in Christian discipleship, the matter I have here named as life structure.

In a reflection on Romans, Juan Luis Segundo expresses convictions very similar to those of Ellul, although giving greater attention to the ongoing dilemma of achieving the integration of hearing and

doing. After citing Romans 14:23: "Everything that does not proceed from Faith is Sin," Segundo adds that

> In Romans, Sin and Faith seem to measure *the gap or distance*
> that is always there between what a human being *intends* and
> what he or she *actually performs or accomplishes*. It is the distance
> between the human project that arises in our "inner humanity"
> and the project we actually accomplish, given that our project
> must go by the way of "the law of the members" to become a
> reality. The effect of sin is to put *greater* distance between the
> two, so that human beings find their own actions incomprehen-
> sible and unrecognizable. The effect of Faith is to put *less*
> distance between the two . . ."[27]

Segundo goes on to point out the kind of sin he describes here is not
so much based on serious, conscious faults but on a kind of perva-
sive bad faith tied to self-deception.

While serious faults can jolt us to face our self-deception, bad
faith "remains impervious to the gradual degradation of all human
relationships," conditioning us in a way that "dehumanizing injustice does not attract our attention because our inner truth has been
neutralized and shackled."[28] Though not using the same language,
Segundo here seems to be making a distinction similar to my earlier
one, between notional and actual spiritualities, with the possibility
that the actual spirituality is an active way of ignoring God and the
implications of God's presence.

Life Structure and Life-Orienting Images

The question of the way one walks as the expression of one's lived
spirituality cannot be dealt with by treating life structure as an
isolated matter. Life structure itself is influenced the life-orienting
images that dominate our consciousness. The reason certain lines of
behavior are acceptable to us is that they fit in with the images we
have internalized from family, peers, and/or society. These images
are not mental pictures such as one might have in a fantasy. Rather
they are the non-iconic images that precede knowledge. Charles
Davis explains this kind of image as that which selects the aspects of
knowledge we choose to pay attention to and arranges them into a
pattern.[29] The example Davis uses is the image of woman a particular
person might have, as already noted in Chapter 4. This image is not
based on a specific imaginal representation of a particular woman;
nor is it tied to knowledge of physiology or even anatomy. This

"idea" of woman is based on associations and expectations closely tied to feelings and most probably tied also to early socialization.

To repeat, the image one has of woman effectively directs that person's attention to particular women who fit the image and away from others who do not. It also serves as an evaluative norm, by which a particular woman's behavior is judged "womanly" and another's judged as "unwomanly." Women themselves operate out of such images, which explains why a particular television ad depicting women as unable to make simple household decisions without outside advice will enrage one woman, while being hardly noticed by another. What fits in with our image tends to be unnoticed; what is in direct opposition to it will be actively rejected.

Much has been written over the past twenty years about the imaginal structure of life, some of it with important implication for understanding spirituality.[30] For my purposes here, I wish to focus on the significance of life-orienting images for Christian spirituality. Succinctly, I could state the following theorem. If it is impossible to effect a renewal of one's Christian spirituality without a shift of life structure, so it is not possible to renew life structure without a change in life-orienting imagery. *If life structure is the vehicle in which spirituality moves, life-orienting images are the tracks or road along which it runs, giving it direction.* One of the tasks of a catechesis of spirituality is to help people become conscious of the images that in fact underlie their consciousness, direct their attention, and offer plausibility to their life structure; and to encourage them to shift those not suitable for disciples of Jesus. Conversely, to seek to renew spirituality by focusing only on prayer is doomed, if only because prayer is all too easily subverted by ways of imagining the world that are at total variance with Jesus' way. I once heard James Fowler incisively name this subversion thus: "The churches are the cheering squads leading the cheers for the dominant culture."

If one wishes to get at the images that dominate a person's life structure and way of paying attention, find the matters that dominate their ordinary speech. The topics that come up spontaneously are what is closest to a person's heart, as Paulo Freire, for one, has so well reminded us. Also, notice the data available in the analogies everyone spontaneously uses to explain reality. The habits of the heart are in part disclosed by what we say after "like" and "as." Another clue would be to find the depictions of life they find significant in films or video, for these are a ways of imagining the world that fit in with a particular person's images. This fact is what makes the preference of young men for the Rambo and Rocky rendition of the world so frightening.

In the consumerist societies of North America, I find two networks or clusters of images worthy of analysis, both for their prevalence and for the way they run counter to the thrust of the Gospel. These are: (1) images of enhanced personal economic position, and (2) images of enhanced personal growth. Both are individualistic in the sense that each, in the pursuit of enhancement, tends to absolve one from wider group concern. Both tend to be competitive, judging personal enhancement over against that of others. John Kavanagh has pointed out in many places how such attitudes are related to consumerist capitalism.[31] So deeply accepted are such "habits of the heart," that it is even difficult to disclose their inappropriateness for those who would follow Jesus.

I presume that one of the reasons preaching so seldom deals with these clusters of images is that the preachers themselves have been formed in the same culture of acquisition and competition, and tend, not to evaluate the images through the lens of the Gospel but to evaluate the Gospel through the lens of the images. It is all too possible for a preacher to have adopted, not the biases of Jesus, but those of the social class in which the preacher grew up.[32] Still, once one sees the challenge to the Gospel in these images, one will find them everywhere, in what we hear and what we see.

The Gospel itself directly challenges both these image-clusters. The Gospel's good news is clearly not about being one step ahead of or one leg up on our neighbor, but about our unity in God, which calls us to the compassion of Jesus: "bearing one another's sorrows." That good news is also about overturning structures fostering injustice among the powerless. Such a programme brings with it an entire new way of living, of paying attention, of judging, and of deciding. Here prayer is not a form of escape but of engaged attention. Such a programme has within it the seeds of the transformed life structures noted earlier in this essay.

The question of course is whether the Gospel's imagination of the world is able to challenge even, or override, the imagination incessantly offered through the printed, visual and aural word. My own sense is that for most persons, it cannot, at least not without the help of groups of disciples actually living out the risks of fidelity. Without the countervailing help of a visible, audible chorus, most persons in our society will not be able to sing the song of good news. They are hardly able to hear the melody. Ultimately, a spirituality is properly not an individual reality, but a cultural reality. It is a zone of signification and consequent life structure located in some social group and visible to others.

In any catechesis of spirituality, the way of life of a group living out gospel fidelity is both the great message and the great communicator of that message. Whether in a consumerist culture such a group can be an entire congregation is open to question. Yet, for those who wish to live a spirituality of discipleship in our day, finding a group of like imagination and commitment seems to be essential.

This point brings me to the irony of a catechesis of spirituality, alluded to at the start of this chapter. In a sense every community embodies a spirituality, in a deep, taken-for-granted way. It *is* a spirituality, and its way of life is the key catechetical agent, not the words or any individual catechist. So the catechesis is always proceeding, since the group is always behaviorally saying to its members: This is what we actually stand for; these are our values and our priorities. True, this "lived" catechesis is not always consonant with the formal catechesis, which may verbally suggest lines of action and attention quite at variance with the lived reality. Any ministry to spirituality as I have described it here will have to take account of this wider and inevitable catechesis of spirituality. What I have described here is a kind of problem-posing catechesis of spirituality that puts under scrutiny the lived spirituality of a group, judging it by its notional, verbal spirituality and of course by the Gospel. One goal of such ministry is to give many in our communities a language by which to name their own spirituality and by which to question that of their community. Basically, a catechesis of spirituality is like all catechesis, a catechesis of liberation.[33] This entire book makes the claim, as alert readers will recognize, that *catechesis is about spirituality*, and it will never assume its proper place in the churches until that connection is actually lived out in local communities. My intention is to encourage such communities to work towards a communal spirituality of justice and liberation.

Notes

1. Aloysius Pieris, "Spirituality in a Liberative Perspective," in *An Asian Theology of Liberation* (New York: Orbis, 1988) 3. A study of some of the books on spirituality produced in the 1940s and 1950s shows how they set out the tradition three stages of the spiritual life: the purgative,

illuminative, and contemplative. These stages corresponded with the various steps of the ancient catechumenate, which even after its demise in the west were retained by monastic life in its initiation process. However, in books like Edward Leen's and Eugene Boylan's, these spiritual stages were presented as stages of prayer, or at least, as having their true meaning, not so much in a way of living one's life as in a way of praying. Pieris seems to agree [p. 144] with my analysis here.

2. It would be a serious error to see in my analysis here and below any attempt to reduce the importance of prayer—both private and public—in a disciplined search for God. In giving an overview of spirituality here, I am not dealing with the complex question of prayer, which deserves separate and lengthy attention. My point here is that spirituality should not be equated with prayer, which is an aspect of it.

3. Jon Sobrino, *Christology at the Crossroads* (New York: Orbis, 1978) 146-178.

4. A helpful account of this effort, but in the context of a survey of the denotation of "spirituality" through the ages is Sandra Schneiders, "Theology and Spirituality: Strangers, Rivals, or Partners?" *Horizons* 13:2 (1986) 253-274.

5. Gustavo Gutierrez, *A Theology of Liberation* (New York: Orbis, 1973) 204.

6. Gustavo Gutierrez, *We Drink from Our Own Wells: The Spiritual Journey of a People* (New York: Orbis, 1984). Gutierrez never actually uses the term, religious culture, but I find the idea as an important assumption throughout the book. The explicit way he describes spirituality is as a "way," one that he equates with discipleship: "Discipleship is rooted in the experience of an encounter with Jesus Christ . . . in which the Lord takes the initiative, and it is the point of departure for a journey . . . A spirituality is the terrain on which `the children of God' exercise their freedom" (pp. 35-36).

7. Pieris notes how the integral dialogical contact of Christianity with Greek culture found in the first five centuries of Western Christianity diminished when Christianity moved into Europe, not through the power of dialogue and incarnational praxis but through the power of law and governmental authority. Authoritarianism had replaced the dialogue with people's actual lives needed to lead them to discipleship as a way of life. The practice of the people was not considered as important as the theory of the theologians. It took another eleven hundred years for Europe's religious leaders to recognize that the living practice of the old folk religions had perdured in the religious ways of the common people. Thus the Reformation and Counter-Reformation were basically programs of *conversion*, i.e., of entire life orientation. This point is found, of course, many places in the literature dealing with the period leading to the Reformation, for example, Albert Mirgeler's *Mutations of Western Christianity* and John P. Dolan's, *History of the Reformation*.

Pieris traces Christianity's mistake of being more interested in religious thought than in religious practice and way of life back to the early Christian apologetics of Iraneus and many others. Pieris' argument is worth close study; see Aloysius Pieris, "Western Christianity and Asian Buddhism: A Theological Reading of Historical Encounters," in *Love Meets Wisdom* (New York: Orbis, 1988) 17-42, esp. 18-23.

8. Carolyn Osiek, "Reflections on an American Spirituality," *Spiritual Life* 22:4 (1976) 230-240.

9. "The great paradox of finding one's identity in wealth is ultimately the paradox of all idolatries: entrusting ourselves to our products, our silver and golden gods, *we become fashioned—re-created—in their image and likeness*. Bereft of personhood and human sensibility, we lose our vision. We become voiceless, unable to utter words of life and love . . . To make wealth one's god, is to become brittle and cold, to become like unto a thing, to become invulnerable, impenetrable, unloving." John Kavanagh, "The World of Wealth and the Gods of Wealth," in L. Boff and V. Elizondo, *Option for the Poor: Challenge to the Rich Countries Concilium* 187 (1986) 17-23, at 23.

10. The description is not original and can probably be found in various versions in many works on spirituality. I first came across it when leading a series of sessions for adults on prayer and using as background reading James Carroll's little book, *Prayer from Where We Are* (Dayton: George A. Pflaum, 1970). Chapter 3, entitled "Tending the Presence of God," started me on a long road of reflecting on the question of spirituality behind the question of prayer and on the key matter of attention. Some sense of the book can be gotten from the titles of Chapters 5-7: "The Tending Silence"; "The Tending Solitude, The Tending Group"; and "The Tending Imagination."

11. Schneiders deals with this matter well in her essay cited above.

12. See for example, Karl Rahner, "The Church's Commission to Bring Salvation and the Humanization of the World," *Theological Investigations*, vol. 14, pp. 295-313.

13. There are many ways of effecting this split. In a review of a recent book on spirituality, Vincent Rush takes issue with its unacknowledged assumption that there is some stable world beyond change accessible through spirituality. See Vincent Rush, "Steps Along the Way: Review of Benedict J. Groeschel, *Spiritual Passages: The Psychology of Spiritual Development*," *Cross Currents* 33:3 (1983) 377-379. In "Spirituality in a Liberation Perspective," Pieris cites a study of John Paul II's exhortations to priests and religious (up to 1982) that claims he makes this same disjunction; see p. 8, note 2.

14. Matthew Fox, "Religious Education and Spirituality: Parts I, II, III," *The Living Light* 12:2 (1975) 167-199, esp. 176-178. It is important to note that this disjunctive approach differs from the time-honored move by both Christian and non-Christian spiritual masters into the desert or into

monastic retreats apart from "the world." Yet, the matter of these various forms of separation is complex and needs sophisticated analysis. For some insight on this matter, see Aloysius Pieris, "A Theology of Liberation in Asian Churches?" in *An Asian Theology of Liberation* 111-126, esp. 117-120. Some of Thomas Merton's reflections on modern monasticism are also helpful here.

For an account of the historical factors that led to such a strong disjunction of the realm of the spirit from the realm of the world, see the chapter "The Mission of the Church," in Francis Schüssler Fiorenza, *Foundational Theology: Jesus and the Church* (New York: Crossroad, 1984) 197-212.

15. Pope John XXIII, *Journal of a Soul* (New York: McGraw-Hill, 1964) 41-42.

16. Ibid. 16.

17. Abraham Heschel, *The Insecurity of Freedom* (New York: Schocken Books, 1972) 92-93.

18. Daniel Levinson, *The Seasons of a Man's Life* (New York: Alfred A. Knopf, 1978) 41-42.

19. Ibid. 43.

20. A telling example of this claim is the following ad that appeared in *The Scholar's Bookshelf Catalogue* Fall/Winter, 1981:

A Catalogue of Horace Walpole's Library by Allen T. Hazen
3 volumes $150.00

At first I puzzled over why anyone would want to catalogue Horace Walpole's library, let alone purchase the catalogue—and at such cost. Then I realized that those wishing to know what shaped the mind of this historical figure would find important clues in his library, containing as it would the works he paid attention to. Find what a person attended to and you find out a major influence on the person's life.

21. Both quotes are found in D. Capelle, "L'Introduction du catéchumenat à Rome," *Recherches de théologie ancienne et médiévale* 5 (1933) 151, notes 38 and 39. Capelle gives the original references as: 1) Hom.V, 6 in Iud. 2) C. Cels. 3, 59. Regis Duffy first called my attention to this source.

22. Regis Duffy, *On Becoming a Catholic: The Challenge of Christian Initiation* (San Francisco: Harper and Row, 1984) 44.

23. As I understand it, *lex vivendi* was the whole point of the literature on the ascetical life that goes back to early Christianity but which assumed almost a literary form in the eighteenth and nineteenth centuries. See Schneiders, "Theology and Spirituality" on this point.

24. See, Chapter 2, note 23.

25. Jacques Ellul, *The Subversion of Christianity* (Grand Rapids, MI: Eerdmans, 1986) 4.

26. Ibid. 4-5.

27. Juan Luis Segundo, "Christ and the Human Being," *Cross Currents* 36:1 (1986) 50-51.

28. Ibid. 51-52.

29. Charles Davis, "Religion and the Sense of the Sacred," CTSA *Proceedings* 31 (1976) 87-105, esp. 87-91.

30. A single title among the many would be, Gibson Winter, *Liberating Creation* (New York: Crossroad, 1981).

31. For example, John Kavanagh, "Capitalist Culture and Christian Faith," *The Way* (July 1985) 175-185; "Capitalist Culture as a Religious and Educational Formation System," *Religious Education* 78:1 (1983) 50-60; "Challenging a Commodity Culture," *Commonweal* (2-16 November 1984) 606-612.

32. Of course there is much more to this problem than I can get at in this chapter. It is possible that church polity itself apes the dominative power of social rule rather than the mind and heart of Jesus. For a well-stated critique of church order from this angle, see Leonardo Boff, "Theological Characteristics of a Grassroots Church," in Sergio Torres and Thomas Eagleson, eds., *The Challenge of Basic Christian Communities* (New York: Orbis, 1981) 124-144.

33. See Pieris (1988) for a explanation of why every theology is a theology of liberation. By extension—and also from varied angles—every true catechesis is a catechesis of liberation.

6

The Catechumen in the Kitchen: A Catechetical Case Study

In this chapter I wish to present a kind of case study of the process by which evangelization moves to catechesis. The case involves young people around the age of twenty, though I believe that the principles hidden in the actual case are applicable to any age group. Also, the case describes an effort to reach out to young people in Dublin, but again, it still can be helpful in shedding light on some principles that affect catechesis in not only Ireland but in the U.S. as well.[1] Studying a specific catechetical initiative through my own participation in a single event should make my reflections on catechesis more specific and practical.

The event, which took place in the Sandyford section of Dublin, was a eucharist whose participants were all unemployed men and women in their early 20s, most of whom were on welfare or what the Irish call "the dole." As one might suspect, since this class of persons is widely known in Ireland to be alienated from the church, there was a history to their coming together, and it is important that I explain it. A woman in their neighborhood had been paying attention to these young people and the way they spent so much time aimlessly on the streets. She noticed in them an edgy disgruntledness and frustration that took bizarre forms of behavior: drinking to excess, vandalism, and even violence against one another.

She took a further step in her interest by getting to know these young people through casual conversation. She did not have any unsolicited advice for them, but simply took an interest in them as persons and paid attention to what they paid attention to. She listened, tried to understand, gave advice when asked. There was a fair amount of trouble among them, and some of it they brought to her for help, usually when things reached a crisis point. She was occasionally called on when there was family trouble, trouble with the law, or when someone went on a drinking or drug binge. After a while, a small group began to meet once a week in her home to discuss their frustrations, both social and personal. They met for months, and the group grew. Drugs, unemployment, boy-girl relationships, marriage, trouble with the law—all these came up during those months, and almost always without any explicit reference to religious matters. It seemed to have been assumed by them that their faith had nothing to do with any of these difficulties.

Eventually, however, these young people directed their attention to Geraldine, the woman who had been giving them her attention for so many months. She was not married; she had a job with the government, and a comfortable living. Why did she give them her attention and time when she could be occupied with matters less stressful than their problems? And so it was that she came—at their request—to speak about herself and the religious commitments at the core of her life, which led her to be concerned about these young people without any hidden agenda about getting them to practice their faith. They were intrigued and for a couple of weeks they had questions about the church and about various aspects of their own childhood faith that made no sense to them. They began to start each weekly meeting with a short reading from Scripture and a discussion of what it meant, and to end each meeting with prayer for the ones among them most in trouble.

To make a long story longer, eventually they—none of them a Mass-goer—decided they wanted to celebrate the eucharist together. It might have been a year and a half after they had first started to meet, but eventually, there in Geraldine's home the eucharist they did celebrate, with a priest who had joined in their discussions from time to time. Though all had been to Mass before, for many it was the very first time they celebrated the eucharist. And so the night when I was there was one of those times every month or two when they broke bread and passed the cup to remember that in Jesus the Father had turned injustice inside out.

But this account of how the whole thing had come about, I myself learned only afterward. I had been invited that night by a priest I admired to share in a home Mass with a group of young people. All I knew was that they were older and that they were not of the privileged classes. Looking back now, I see I was not ready for most of it. I was not ready to be squeezed into a small living room with more than fifty young people. I was not ready for the quality of the care they showed for one another, in their awareness of one another's pain, combined with a feisty lack of self-pity. I was not ready for the high colorful, earthy language they used to express themselves. I was especially not ready for their insights into the meaning of the scripture readings for their own lives, insights juxtaposed with silence that got deeper and deeper as the reflection continued. Having been invited to a home Mass with some young people, I was not expecting all this. I was surprised and delighted.

I hope the event I have been describing does not sound pious and warm and wonderful, because it was not. There was a tone of very real anger, both at the social situation they were in and at the church. Their social anger made a great deal of sense to me. Here were young people, young and vital, capable of work and clearly eager to work, showing their bitter scorn for the dole, both the fact of the dole and the meager size of it. Among the group were couples who wanted to marry but who judged they could not, for lack of a living wage. They wanted to get on with their lives and with their loves, to have homes and children, and to have the financial basis necessary for life together. However, all this was lacking to them.

I have thought many times afterwards what it must mean to have no place, to be told you have no place in your own land, the country of your birth. You are excess baggage. We do not need you. Not only do you have no contribution to make to the social project, you are an actual burden on that project. What must it seem to these young people, to have energy and eagerness to work and to be told you have no place, even before you have had a chance to prove yourself.[2]

To find an example from Irish history that illumines the injustice of this situation, one would have to go back to the time of the Irish famine and look at certain proposals the British overlords had for the starving peasants. One account of this period notes how

> The idea that the peasantry had become superfluous in Ire-
> land, that more attention should henceforth be given to rid-
> ding the land of people and stocking it with cattle, gained more
> and more adherents among Ireland's landlords as the famine's

ravages continued. It was an idea set forth repeatedly by Lord
Carlisle during his visits to Ireland, in words like these:

> Here we find, in the soil and climate, the condition best
> suited for pasture; hence it appears that cattle, above all
> things, seem to be the most appropriate stock for Ireland ...
> Corn ... can be brought from one country to another from a
> great distance, at rather small freights. It is not so with
> cattle, hence the great hives of industry in England and
> Scotland can draw their shiploads of corn from more south-
> ern climates, but they must have a constant dependence on
> Ireland for an abundant supply of meat.

> Great Britain wanted a pastoral country nearby to produce
> meat for its industrial workers, and since a pastoral country
> could not be a populous one if its flocks and herds were not to
> be eaten at home, the Irish people were being told, by way of
> evictions and the pulling down of cabins, to clear out of Ire-
> land.[3]

Obviously in this sort of thinking, there was no place in Ireland at
the time of the famine for its own people. What does it mean today
for its young people to face the prospect of never in their lifetimes
having a permanent job? What does it mean to be young and to be
told in various behavioral ways that you should think twice about
marrying and having a family, because you will spend your life not
knowing from one day to the next where the next meal is coming
from?

I began to see that, in this religious place and at this holy event,
their social anger was religious. Citing Chrysostom, Aquinas notes
that "he who is not angry when there is cause for anger, sins."[4] In
this sense we can speak of the virtue of anger and claim that "a lack
of anger in certain situations means a lack of willed commitment to
the good of justice."[5] I wish these young people had known how
much on their side was church teaching, as found for example in
the three principles set forth by the Bishops of Canada in a pastoral
on economic justice.

> 1. The basic rights of working people take priority over the
> maximization of profits and the accumulation of machines.
> 2. In a given economic order, the needs of the poor take
> priority over the wants of the rich.
> 3. In effect, the participation of the marginalized takes prece-
> dence over an order that excludes them.[6]

However, as I have already indicated, their anger in that eucharist was also directed against the church or at least against a particular understanding of the church. They seemed convinced that the church had taken sides and sided with the well-to-do and not with them. Though nobody cited particular policies favoring the children of the wealthy over the children of the poor, still this conviction was strong. I was especially intrigued with what I will call their catechetical anger, which scoffed several times at various teachings learned when younger but which now seemed ridiculous. I cannot remember the specific points ridiculed, but they all seemed to be the hortatory teachings, the oughts and musts. Freely assembled around bread and wine, engaged in intense discussion of Jesus' place in their lives, these young people had the wit to make these disembodied "thou shalts" seem ridiculous indeed.

Catechesis in the Framework of Ministry

Eventually I came to see in this eucharist and in the events leading up to it some important aspects of ministry and of the relation of catechesis to pastoral ministry, already noted in Chapter 1. I realize, of course, that there are some who might question whether a eucharist with Dubliners on the dole has any catechetical significance at all. I presume there are still those who limit catechesis to instruction in doctrinal formulations and who tend to see it as something that passes between teachers and students in classrooms. I, however, prefer to view catechesis within pastoral ministry, rather than within education. As a form of the ministry of the word, catechesis cannot function properly unless it is integrated into a total work of the church that includes the three other ministries: the ministry of worship, the ministry of guidance and counsel and the ministry of healing. Among all four ministries: word, worship, guidance/counsel, and healing, there is to be a kind of balance of nature, a symbiosis, with the various forms in harmony with one another.[7] What happened in Sandyford illustrates this point well.

It is worth noting that *in her initial approach* to these young people, Geraldine did not do catechesis at all. At the start there was no explicit religious message. She instead took the stance of guide or counselor and of healer. In other words she did what she did because it was part of her integrity as this kind of Christian person.

She might not have named it as such, but her work with these
young people comprised two of the four fundamental aspects of
ministry: the ministry of guidance and the ministry of healing. Both
these ministries are action-oriented but rooted in the primal action
of noticing, of listening, of trying to discern. Here we have the
ministry of those who are wise enough to be literally dumb. If they
will know we are Christians by our love, one of the sure signs of
love is attentiveness.

Perhaps we could call these two basic ministries: guidance/
counsel and healing, the ministries of credibility. At least for those
who stand outside the circle of faith, these are the works that make
the community's life believable and inviting. They cannot be feigned,
because they either make the good news seem like good news or
they do not. It was when these young people realized that Geraldine
herself was good news to them, that they inquired about the sources
of her good news. And it was when they inquired that she gave
them an account of the faith that was in her. She had at that point
moved into the ministry of the word, which is a ministry of ac-
countability, in the sense that it gives an account of the roots of
one's action. These young people knew that she did not love them
as potential church-goers because she had not proposed church
attendance to them. She loved them because they glowed with the
goodness of God. Geraldine did not want to bring them to God.
What made the difference (I suspect) to these young people is that
Geraldine had already found God present in them.

I have gone into this in some detail, because Geraldine's work
with these youth exemplifies so well the work of evangelization.[8]
Because evangelization is an aspect of the ministry of the word, its
chief form might seem to be the verbal, but its foundation is in
deeds; and those deeds begin not so much in an attempt to influence another as in an attempt to be true to one's call to discipleship.
The first form of evangelization is not a verbal announcement at all,
but a commitment to justice and to solidarity with the oppressed, to
the point of being with them in their efforts to have their injustices
redressed.[9] The first form of evangelization is the good news
enfleshed in a person or community.

Another way to say it is that Geraldine did not begin by "talking
the way" with these young people but by "walking the way" with
them. Eventually the whole process reached the point of words,
talk about the realities of Christian faith. Gradually those who
presumed those realities meant nothing to them came to judge that

they meant everything to them. When they came to see that they stood inside the circle of faith or wanted to stand there they had crossed over into the zone of catechesis, which always presumes faith. From there they proceeded to worship, which itself continued their catechesis because it was in the context of worship that they struggled to understand further what faith was calling them to, what it meant to them.

Catechesis and worship, then, were not the first steps in this journey at Sandyford; they were the final but continuing steps. Geraldine presumed little (except the possibilities) and started where the young people were; together they took a kind of exodus journey out of alienation to the eucharist. I would like to stress, however, that this journey was one they entered into themselves and then progressed in a step at time. They were not marched along to an alien beat like prisoners of war. Evangelization and catechesis can only take place in an ambience of freedom and choice.

Two Catechetical Dilemmas

If you have followed carefully my story of ministry in Sandyford you have seen in it special problems for the church in its exercise of its own fidelity. First of all, the church in its ministries of credibility needs to be present on the side of the most disadvantaged or marginalized. If the church in its organized "official" life had been on the side of these young people, it was not apparent to them, nor was it apparent to Geraldine. Among the followers of Jesus, systemic unemployment which denies any persons their fundamental human rights must not be met with either the silence of words or the silence of deeds. As has the U.S. church, the teaching church in Ireland has well pointed out that the horrors of Latin America at root stem from economic inequities, with the haves in the position of privilege and power, not willing to give an inch of their comforts, and the have-nots being in a position of desperation. Possibly the same teaching needed to be applied to Ireland, geographically far removed from Guatemala and EL Salvador, but morally much closer than many might like to admit.[10] "Quite recent research has shown that while the top 10% of Irish households have 42% of the income, the bottom 19% have little more than 4%—the biggest inequality in the European Economic Community."[11]

I stress this point because at issue here are catechetical matters in several layers. If there are structural inequities present in Irish society, then colluding in them are managerial-class and invest-

ment-class persons who name themselves as followers of Jesus and
on whom has been lavished the best talent and the best facilities the
church has to offer.[12] These persons have a special responsibility to
be on the side of the have-nots, though they may not all have heard
the Gospel preached as good news of justice. Even further, if it is
true, as some would claim, that adult catechesis in general has been
ignored in Ireland, because it was expected that the "traditional
faith" of the family and neighborhood was sufficient to keep faith
alive, can it continue to be ignored in a time of orchestrated consumerism? Have catechetical leaders fully accepted the fact that the
days are gone when Christian faith could be passed on through
family traditions and through socialization in village or neighborhood values? In the age of television, could it be that expressions of
robust faith like the following hymn of Peig Sayers, the famous
Irish storyteller, can only be continued through deliberate nurturing, which will include careful catechesis?

> My love my Lord God! Isn't it straight and smooth life goes on
> according to His true holy will! Shouldn't we be joyful for His
> glorious light to be lit amongst us! Isn't there still many a
> person lying in the dark! God with us, Lord, isn't that a pity I
> understand that there is no more valuable jewel in life that to
> have love for God of GLory . . . for I see a lot that reminds me of
> the great power of God.[13]

As lovely as this hymn is, to be appropriate to our time, the second
sentence would need a corrective to point out how evil systems can
spin on, smoothly countering every aspect of God's will.

The second dilemma hidden in my tale of Sandyford is one of
finding the proper relationship between catechesis and ministry. In
its ministry, the church, while on the side of the victims must also
be at their side, as a guiding, healing presence among the people.
Establishing such a presence may be a particular problem in Catholic Ireland where some might expect certain of the church's ministries to be institutionalized in services provided by the state. I
realize that I am alluding here to a large theoretical question which
needs careful analysis. Still, the parish that gives the impression
that its one and only ministry is that of worship has already begun
to die, because it has ignored its wider mission.

A good example of a ministry that can function properly only in
the local believing community is the ministry of catechesis. As an
ecclesial activity, catechesis cannot, of its very nature, be relegated

to the schools. The General Catechetical Directory makes clear that the chief catechizer is not a teacher, even one called a catechist, but the believing community itself. I repeat here the passage cited earlier.

> Within the scope of pastoral activity, catechesis is the term to be used for that form of ecclesial action which leads both communities and individual members of the faithful to maturity of faith. With the aid of catechesis, communities of Christians acquire a more profound living knowledge of God and of his plan of salvation centered in Christ.[14]

Notice the communal stress here. Catechesis is not for children only; in fact it is not even mainly for children. It is primarily adult activity, that is, a lifelong struggle to make sense of death, evil, injustice, and suffering, a struggle that emerges with something to celebrate.

If catechesis is mainly done apart from the local community of faith and mainly in schools, what happens to a young person who leaves school at age fifteen or sixteen, as many in Ireland do? Is that person, who is apt statistically to be from the poorest sectors of society,[15] to live the rest of his or her life with a primary school understanding of faith? Are there not understandings of faith appropriate or even accessible only at later moments of life, including some of the more complex issues of justice and peace? Who then will be the catechist for this fifteen year old no longer in school? Or who for example will catechize the business executive in Cork, whose decisions may worsen economic injustice in Ireland?[16] Of course these questions can be applied to the church in any country. If the local church does not face up to catechesis as its own work, then we leave our people with the "catechesis of the tube," with the catechesis of the latest television sitcom, a religion geared to the ever greater fulfillment of consumer fantasies. We no longer have a choice in this matter. We either, like the third world churches, ground our work of religious transformation in slow and careful catechetical ministry or we abandon our people to oppressive systems, in this case to the marketeers.

If the abundantly researched erosion of faith in Ireland is a symptom of the lack of adult catechesis,[17] then possibly that symptom will begin to disappear when more persons take their places as fulltime pastoral assistants providing catechetical leadership in parishes. Not every priest is a good catechist, just as not every

priest is a good preacher. Some who preach poorly are good coun-
selors or in other ways gifted at works of compassion and healing.
Above all, a priest in our day is called to be the affirmer and
nurturer of the gifts present in the community. When gifts are thus
nurtured, then we will find those who are to be the presence of our
community at the sides of the alienated, the way Geraldine was for
the young people at Sandyford.

Perhaps the possibilities of a broader approach to ministry in
local parishes can be illustrated with what a young man told me
one night in a pub in Maynooth, the town where the major national
seminary is located. He had left the seminary and was then studying at St. Patrick's College. He said something like this:

> If I went to my bishop and told him that I was thinking I might
> have a vocation to be a priest and that I was willing to begin
> studies for the priesthood, I would get every sort of open-
> handed encouragement. If I didn't have the means, I would
> receive financial help. My summer employment would be
> aided, partly because I was studying to be a priest, partly
> because I had good connections through the church. I could go
> on and be ordained; and yet a year after ordination I could
> throw the whole thing over and go sell insurance. However, if
> I went to my bishop and told him that I had been in the Young
> Christian Students and Young Christian Workers since I was
> fifteen, and that I had been spending almost twenty hours a
> week working to develop a Christian understanding among
> the unemployed in Dublin; and that I was finishing a degree in
> religion at St. Patrick's College and wanted to undertake a
> fulltime ministry with young people in the church, I would
> receive the bishop's good wishes and no more.

He also claimed that the bishop was likely to tell him that he should
become a teacher. He was quite clear however that he did not wish
to serve in that structure.

Religious Education in the Schools

I have stressed here the catechetical importance of the church's
being on the side of the most marginalized and of placing catechesis
within ministry. In this concluding section, I wish to comment
explicitly on the role of the school in dealing with religious understandings. To be blunt, I have great doubts about the possibilities of
catechesis in the schools, especially in the high school years. In my

view, schools should be doing religious education and leaving catechesis to be done by and within the local church community. Serious discussion of this matter is underway in many places, among them, the U.S. and Canada.[18] Three points should be included in that discussion.

1. A fundamental question, often overlooked by teachers but fundamental to understanding the social reality of a school, is the following: Under what circumstances and auspices do those who assemble in schools come together there? And what sort of institution is it in which they assemble? I would love to believe, as one whose profession involves teaching in a school that the young who assemble there do so willingly because of my skill as a performing artist and because of the luminous quality of my reflections. Yet I know students do not assemble in a university for the reasons people assemble in a theater. The forces in the university are complex and even contradictory.

In a primary or secondary school, however, the forces are much more direct and compulsory. Those who assemble in those places do so because not to do so would mean the intervention of the state in their lives. Since civil law mandates schooling up to a certain age, those who assemble in schools do not do so out of a full choice on their part. To admit this fact is not to deny that many children and youth actually enjoy various aspects of life at school. In fact, Irish youth rank teachers at the top of the list of those who understand them, just after parents, a wonderful tribute to the teaching profession.[19] Still, the primary and secondary school does not exist as a zone of full choice, as becomes clear when we contrast the school with the worshiping community.

The worshiping community is meant to be the place of free assembly. Why? Because it is in the nature of human beings that celebration can only be proposed; it can never be imposed. At the moment of imposition, celebration ceases to be true celebration and becomes something else. It might superficially look like celebration but the heart has been cut out of it. Celebration works from the inside out; compulsion works from the outside and never fully gets in.[20] Not all in the church like to face the implications of this fact, i.e., that obligation subverts the act of worship.[21]

I have already noted that catechesis is a cousin of celebration. In the early church, full catechesis could only take place after the ecstacy of both having gone down into the water of baptism and shared in the broken bread of the body. This fullest form of catechesis was mystagogic catechesis, a pondering of the wonderful things that had happened.[22] Mystagogic catechesis was the final step in the catechumenate, a process every step of which the community insisted be free.

If freedom and choice is a central aspect of catechesis, then that aspect is masked somewhat when catechesis is done in the zone of obligatory attendance, i.e., the school. In catechesis the person is actively pursuing his or her own understanding. The catechist presumes that the person has already embraced Jesus' way and stands inside the circle of faith. In a school that presumption of choice is not so possible as it was, say, in Sandyford. Everyone at the eucharist in Geraldine's parlor was there actively seeking an enrichment of his or her faith life. What was interesting to me was that not every person was in the parlor. In the kitchen was a young man who had decided he could not celebrate the eucharist until he had stopped his compulsive and destructive drinking. How he came to that decision I have no idea, but all understood and accepted that he was not fully ready. So all the time we were there at the eucharist we were aware that there in the kitchen was someone not fully ready, our "catechumen," who was a full member of the group through friendship but whose lifestyle needed more work before sharing the cup.[23] That incident illustrates for me the choices so central to catechesis, but not necessarily central to a school.

2. Religious education, on the other hand, falls not within ministry as does catechesis, nor is it a cousin to celebration.[24] It rather falls within education and involves, not a way of walking like catechesis but a way of studying. It is a kind of inquiry and is more similar to the study of science and literature than it is to catechesis. If I could play with my words "impose" and "propose," I am not even sure one can propose literature. The study of literature is a process of exposing it rather than proposing it, that is, of looking at the history of various literary forms and of the ideas and emotions contained in them. To be educated does not mean having come to adopt any of those forms oneself but to understand them as part of the legacy of human expression. The possibility of such understanding is of course itself a great gift.

Similarly, religious education is also a great gift, which examines religious questions, including Christian ones, not so much from the point of religious commitment, which is the perspective of catechesis, but from that of intellectual inquiry.[25] What seems especially important about religious studies or religious education is that it can dispel multiple illusions young people can develop about religious matters: that the religious is limited to the Christian; that the religious is something imposed on them by an institution called the church, rather than an area of human achievement pursued in all cultures of all time; that other religious forms are "wrong" in the face of our "right" way. Religious education seeks religious literacy that is, a broad understanding about how religious forms work, especially about how religious language works.[26]

In doing religious education, we need not exclude the examination of Christian and Roman Catholic matters, but we examine them from a much more objective stance than that used in catechesis. Catechesis presumes conversion; religious education presumes some willingness for disciplined inquiry. Its goal is not growth in commitment so much as growth in understanding. The fulfillment of catechesis is worship and action for justice. The fulfillment of religious education is mastery in an intellectual sense.[27] I claim that such an approach to religion is especially important after about age 14-15, when many young people need a chance to re-think religious questions from new standpoints and in doing so actually re-think their own religious commitments. Admittedly I am drawing rather bold lines between catechesis and religious education, much bolder than they exist in practice. I do so as a device to call attention to certain distinctive features of each.

One of the reasons I stress the value of religious education is my commitment to catechesis. We will never move to religious education until catechesis is more properly situated in the local church, as a lifetime pursuit of fidelity to discipleship. The pursuit of fidelity certainly has its ups and downs, which is one reason we have a sacrament of reconciliation at all. If we knew that the catechesis necessary for a lifelong pursuit of discipleship was going on in our local churches, we would then be able to broaden our approach to religious matters in schools, where intellectual inquiry is the appropriate mode. However, where there is little lifelong catechesis going on, I can see how persons in charge of church schools might be reluctant to move toward religious education.

3. A further aspect of schools deserves a word: the issue of freedom. If Christian faith cannot be imposed, neither can education, because in its deepest sense education also comes from inside out. A key problem schools have to grapple with is that of establishing a consensual climate. When a person reaches the age for secondary school there must be sensitive attention to the establishment of such a climate. In schools there is an educational triangle among whose parts must be developed a harmonious balance: the

faculty, the students, and the subject matter.[28] The relation among these parts needs to be negotiated between students and teachers. One does not establish consensus by incessantly asking students, "What would you like to do today." Yet if students have not agreed to a particular line of disciplined inquiry, there will be little learning. In modern societies with ready access to information via television, young people are more and more resisting the imposition of education forms in which they have no say.[29] At all levels of education, dialogue is the appropriate form, not communiques from on high. Communiques undermine communication, though they are the death of catechesis. In dealing with religious issues, schools need to be especially open places.

Conclusion

In this presentation I have tried to illustrate one approach to catechetical method. Instead of beginning with a discussion of theoretical matters, I chose to begin with a concrete incident focusing attention on the marginals in our society. I did so out of a conviction that the option for youth should be fused with the option for the poor. If our entire program of ministry, including catechesis, begins among the marginals, at their side and on their side, that position provides us with the radical questions for discipleship in our time. I have also chosen as seminal the image of the catechumen in the kitchen, because it highlights the catechetical questions of choice and readiness. It also draws attention to the life-giving but tolerant posture of those who gather in faith, who are secure enough in their own continuing search for fidelity to allow time and space for the one who does not quite fit. Irish kitchens have been the places that for eons have welcomed openhandedly the wanderer, and perhaps they symbolize the warmth offered by a people sensitive to the marginal and displaced because they themselves as a people have been marginalized and victimized.[30] Perhaps in that fact lies a lesson of catechetical significance for the church at large.

Notes

1. Brendan Fay of Drogheda, Ireland, graduate assistant in the Theology Department, St. John's University, Jamaica, New York, provided valuable leads in my preparation of this chapter.

2. The particular compassion John Paul II has shown to unemployed young people is worth noting, as well as the way he connects unemployment with justice; see John Paul II, "Speech to Youth," Memorial University, Newfoundland, Canada, 12 September 1984, *Canadian Catholic Review* 2:9 (October 1984) 345-346.

3. Thomas Gallagher, *Paddy's Lament: Ireland 1846-1847* (New York: Harcourt Brace Jovanovich, 1982) 145-146.

4. Cited in Daniel Maguire, "The Primacy of Justice in Moral Theology," *Horizons* 10:1 (Spring 1983) 72-85, at 78.

5. Ibid.

6. Canadian Conference of Catholic Bishops, *Ethical Choices and Political and Political Challenges: Ethical Reflections on the Future of Canada's Socio-Economic Order* (Ottawa: Concacan Inc., 1984) 5-6.

7. See "Youth Ministry in Transition," Chapter 1 of Michael Warren, *Youth and the Future of the Church* (Minneapolis: Winston-Seabury, 1985) 8-16.

8. For an overview of the centrality of evangelization in contemporary catechetical thinking, see Michael Warren, "Evangelization: A Catechetical Concern," in Michael Warren, ed., *Sourcebook for Modern Catechetics* (Winona: St. Mary Press, 1983) 329-338.

9. An important treatment of this key aspect of evangelization is Jon Sobrino, "Evangelization as Mission of the Church," Chapter 9 of *The True Church and the Poor* (New York: Orbis, 1984) 253-301.

10. According to Peader Kirby, many working for justice in Ireland have made the same comparison; see Peader Kirby, *Is Irish Catholicism Dying?* (Dublin: Mercier Press, 1984) 90.

11. John McGrath, cited in Denis Carroll, "The Option for the Poor," *The Furrow* 33:11 (November 1982) 672. Another way of stating the same inequality is: "The top 20% of Irish income earners take in 43.4% of all income earned; while the bottom 40% receive only 15.7% of all income earned in the country." Peter McVerry, "A House Divided," *New Creation* (August 1982) 27.

12. There are, of course, two sides to collusion in unjust systems. The poor can also collude when they do not take seriously their own need to participate in the formulation of social policies. Without popular participation, no re-distribution of power is possible. See Richard Quinn, "Economic Development and Christian Faith," *The Furrow* 35:4 (May 1984) 306-318.

13. Peig Sayers, *An Old Woman's Reflections*, trans. Seamus Ennis (New York: Oxford University Press, 1972) 29.

14. Sacred Congregation for the Clergy, *General Catechetical Directory* (Washington, D.C.: United States Catholic Conference, 1971), par.21, p.21.

15. The statistical evidence for this claim can be found in "Aspects of the Education and Employment of Young People in Ireland," Chapter 8 of

National Youth Policy Committee: Final Report (Dublin: National Stationery Office, 1984) 73-93.

16. A nuanced presentation of the need for adult catechetical work in Ireland, though not stressing the justice perspective, is Liam Lacey, "Adult Catechesis in Ireland: A Way Forward," *The Irish Catechist* 7:3 (October 1983) 31-41.

17. For an overview see Liam Ryan, "Faith Under Survey," *The Furrow* 34:1 (January 1983) 3-15.

18. See James Dunning, "Words of the Word: Evangelization, Catechesis, and the Catechumenate," (Washington, D.C.: North American Forum on the Catechumenate, 1984).

19. *National Youth Policy Committee: Final Report* 54.

20. In a recent study of the doctrinal understanding of Irish youth, Bernadette MacMahon uncovered some astonishing evidence of the ineffectualness of compulsion. Of two groups one of which had received ten full years of compulsory catechesis in school, the other twelve years, she writes: "The number [sic] of fifteen-year-olds giving `very good' answers to eleven questions varied from 0.1% to 2%; and among the seventeen-year olds from 1% to 3% according to the questions under consideration." Bernadette MacMahon, *Listening to Youth: The View of Irish Youth on Their Religion* (Dublin: Dominican Publications, 1987) 15.

21. See Josef Pieper, *In Tune with the World: A Theory of Festivity*, (Chicago: Franciscan Herald Press, 1973).

22. An excellent account of mystagogic catechesis can be found in Hugh M. Riley, *Christian Initiation*, Studies in Christian Antiquity, vol. 17 (Washington, D.C.: Catholic University of America Press, 1974).

23. The importance of change of lifestyle in the early catechumenate was highlighted by Regis Duffy, "Liturgical Catechesis: Catechumenal Models," The First Annual Mary Charles Bryce Lecture. Washington, D.C., Catholic University of America, 1983.

24. An attempt to compare and contrast catechesis and religious education is Michael Warren, "Catechesis: An Enriching Category for Religious Education," *Sourcebook* 379-394.

25. See Michael Grimmitt, *What Can I Do In R.E.?* (Great Wakering: Mayhew-McCrimmon, 1973) esp. Chapter 5, "A Conceptual Framework for Religious Education in Schools," 49-87.

Contrast Grimmitt's treatment with the jumbled categories used in the following news report, Christina Murphy, "Education is Secular, Says Teacher Priest," *Irish Times* (26 June 1982) 15.

26. See, for example, Grimmitt's treatment of this matter, *What Can I Do* 59-75.

27. Still deserving close attention is the following treatment of the religious studies question in third level education, Cosmas Rubencamp, "Theology as a Humanistic Discipline," in George Devine, ed., *Theology in Revolution* (New York: Alba House, 1970) 185-197.

28. "A major concern of this Committee has been the provision of opportunities for young people to participate in their society. To this end, we asked young people if they see it as important that they be involved in the decision making procedures of their schools and colleges. The vast majority (82%) felt they should, and the suggestions received particular support among the under 17's and those still in school. Young people in urban areas, and females, also saw this as being particularly important." *Youth Policy Committee: Final Report* 84. See also Theodore Sizer, "A Study of High Schools: A Proposal" (Washington, D.C.: National Association of Secondary School Principals, March 1981).

29. See the fascinating analysis of the new "hunters and gatherers" in the new information age in Joshua Meyrowitz, *No Sense of Place: The Impact of Electronic Communications on Social Behavior* (New York and London: Oxford University Press, 1985) 307-329.

30. See Diarmuid O. Laoghaire, "Old Ireland and Her Spirituality," in Robert McNally, ed., *In Old Ireland* (New York: Fordham University Press, 1965) 46-47; also Gallagher, *Paddy's Lament* 14.

7

Catechesis and Social Justice

Those of us who have read the Roman Martyrology, the book containing the lives and martyrdoms of the earliest Christians, know that some of those killed for their faith were catechists. These catechists were sort of travel guides delegated by the community to help the community understand what it means to be followers of Jesus and to help point out the route a faithful follower might have to take in one's daily journey. The martyrdom of these persons meant that the very ones who called the members of the community to fidelity to Jesus' way sometimes were called upon to show their own fidelity unto death. And yet, early catechists were rarely martyred because they were catechists but simply because they were Christians.

However, there is on record the martyrdom of a very large number of persons killed not just because they were Christians but exactly because they were catechists. Neither were these catechists rounded up for a mass execution. Rather they were killed one at a time, mostly in isolated, hidden incidents. To repeat, these catechists were not martyred just because they were Christians but because of the fact that they preached to others the Gospel, which civil power found to be quite dangerous.

What may be most interesting to us is that these martyrs were not from Macedonia, Pamphylia, Cappadocia or Syria. Neither did they live twenty centuries ago. They were all from the province of Huehuetenango in Guatemala, the same catechists I discussed briefly

in Chapter 4. Obviously, and I would add, appropriately, the significance of their story has seized my catechetical imagination.
Murdered between 1978 and 1987, most were married men with
families. Currently the widows and orphans of these catechists live
in poverty and hardship in refugee camps in Mexico, living testi-
monies to the extreme risks of catechesis.[1]

In the face of these facts, some catechists may ask themselves
why anyone would want to kill people like them, for proclaiming
the Gospel. In those countries where catechists find little opposition
to their catechetical ministry, the very idea that someone might
want to take their lives because of their catechesis is a shocking,
almost ridiculous one. Yet, fewer than four hundred miles from
Brownsville, Texas, three hundred adult married men have all too
recently been assassinated for taking the message of Jesus to their
people. Why this horror? The reason they were killed is actually
quite simple: the Gospel these catechists proclaimed included the
call to social justice so integral to Jesus' message. As I pointed out in
a previous chapter, in Guatemala, Jesus' good news about justice is
also dangerous news. Preach it and you could lose your life. Preach
it and there is a good chance you could be called a communist and
put on someone's death list.

My own conviction is that the martyrdom of the Guatemalan
catechists has something to teach us about the relation of catechesis
and social justice in our day. That relationship, however, is not one
that has become evident only in Guatemala or only in our century.
From the beginning, the characteristics of catechesis in the church
disclosed the connection between justice and the sharing of the
secret Christians had discovered in Jesus. An examination of these
characteristics of catechesis in the early church will be helpful for
understanding both the catechesis of justice today and for appreciating how unsettling good catechesis can be. Thus catechesis involves (1) a particular kind of message, (2) directed to particular kind
of lifestyle, (3) embodied in living ecclesial groups.

Before going on the elaborate this catechesis I acknowledge that
my method in setting out the catechesis of the early church is
limited by lumping several centuries and the witness of varied
communities together. In claiming to find in the life of the early
church evidence of a particular position, it would be most accurate
to specify particular periods and particular churches. However my
own study shows me that like most historical matters, this one of
justice in the early church becomes more complex the more closely
one studies it; and limits of space bar my undertaking a review here

of these complexities. Ranier Kampling has set out some of these complexities in a helpful overview of the question of rich and poor in the early church. Kampling writes:

> Wealth and poverty are concepts that need to be seen in their *social context* [All emphases his] for their precise meaning to become clear. The poor man or woman of the *Roman empire* is characterized by lack of food, education, freedom, often also health and power. The poor included both those who had to toil for their living and also those who were dependent on the contributions of others. Their social status was zero. Rich persons on the other hand had possessions and thus power. They had the opportunity to assert themselves and their interests over against the State and the society whose respect they enjoyed . . . The social crisis of the Roman empire that began in the third century and accelerated in the two following centuries led to the impoverishment of great masses of people throughout the empire and to the accumulation of wealth in the hands of a few who for their part ruthlessly exploited those without property. Because of this social reality that was reflected in its own composition the Christian community saw itself obliged to consider the relationship between rich and poor against the background of the claim to be a *community of equals* (see Gal. 3:28, 1 Cor. 12:13) and to strive to reach a solution that could prevent social differences and tensions becoming repeated within its own ranks and stop those who were discriminated against socially because of their poverty being neglected in the church too.[2]

Still, as doctrinal controversies intensified in a spreading church and as the kingdom came more and more to be identified with the church itself, concern for such justice-related matters as hospitality devolved to hospitality *for Christians.* To admit this fact is not to deny that the New Testament remained normative and that such key justice passages as Matthew 25, Luke 6: 27-49 (on the love of enemies), and the parable of the Good Samaritan called for radical positions, even when those positions were not taken by whole communities. Just as John Chrysostom, cited here in detail, did for his time, current scholarship, such as that of Sobrino, also noted here, tries to recover the radical message of Jesus.[3]

The Message

The reason people of the early churches were put to death, not so much because they were catechists but simply for being Christians, was that Christians stood for a range of values that went against the social system of their time. Of course, the individual catechists proclaimed and carefully explained that message, but the entire body of the followers of Jesus stood for that message in the sense that their lives embodied it or at least the attempt to follow it. Christians proclaimed a new order of reality which they claimed had already begun in the person of Jesus. An integral aspect of this new order of reality was a new social order based on the message of Jesus.

The way Jesus himself preferred to speak of this new reality was as the Kingdom of God.[4] For Jesus, the Kingdom of God did not mean a political kingdom but a time when what would reign was sisterhood and brotherhood among all people, a time when fairness and kindness would replace greed and cruelty in the way people dealt with one another. The only king would be God and the only way of doing things would be God's, which was the way of love for one another.[5]

Jesus preached reform of life, because the new times were right at hand, and the only way to be ready for them was by changing one's life toward more compassion, greater justice, and less greed. Everybody was invited to be part of the Kingdom but the invitation by itself did not qualify one to be part of it; change of outlook and of lifestyle was also required. Jesus suggested the radicalness of the change in his metaphor of the dinner party to which those who had invitations were not admitted because they had on the wrong clothes. The key to understanding this metaphor is the fact that these persons had not changed, and change was a must for being welcomed to that table.

Jesus kept insisting: change your ways to God's ways. Love your enemy; protect those with no protection: the widow, the orphan, the sick; give some of the food you have prepared for yourself to the hungry person whose name you do not even know. On Jesus' lips the Kingdom of God was not pie-in-the-sky but involved specific ways of dealing with problems of human relatedness, which today we call "social questions."

Jesus claimed that the coming of the Kingdom was good news. Such a claim was ironic because it was clearly understood as very bad news by those who first killed Jesus and later his followers because they preached the Kingdom of God. This good news was evidently news they did not care to hear. Jesus said the Kingdom was good news especially for the poor, because under God's new order the injustice and oppression they suffered would be corrected. Actually, Jesus preached that the new way was good news for the rich too, because it would free them to become the kind of human beings God wanted them to become, instead of being persons who inhumanly took advantage of the powerless or just as inhumanly ignored them.

Still, Jesus' coming Kingdom was a special delight to the poor, because they were to have a special place in it. Jesus was announcing a fullness of human life to those who had it least. Notice though that Jesus' concern for the poor was not just in some future time. His own ministry and preaching offered hope and healing to the poor in the here-and-now. Apparently the poor recognized that though he mingled with all, rich and poor alike, he was clearly biased, siding with the poor, with the outcasts, the sinners, the physically impaired. Basically, this "siding" meant that he saw life through their eyes and called for social changes that would benefit those beaten down. Thus to the powerful or "rich," he proposed the following changes: instead of hoarding, sharing; in place of domination, helping and compassion; instead of ambition, equality.

If these features of Jesus' message were once clear to his early followers, their clarity may be somewhat diminished in our own time. A friend of mine who recently tried to explain Jesus' taking of sides to several groups of teen women in a Catholic high school ran into resistance to the idea and outright denial. The sticking point in the minds of these young people seemed to be that God loves all persons equally. They did not seem to be able to hold onto the paradoxical truth that God has an unconditional love for all persons and at the same time, a special love for the oppressed poor.[6] So this teacher took pains to elaborate, showing how this special love is affirmed again and again in our Scriptures, both Old and New Testaments. According to the Scriptures, and particularly according to the words and deeds of Jesus, God demands justice for those beaten down, for the victims. In fact, not only does he take the side of the poor but he calls those who love him to do likewise. To deny this aspect of God's message to us is to make God in our own image, whereas we are called to be made over in God's image.

At this point the young women in my friend's classes still do not fully accept this aspect of the Christian message, but they are thinking about it and what it might mean in their own lives. My friend claims that these have identified the message of Christianity with the American dream of "making it" through one's own initiative and then of being loved by God for one's personal industriousness. Some of these students said straight out that those who do not make it, those in the streets whom they name the poor, do not make it due to their own fault, their own personal failure.

From a catechetical point of view what is interesting about these particular young people is that they claim to have never, in eight to ten years of previous catechesis and in about ten years of Sunday homilies, heard of Jesus' preaching of a new order in which the poor would rejoice most. The new time of justice proclaimed by the early disciples of Jesus, which got them into such hot water (or boiling oil) seems to have been omitted in any catechesis they can remember. Instead, the catechesis that stuck with them is one that affirms middle-class values. In this catechesis, "God helps those who help themselves" carries much more weight than "God hears the cry of the poor." What seems to have happened in our churches is that the cultural message of our own social arrangements has over-ridden Jesus' message in the gospel. So effective has been such an over-riding that one can rarely talk about the good news of justice found in our Scriptures, even in groups of catechists without stirring up in a least a few listeners, intense denial or opposition. Here, of course, this opposition does not have the fanaticism it has in Guatemala, where, if you as a catechist try to share with your fellow Christians this message about a new day of justice called for by God, you are likely to be shot in your bed or macheted on the footpath.

For catechists striving to be faithful to the message of Jesus and to devise ways of sharing that message with others, the problem of discerning exactly what is the good news of our tradition becomes an important task. For some that task will involve learning to read the Scriptures in quite a new way. Some may find they cannot be faithful to the ministry of catechesis without doing special background reading.

The ministry of catechesis is both more demanding and more radical than the unfortunate caricature of it still found in some places: instilling in children disembodied doctrinal positions. Catechesis, with its chief form being catechesis for adults,[7] speaks to the most pressing issues of our time, not, certainly, offering easy answers but asking very probing questions about our responses to these issues. I myself do not believe a person who is glib about the significance of the Gospel in our time should be a catechist. Instead of glibness, a catechist should have a kind of stutter, a sort of hesitancy in the face of the possibility that she or he could trivialize the gospel message.

Lifestyle

Another feature of the catechesis of the early church, one that keeps surfacing throughout this book, was that it was directed ultimately, not to ideas in the head or to notional understandings of the message, but to lifestyle, that is, to ways of living. The lifestyle of the individual was important but not just in itself. The individual's lifestyle had to fit with that of the community. The community's way of life as an embodiment of the Gospel was the deeper issue. We can see this concern with lifestyle at its clearest in the practice of the catechumenate in the first three centuries of the church. The catechumenate was certainly a time for learning what the followers of Jesus actually believed, but it was even more a time for re-directing the way one lived one's life. Nobody was allowed to enter the last stages of the catechumenate until it was clear to the community that the person was living the way Christians were supposed to live. It was not enough to know the way; one had to be able to go the way.

The catechumen seeking baptism had to find witnesses to attest to his or her change of lifestyle and a sponsor who would assume a special responsibility for the continued progress of the new Christian. Candidates had to be willing to give up jobs that would hinder the practice of Jesus' teaching. Basically, when the person had come to live as a Christian, then and only then could the person be baptized and welcomed as a full member of the community.

These demands of the early communities may seem stringent; yet, in a time of intermittent persecution, living in a environment hostile to the teachings they tried to follow, Christians were concerned with their credibility as a community. They were consumed by concern for the sign of living deeds, rather than the sign of words. The community claimed it lived by the values of love for one another; the only proof of that claim they had was in the actual doing of it. "They will know we are Christians by our love." In one of his homilies, St. John Chrysostom put it this way:

> If we hope to win the victory over them (learned persons), let us strive to conquer, not with words, but through our lives . . . we will achieve nothing unless we show them a life which is better than theirs, because without paying any attention to what is said, they examine what we do, and they think to themselves: follow your own teaching first of all, and then exhort others.

Chrysostom goes on to illustrate what he understood by right living by giving an example that has to do with sharing possessions. "If you say that there are immense riches in the other world, while we see you attached to those of this life as if the other did not exist, we are more inclined to believe your deeds than your words."[8] The deeds Chrysostom was concerned about were very much the deeds of justice.

Living in the latter part of the fourth century, with the persecutions over, Chrysostom constantly reminded his fellow Christians that if they would be faithful to the person of Jesus, they had to find him in the poorest and most afflicted members of his body. To the comfortable Christians of Antioch and Constantinople, he offered the following challenges:

> Your dog is fed to fullness while Christ wastes with hunger. Christ has nowhere to lodge, but goes about as a stranger, and naked and hungry, and you set up houses out of town, and baths and terraces and chambers without number, in thoughtless vanity; and to Christ you give not even a share of a little hut.[9]

For Chrysostom, care for victims is not an option but a duty. In another place he exhorts, "If you see anyone in affliction, do not be curious to enquire further who he is. His being in affliction is a just claim on your aid. He is God's, be he heathen or be he Jew, since even if he is an unbeliever, he needs help."

In many of his sermons, Chrysostom contrasted the self-indulgence of wealthy Christians of Antioch with the abject misery of the homeless who slept in open public places, under the colonnades of the public baths and temples. Further he challenged their view of private property, saying:

> The possessions of the Lord are all common. Is not this an evil then that you alone should have the Lord's property, that you alone should enjoy what is common? Is not the earth God's, and the fullness thereof? If then our possessions belong to one common Lord, they belong also to our fellow-servants.

Notice the similarity of this teaching with that of Pope Paul VI in the encyclical *Populorum Progressio*: "No one is justified in keeping for his exclusive use what he does not need, when others lack."[10]

Were he living in our day and speaking to use, Chrysostom might have used the following tale told by Sr. Joan Chittister.

> Consider the world a village of 100 people. Six of the people
> live in Western Europe and North America in a glass house
> where they eat and drink and wear and collect for themselves
> two-thirds of everything that is made in that village while the
> other 94 sit on the lawn and watch. And it is getting intolerable
> to them. No wonder those six buy so many guns.[11]

Obviously these questions about our lifestyle are hard ones. As I
have said, one cannot raise them in public in the U.S. without some
persons getting quite angry. If you raise them in Guatemala, you
could very possibly be killed. They are questions about what in the
gospels we should be concerned about. They are questions that
relate the Gospel with the way we live.

The Catechizing Community

Unfortunately, there is a kind of catechesis very much cut off
from these questions. It focuses on doctrinal matters abstracted
from life and on information to be mentally stored. This approach
to catechesis is disembodied because the gospel message it pro-
claims is not found in the life of the community. Quite different
from such an approach is a third feature of catechesis in the early
church. The chief catechizing force was not the individual catechist
but the life of the community.[12] Because this communal feature of
catechesis so integral to the community's message and lifestyle has
already been explored above, my treatment of it here will be very
brief.

The hope that catechesis can be done by a small group of well-
trained persons hard at work with children and with adult catechu-
mens is an illusion, but a stubborn one. Sacred texts are essential to
all religions and adherents of any religion need to ponder these
texts. However, the question facing Christian groups today is:
What are the significant religious texts? Are all the significant texts
found in the written Scriptures? Or is it true that those written texts
take on meaning only insofar as they are embodied in the text of a
community's life? As previous examples have shown, the early
church recognized that its own life was the gospel message proclaimed in a way far more powerful than verbal proclamation
alone. In fact, the modern catechetical renewal has been based on an
attempt to reclaim the early Christian understanding of the importance of communal witness. I have already pointed out in several
places how the General Catechetical Directory envisions catechesis

as a form of ecclesial action, that is, as the work of the community.[13] When not integral to the lived life of actual communities, catechesis is a puny endeavor, imposed by those with power and only endured by those who must submit. The community's life is a text, the good news embodied in legible deeds.

What are the possibilities of such a catechesis today? There is evidence that these possibilities exist. In some dioceses there has been an intense effort to renewal of communal life in local parishes, through involving adults in exploring the Scriptures and their meaning in our time. In every diocese there are communities that have come alive through the struggle to understand and accept what being a disciple of Jesus involves in our time. For many persons in these communities, a new kind of discipleship has required re-imagining what being a follower of Jesus involves. Such a reimagining leads to transformation in understanding and lifestyle.

However, such catechesis cannot succeed without a willingness to face controversial questions which are the cutting edge of the problems facing those willing to follow Jesus. Catechists facing justice issues will need some of the courage of the Guatemalan catechists, since it is all too possible to deal with questions of faith in general ways that avoid central but controversial issues. To face these issues, however, more than courage is required, and any catechist will have to work to be better informed.

Behind the issues I have in mind there are complex problems that do not lend themselves to simple (or simple-minded) conclusions. When we take a position—and I claim we have eventually to take a position—we will have to be well-acquainted with the other side. Further, in taking our positions, we will have to leave room for others of good will and serious conscience to take their own positions that may differ from ours. The issues I am referring to are those involving weapons' production; involving our country's relations with other nations as far as the rights of other nations are concerned; involving military service and the right or the duty to object in conscience to military service or even to registration for possible military service; involving the non-payment of federal taxes that go to support militarism; involving state and federal policy affecting various populations below the poverty line; involving abortion and the various positions to that question now emerging among our fellow Catholics; and the exclusion of women from ordained ministries. Obviously we cannot deal with all these and other important questions in any one parish in a single year. But what does it mean when a particular parish is willing to deal with none of these questions or when our catechesis is limited to sacramental and liturgical questions set out before children, confirmands or pre-cana couples? It means our approach to catechesis is too limited and not one that can nourish the whole community.

In actual fact, the community cannot avoid the issues I have outlined, for reasons pointed out by a Protestant religious educator, as follows.

> After seeing that the group of believers is the unity with which we must work, we must then see that whatever is done or said, or not done or not said, is teaching. There is no such thing as postponing the solution to a problem. The   decision to postpone is a decision; it teaches that the issue is too hot to handle, that such issues are not appropriate for the church, or that the tactic of postponement is more important at this point than a resolution to settle the matter. People learn from the way events are handled. There is no neutrality. If a congregation attempts to be neutral, it teaches that on the issues at hand it can't make up its mind, it is fearful of the result of a decision, if it is confused about how to proceed. There is no avoidance of an issue. Not to see an issue is to teach that Christians do not see issues. Christians who avoid problems in social ethics— such as involvement in racial relations, war, or the distribution of wealth—are saying that the christian faith does not operate in these areas.[14]

Many readers will already have noted that behind my claims here about the close connection between catechesis and social justice are disturbing questions about the sort or gospel commitments found in our local churches. At the heart of those disturbing questions is the question about the sort of Jesus we are following. All Christian communities proclaim Jesus as Lord, but it is impossible that all follow the same Jesus. Guatemalan Roman Catholics who are ready with equanimity to "kill a communist for Christ" cannot be following the same Jesus as the catechists they slaughter. This problem, however, assumes much subtle forms. In a previous chapter[15] I explained how a recent study of youth retreat programs in the U.S.[16] led me to conclude that these programs tend to offer a Jesus so tied to personal self-affirmation and even self-aggrandizement as to be a religious analogue of Reaganomics.

Reflecting on the many gospel passages where Jesus' message of justice results in plans to get rid of him,[17] I have come to ask myself if it is quite possible for our middle and upper class churches also to work towards eliminating this Jesus. Note that this effort is not totally to eliminate Jesus but rather to eliminate this Jesus who announces a new day of justice. Having died once, Jesus obviously cannot be killed, but this Jesus who stands with the poor is effectively eliminated by being ignored. Ignoring Jesus is perhaps the most effective way of getting rid of the One who loved justice. An examination of Sunday homilies, of catechetical materials for children and youth, and even of graduate religious education curricula shows how it can happen that, though Jesus has not disappeared over a cliff, the heart of his message can be eliminated. The special danger of this situation is that we are left with a Jesus made over in our own image compatible with the worst features of our culture.

We end up with a Jesus who affirms our culturally-conditioned aspirations, not the Jesus who embraced the lepers and who was condemned and eventually criminalized for healing the blind on the sabbath. All of us, but particularly those who are catechists need to embrace, not just any Jesus but Him who calls us to the hard choices of discipleship on our day. In the face of these choices, perhaps we all can find encouragement in the peasant catechist martyrs of Guatemala.

Notes

1. For documentation see Allan Nairn, "The Guns of Guatemala," *The New Republic* (11 April 1983) 17-23; Virginia T. Johnson, "Agony in Guatemala," *The Sign* (February 1981) 7-11; and especially Gordon L. Bowen, "No Roadblocks to Death," *Commonweal* 111:12 (15 June 1984) 361-364; James LeMoyne, "Central America's Arms Buildup," New York *Times* (19 April 1987) A1, 16.

2. Rainer Kampling, "'Have We Not Then Made a Heaven of Earth?' Rich and Poor in the Early Church," in Leonardo Boff and Virgil Elizondo, eds., *Option for the Poor: Challenge to the Rich Countries Concilium* 187 (Edinburgh: T and T Clark, 1986) 51-62, at 51.

3. Some sources are: Raymond Brown, *The Churches the Apostles Left Behind* (New York: Paulist Press, 1984) esp. 50-55 and 118-119; Edward Schillebeeckx, *Ministry* (New York: Crossroad, 1981) 1-37; R. Schnackenburg, *God's Rule and Kingdom* (New York: Herder and Herder, 1963) esp. 99-258; Bernard Pruzak, "Hospitality Extended or Denied: Koinonia Incarnate from Jesus to Augustine," *The Jurist* 36 (1976) 89-126;

also Michael McDermott, "The Biblical Doctrine of Koinonia," *Biblische Zeitschrift* 19 (1975) 64-77 and 219-233; William Walsh and John P. Langan, "Patristic Social Consciousness—the Church and the Poor," in John Haughey, ed., *The Faith That Does Justice* 113-151.

In an important essay Aloysius Pieris notes that the Christianity that grew up in the Roman Churches adopted what he calls a "stoic" approach to liberation, which involved dealing with social problems, not through social transformation, but through spiritual transformation, that is, attitudes of mind and heart that allowed a person to transcend the unjust structures. Pieris' analysis is worth study; see Aloysius Pieris, "A Theology of Liberation in Asian Churches;" see also Aloysius Pieris, "To be Poor as Jesus Was Poor?" *The Way* 24:3 (July 1984) 186-196, an essay on Christian spirituality as a spirituality of poverty.

4. See Jon Sobrino, "Jesus in the Service of God's Kingdom," Chapter 3 of *Christology at the Crossroads* (New York: Orbis, 1978) 41-78.

5. To state that Jesus did not establish a political kingdom is, obviously, not to deny that his message has implications in the public-forum-on-social-choices (politics); see Segundo Galilea, "Jesus' Attitude Toward Politics: Some Working Hypotheses," in José Bonino, ed., *Faces of Jesus: Latin American Christologies* (New York: Orbis, 1984) 93-101.

6. See the explicit embracing of the preferential option for the poor in the "Puebla Document": *Evangelization at Present and in the Future of Latin America, Conclusions of the Third General Conference of Latin American Bishops* (Washington, D.C.: United States Catholic Conference, 1979) Pars. 382, 707, 769, 1134, 1153, 1165, 1217.

7. "... Catechesis for adults, since it deals with persons who ae capable of an adherence that is fully responsible, must be considered the chief form of catechesis. All the others forms, which are indeed always necessary, are in some way oriented to it." *General Catechetical Directory* Par. 20.

8. *Homily on 1 Corinthians.*

9. All the citations from John Chrysostom in this section are from Dolores Greeley, "St. John Chrysostom: Prophet of Social Justice," *Studia Patristica*, vol. 18, in Three Parts, ed. Elizabeth Livingstone, 1163-1168.

10. Paul VI, Populorum Progressio 23, in O'Brien and Shannon, eds., *Renewing the Earth: Catholic Documents on Peace, Justice, and Liberation* (New York: Image Books, 1977) 320-321; see also A.M.C. Waterman, "Theology and the Redistribution of Wealth," *The Ecumenist* 22:5 (July-August 1984) 75-78.

11. Joan Chittister, "No Time for Nicodemus," *Origins* 14:4 (7 June 1984) 49-55, at 53.

12. Someone might object that my earlier example of Geraldine working with the disaffected young people in Dublin belies my claim here that the community is the chief catechizing force. While it was true that the young people she dealt with had broken with their local churches, still her genius was in herself assembling the community, and *that group of young*

people became the catechizing community. They were a local church. When I met them they were in the first stages of establishing connections with the other local churches.

13. *General Catechetical Directory*, Par. 21.

14. C. Ellis Nelson, *Where Faith Begins* (Richmond: John Knox Press, 1967) 184-185.

15. See Chapter 4, p. 56.

16. Michael Warren, "Twenty Years of Youth Weekends: A Revised Appraisal," Chapter 11 of *Youth, Gospel, Liberation* (New York: Harper and Row, 1978) 107-117.

17. See the following provocative essay: Jon Sobrino, "The Epiphany of the God of Life in Jesus of Nazareth," in Richard and others, *The Tools of Death and the God of Life: A Theology*, trans. Barbara E. Campbell and Bonnie Shepard (New York: Orbis, 1983) 62-102.

8

Social Justice Catechesis and the Problem of Action

I have argued here that the role of catechesis is to influence not only individuals but communities, and to influence them in the direction of transformed life structure and action. The life structure and action of the community is the ultimate influence on its members. Still, in many cases the process of leading local churches to take active corporate stances toward justice and peace starts with catching the attention of individuals who will later gather in small groups to struggle together over naggingly complex matters. After all, the individual members of a local church inhabit, not only the world of the community's religious vision, but also the world of the dominant culture, whose vision is often enough counter to the religious one. Further, the individuals inhabit the secular culture in ways varied by their life circumstances: job, family-size, use of money, reading habits, and ways of using electronic media. For some this wider secular culture has the actual ultimacy and is much more directive of their total lives than their religious commitments. For others the opposite might be true, though in the face of the massive influences of the dominant culture, holding fast to a religious vision will never be easy and automatic.

The difficulty for most persons is not one of coming to a new, religious vision of the world, i.e., conversion; the problem is maintaining that vision. Through the catechetical process, the clash of visions needs to be examined; the religious vision needs to be highlighted and justified and then explored for what it means in the face of the dominant culture. Achieving such a goal is not an easy matter, especially because, as we have seen, of the influence of the ideology of the dominant culture. The problems this ideology causes for catechesis can be seen clearly when ideology—a word with seemingly endless definitions—is understood the way the social philosopher, Louis Aththusser, describes it.

Althusser's approach to ideology removes it from both intention and consciousness. Ideology is not even directly willed by a person under its influence. It is pre-conscious and emerges from the systems of meaning, images, and values embedded in the concrete practice of a society. These are what shape our deepest way of understanding ourselves. According to Althusser:

> It is customary to suggest that ideology belongs to the region of "consciousness" . . . In truth, ideology has very little to do with "consciousness" . . . It is profoundly unconscious, even when it presents itself in a reflected form. *Ideology is indeed a system of representation, but in the majority of cases these representations have nothing to do with "consciousness"*; they are usually images and occasionally concepts, but it is above all as *structures* that they impose on the vast majority of men, not via their "consciousness" [Italics mine].[1]

When this description is applied to catechesis, one better understands the difficulties catechesis encounters when it counters or even questions the dominant ideology of a culture. Catechesis, as I have repeated so often here, is primarily an activity of the community and for the community; but as a kind of clarification of what the community in fact is called to, it often has to clarify for particular persons what they hold in "profoundly unconscious" ways in their heart of hearts and how they actually structure their lives.

In the face of unacknowledged ideology, catechesis finds an especially "hard case" in dealing with questions of justice and peace. For individuals or groups, a catechesis of justice and peace calls for the patient clarification of misunderstandings and the gradual pursuit of new information, sometimes in a highly charged, even confrontational atmosphere. Those who have absorbed the worldview of the culture but reflected little on the deeper meaning of Jesus' call for a new day of justice can be expected to resist what for them may be a radically new idea. This catechesis cannot succeed without painstaking attention to the persons involved and to their struggles to understand the connection between their commitment to Jesus and their commitment to justice. Eventually, one would hope, these persons will take their place within a community that embodies a stance of committed action on behalf of peace and justice.

In this chapter I will focus on a single but seminal problem that has risen often in my own efforts to do a catechesis of peace and justice: the problem of action, especially as compounded by guilt and feelings of helplessness. This is the problem that emerges *after* a person's conversion to Jesus has been extended to its consequences for the social structures of our world.[2] As we shall see, because of the very assumptions about power and agency in our wider culture, a catechesis that succeeds in raising questions of justice quickly runs into the dilemma of what should be done about injustice. At the same time that some form of action is essential as a response to a new understanding of peace and justice, hasty forms of action as escapes from helplessness and guilt can be counterproductive.[3] Note that the problem I am dealing with here is not one of action as an aspect of knowing, i.e., the epistemology of action, but rather the problem of action when motivated by an inability to face guilt and helplessness. Some forms of activity should not be classified as action at all, because they are more a kind of *reaction*, not so much to actual situations outside the self that need to be faced and rather to the inner world of emotion.

The Pain of Unwitting Complicity

Persons sensitive to the task of discipleship can experience alarm and anxiety when they discover areas of life they had not been paying attention to but which needed their personal and group focus. A problem they had not been paying attention to sufficiently has now surged into view, and their new attention has a religious urgency. They could have been aware, perhaps should have been aware, but were not. That inattention amounts to a kind of complicity in evil, unwitting perhaps but none the less painful to admit. The recognition of one's place in silently supporting systems of evil creates what I will call "the ache of complicity." Because such persons know the new information is calling them to some sort of response, they can sometimes be tempted anxiously to find quick avenues of action.

When people cross over to a new understanding of their union in God with sisters and brothers they had previously given little thought to, something in their affective response often undergoes a shift. Their imagination has been freed, not simply to identify the sufferings of others but also to identify with them. As a result the injustices of others can become a kind of religious wound, a kind of psychological stigmata, that one carries invisibly in one's body. Like an actual stigmata, the wound comes from identifying with the wounds of another. Someone once explained this process to me as the transformation that comes about from meeting a victim, in the sense of encountering that person's victimhood and all the implications of human victimization.

When the victimization of others is allowed to get through to us for the first time and disturb us at any depth, the result is a kind of shock. The shock is all the more upsetting if we have been used to thinking of our own victimization as the prime one the gospel heals. In many middle-class churches, the good news preached is often the news of one's own goodness. When such news is offered as a kind of smug self-congratulation, it is a perversion of the Gospel. This good news is an analogue of the promises of the marketeers: there is a "you" that is better than the surface you, and the right product can bring it out for all to see. Your human condition can be transcended via the right product, in this case a religious product. Religiously, we are told that we are good, that the great pains the gospel message deals with are *our own* individual pains. God heals our personal troubles, our aches, our grievances against others. The good news that God embraces us is presented so as to take from us any pressing need to face ourselves and our own evil.

The problem here is not outright falsehood but the perniciousness of the half truth. When we name ourselves as the neighbor in Jesus' call to love our neighbor as ourselves, we have perverted that call. The conversion Jesus calls for is a change of heart and a change of social structures, not the conversion to self-affirmation. When the Gospel has been reduced to a message about self-esteem, coming to discover its social justice dimensions and one's unwitting complicity in systems of evil will be a shock. Encountering the victims involves a range of affective reverberations, which are not without their own problems.

In the face of such an affective shift, there is a danger of opting for illusory action, that is, forms of action providing outlets for commitment and energy but little else. If the issue at hand is so complex as to not offer clear lines of response, the anxiety of some may intensify. Touched by the urgency of a particular social problem, these persons have come to a new level of attention. Ironically, however, heightened anxiety leading to hasty plans of action can in the long run lead to a kind of immobility or at least away from significant action.

The Problem of Guilt

As I have already noted, there seem to be two prongs to this anxiety: guilt and helplessness. My chief concern here is with the helplessness side of the problem, but a word about guilt is also in order. In the past I have often found myself exhorting groups considering justice issues to move away from guilt and to focus instead on analysis, that is, on trying to probe deeper into the causes of the social problem in question. In doing so, I was basically trying to help them avoid an immobilizing guilt. I have now come to see that guilt in fact cannot be avoided and that it must be faced. Indeed there are ways of facing guilt that are not immobilizing but rather energizing. One's collusion, albeit unwitting, in unjust structures is uncomfortable to face but must be looked in the eye as a part of conversion. Facing guilt involves facing one's own human condition as a sinner and also as a social sinner, in the sense that one admits complicity in sinful social structures not of one's own creation. Whether one wills it or not, one can admit that one benefits and even profits from unjust structures causing harm and inflicting misery on others. When such an admission is marked by shock at and abhorrence of these wrongs and one's connection to them, it can lead a person—or a group—to oppose these structures with the energy born of passion.

The matter is complex, and its complexity must be an explicit part of a catechesis of justice and peace. If it is true that "recognizing sinfulness means acknowledging both ... Christian responsibility for bringing about change and . . . failure to exercise that responsibility adequately in the past,"[4] it may also be true that there is no concrete exercise of Christian responsibility here and now that is likely to change the unjust situation in the immediate future. Still, facing one's corporate guilt may be an important aspect of the move to persistent action. My complicity in an evil system, once faced, calls me to oppose that system, working to change it. It is important to note here that while I may, as an individual human person, be able to face my complicity, I cannot exercise my responsibility to work against evil systems except with the help—we could call it "the sacramental complicity" —of others. This reminder leads me to another important aspect of action, namely, facing realistically one's limitations.

The Problem of Helplessness

The problem of finding the right action-response against injustice is not solved simply by facing guilt. Helplessness is a companion problem, and a stubborn one. There are two sides to this problem: first, the negative side of naming and owning the true scope of one's helplessness; second, the positive side of naming and owning realistic avenues of one's power, which are either communal or toward communal action. The first aspect of helplessness may be especially difficult in technological societies where persons are used to seeing all problems as solvable. Every technical breakdown can be remedied with the proper tools. Every seemingly insurmountable dilemma can be corrected with planning, work, and money. Out of such a cast of mind, a person can easily move too quickly to action simply as a way of doing something, anything. Action can actually be a strategy for handling one's own anxiety, one's personal distress over the problem one has come to face. It can be a way of reducing an "ache" that must be held on to and managed.

Unfortunately there are forms of action that actually cover up one's true situation of being little able to deal directly with certain intractable problems. One can find, fairly easily, forms of response that actually give individuals or groups a sense of doing something but which in fact are quite illusory and ineffective. It is not uncommon, for example, for those dealing with youth's concern for world peace and disarmament, to encourage young people to focus on inner peace as the first and most important step in taking action for global peace. Confusing peacefulness and peace and then making inner peacefulness a requirement before any action for peace can be undertaken is a sure way to shortcircuit any kind of action in the public sphere.[5] Indeed in a world bristling with weapons of mass destruction, the gift of God may not be peacefulness at all but rather "stirred-up-fulness." There are even ways of advocating prayer for peace as a way of avoiding a keen sense of one's helplessness in the face of escalating weapons production. The problem is put in God's hands, not in a movement of true religious trust but as a way of absolving oneself of any concrete action to counter the culture of militarization.

Ironically, however, facing one's helplessness could be a first step toward effective action. A young woman from the U.S. living in New Delhi with her husband and family has written of her difficulty in dealing with the devastating poverty of so many in her city.

> have lived in India for nearly six years now and I am no closer to understanding poverty than I was the day I arrived. Perhaps I am farther away. Then at least, I was full of innocence and rage, grieved by everything I saw, moved to impossible gestures. Now, a bit jaded, a lot numb, and more and more caught up in my life and its complications (children, a home, work), I notice less.[5]

She writes of meeting a tiny emaciated woman out begging with six-day-old infant and being stunned with the contrast between that woman's situation and her own of relative comfort. In reflecting on her dilemma of what she should do, she writes:

> Growing up in America, with its strong belief in self-sufficiency, is at the heart of the problem. When I lie awake nights berating myself for being such a terrible person, I invariably drop off to sleep resolving to *try harder* to be good, as if the answer lay in my own efforts. Somehow it never occurs to me to give it over to God, to let her provide me with the strength I need. This is not mere sentimentality. It is the greatest strategical error one can make. To even think that one can face all the sadness and injustice of the world without a deep-rooted faith in God is ridiculous.[6]

I would add that in addition to a "deep-rooted faith," one needs also an environing community whose vision of God will enable one to "face all the sadness and injustice of the world."

Guilt and helplessness are not easy problems to deal with. The answer to them lies in the direction of hope. Unfortunately, some who should be announcing the Jesus' good news of justice do not do so because they fear overwhelming their listeners with problems and thus fostering feelings of despair. Such persons confuse optimism and hope. I agree with Matthew Lamb[7] that a follower of Jesus does not opt for either optimism or pessimism. Optimism as an attitude of heart judges that all will be well, and thus no action need be taken; pessimism judges no change is possible and thus action is futile. Hope is a religious category and judges that God has put the world into our hands and calls us to labor for justice and not count the cost. Far from predicting specific results, hope, as a religious virtue, works for justice with the deep conviction that injustice does not have the last word. Though injustice can and does kill and causes unlimited suffering, God revealed in the lifting up of Jesus that injustice does not triumph. Life and goodness do.

Joanna Rogers Macy, a psychologist who coped for years with a kind of despair in her own life, tells of her search for a psychological cure for her despair. She had examined her childhood and her relationship with her parents to uncover the cause of her despair. Some thought her problem might be physical and prescribed drugs for her. Finally she came to see that her despair was not psychically based at all but socially-based. It was a reasonable response to the condition of a world she had been paying close attention to. She decided to face her despair, name it for what it was, and seek in solidarity with others of similar perceptions, forms of action that would offer some hope. She also began teaching others to enter their despair and emerge on the other side in a hope, built on communal support and commitment to action. Though not explicitly religious, her work is an important clue to the question of action in our time.[8]

The Power of Paying Attention

Perhaps, the positive side of helplessness, namely, that of finding realistic lines of action, can be illustrated by another example. A friend phoned one night to discuss the hunger problem in Africa. While recognizing his distress, I feared he would tell me that he had written a check to a relief agency as a way of relieving his affected conscience. However, his action was different from check writing as a total strategy. He had resolved to forego several meals a week and to send that money for relief. His action seemed to me a creative way of letting himself, his stomach, be in physical solidarity with the victims of hunger. He was seeking to make his psychological "ache" somehow physical. His own hunger would remind him each day of the sisters and brothers in other countries. So he was not jumping away from the problem through action taken hastily to relieve him of his own psychic distress. However, did his action go far enough?

This particular person was gifted with a good education and a keen mind. I encouraged him to consider an added action, which would take as much discipline, though of a different kind, as his action of fasting. I suggested he read an analysis of the world food problem that would help him understand the broad political and social policies behind the hunger question. Such information would also enable him to inform his friends on the broader scope of this key issue of our day. In other words, I was suggesting an action of focusing not just on hunger but also on the various causes of hunger and the proposals for long-term solutions to the problem.

Behind this suggestion to my friend lay a conviction that the first action, and a highly significant action, is the act of paying attention to the problem or situation that has come into view. The forces, institutions, or persons profiting from injustice have as a first concern, a fear that people will begin paying attention to the results of their policies. Without such attention no change is possible. So, paying attention to injustice, especially when it involves whole communities, is a revolutionary act and a potentially dangerous act from the perspective of those who profit from injustice. From the other side, the first act of solidarity with the victims of injustice is the act of attending to their situation. Richard Rohr has pointed out, similarly, that documenting the injustices suffered by victims is a fundamental act of fidelity to these people. Documenting is a kind of painstaking, detailed attention. A striking example of the power of this sort of attention is the action of the mothers of the Plaza de Mayo in Buenos Aires in Argentina, who stood for years in a public place, displaying pictures of their "disappeared" sons and daughters, until finally their action helped bring down a criminal dictatorship.

There are, of course, gradations of attention, and though I am not ready to map them, possibly a first level of attention is the level of stewing. By "stewing" I want to suggest that one tolerate the tension of seeing the problem and knowing that one is upset by it at the same time one may not have any clues about what to do. Stewing takes courage because it involves coping with pain, anxiety, frustration, and so forth.

A youth worker from Germany has told me that many young people there in the early 1980s were alarmed about the arms build-up, especially the placing of U.S. Cruise and Pershing missiles in Europe, and they wanted to take action against that build-up. However many of the young people became discouraged and finally abandoned their efforts, and in some cases their interest, when they saw they did not produce the results they wanted. They needed more patience, more stewing and less concern for immediate results. The reaction of these young people is understandable to anyone who has tried to take similar action against a well-entrenched problem.

Those encouraging or taking forms of direct action for social change would do well to remember the importance of paying attention as a significant, far-reaching kind of action. It is the primal empowerment, on which other forms of empowerment build. Systematic attention is the sort of action that can affect a lifetime, because it can lead to a lifelong commitment to justice and to various levels of action for justice. Thus, action to influence the attention of others, which is the action of consciousness-raising, is a forceful kind of action, and a fearful one from the side of the oppressors.

Gabriel Moran tells of attending a meeting on justice questions with a group of educators, who were asked to reflect on what they would do in response. Moran was surprised so few educators saw their educational activity as a key form of action. His own simple and profound response to the question of what his action for justice would be was two words: "I teach." Such action is within the power of many. Handing on printed information to friends and associates, engaging them in conversation, and calling their attention to organizations, events, and film and TV depictions of some social problem may all serve to enlarge the circle of those who understand a particular issue.

Similarly, the kind of direct action taken by persons like Daniel and Philip Berrigan is significant because of its power, through the effective use of symbols, to focus attention on an evil that has been overlooked. Their creative forms of action do not in themselves change structures; rather they change the perception of the problem, a first and crucial step.

Actually there are two transformations called for: the transformation of structures, which will take a long time and which must be worked at consistently; and the transformation of consciousness, which involves coming to recognize the need for the transformation of structures and which is a prior requirement for structural change. The transformation of consciousness as a moral transformation involves a willingness both to face the enormity of the issues but also to adopt patterns of living consistent with one's new understanding. To work for the transformation of structures, while putting the completion of the work in the hands of God calls for both courage and deep faith.

A friend who was spending a day a week washing dishes and serving soup at the Catholic Worker house on the lower East Side of New York City, was asked whether his time might have been better spent doing more research for the book on justice he was editing. He admitted that he did not need his educational background to do the work he found himself doing for the soup line. What he did involved almost no skills. Still, he said, he needed to be with and among the poor in order to keep a sense of personal integrity in his attempt to deal conceptually with issues of justice. He seemed to be saying that his was an action of paying attention to actual persons on the margins of society, of trying to be with them, not just in his mind but in actual minutes and hours spent among them as they came to eat. He said he did not expect to effect much change in the condition of these men of the streets. The significant changes were occurring in his own attitudes and in his appreciation of those on the margins of society.

His was another kind of stewing, involving immersing oneself, even temporarily, in the lives of the victims. His response illustrates the value of probing and deepening our understanding of the various levels of action. Probing these levels will on the one hand help us avoid trivializing the value of even small acts and on the other hand, avoid overstating the value of objectively significant action.

Public Action with Others

One aspect of responsible action for justice needed much more attention, especially in a culture marked by privatization and individualism, is that of public action with others. While public action is appropriate for many people in many different situations, it is very appropriate for the church as a public body publicly committed to the Gospel. Action with others is not possible without the prior dialogue necessary to share mutual perceptions of a social situation and vision of the needed change. Such dialogue ordinarily takes time and involves working through disagreements. It is hard and painful work, which is an indispensable part of a catechesis of justice and peace. At times it might seem to some as if action would be easier and more effective if they simply undertook it alone. And yet, significant action on social issues will have to be social, meaning, involving blocks of persons working together, and public, that is, intended to influence the decisions by which public policy is formed. Violent action done by a very few will, sad to say, attract much attention. The non-violent struggle, however, is much more democratic because it calls for much larger numbers and for the laborious, slow task of networking and dialogue. It is action for the long haul.

I have noticed that when some persons concerned for peacemaking first come to understand the importance of collaborative efforts, they are awed by the task. They are not used to networking with others on issues. The only networks they know are familial ones, which are sometimes difficult enough in their own right. It takes courage to commit oneself to forms of action that involve persons working as a group. This is a commitment, not just to persons, but to persons who have the possibility of being *a people*. If the structure of evil in our day is institutional and corporate, then too the structure of resistance to evil must find its true corporateness in groups of people working together as a body.

Even when working with those of other religious traditions, Christians have a powerful metaphor of "body" to aid them in working with others. Ultimately, the role of catechesis is to provide a kind of "fidelity therapy" to the church seeking to embody the Gospel. When local groups of Jesus' followers embody action for justice and peace, catechesis can finally take the privileged form of inviting others to learn from the community by joining them in their pilgrimage to justice. At issue in matters of justice is not only an individual's fidelity to Jesus' message but the fidelity of the community of followers. Likewise, the most notable failures of Christians in our century have been not so much at the individual level as at the corporate level. What are we who count ourselves as disciples of Jesus called to be in the face of these pressing questions of our time? This is a nagging question that gets at the heart of our togetherness and what it means.

Notes

1. H. Althusser, *For Marx* (New York: Vintage Books, 1969) 233, cited in Henry A. Giroux, "Theories of Reproduction and Resistance in the New Sociology of Education: A Critical Analysis," *Harvard Educational Review* 53:3 (1983) 264.

2. In *Spirituality and Justice* (New York: Orbis, 1984) Donal Dorr explores three levels of conversion: on the personal level of one's relationship with God; on the interpersonal level of relationships with friends and

with those with whom one has personal contact; and on the public level of social and political structures.

3. There is a difference between guilt as a neurotic symptom, a "feeling" bubbling up from our unconscious, and guilt as an appropriate reaction to one's part in acts not appropriate for a human being or at least not proper for this particular human being in this particular circumstance. As I will explain below, even the latter kind of guilt can become tinged with neurosis, as when one is immobilized by it. Philip Rieff warns us of the danger of disposing of all guilt as neurotic and thereby ridding ourselves of a moral sense. For a more recent statement of Rieff position on this matter, see "For the Last Time Psychology," *Salmagundi* 74-75 (Spring-Summer 1987) 101-117.

4. James McPolin and Peter McVerry, "A Missing Link," *The Furrow* 35:4 (April 1984) 239-245, at 244.

5. See Faith Mauro, "Let There Be Peace on Earth and Let It Begin with Me," *Emmaus Newsletter* (Winter 1984) 3.

6. Jo McGowan, "The Poor Break Through," *Commonweal* 114:12 (19 June 1987) 383-386, at 383.

7. Ibid. 386.

8. Matthew L. Lamb, *Solidarity with Victims: Toward a Theology of Social Transformation* (New York: Crossroad, 1982) ix-x.

9. A very helpful succinct statement of her position is Joanna Macy, "Despair Work," *Evolutionary Blues* 1:1 (1981) 36-47. Her longer work is Joanna Rogers Macy, *Despair and Personal Power in the Nuclear Age* (Phildelphia: New Society, 1983). Macy has many important things to say about the work of imagination in fostering hope. Her work on imagination make good sense for Christians for whom Jesus imagines a religiously grounded hope.

9

Catechesis and the Problem of "Popular" Culture

In this chapter I make two claims about the current situation of catechesis in the U.S. in its relationship to culture in its most quickly changing form, that is, as seen in electronically communicated images. The first claim is that the electronic transmission of meanings presents us with a new kind of culture and a new way of living in culture. The second is that the new condition of culture poses a special problem for catechesis, a problem that does not have ready answers. Both claims are complicated by the difficulty of finding a language that will cogently describe these new situations and coherently set forth ways of addressing them. As a first step, I wish to deal with the notion of culture itself.

The Meaning of Culture

According to the Welsh scholar, Raymond Williams, "Culture is one of the two or three most complicated words in the English language."[1] If one accepts as true that what one cannot name one cannot see or be aware of, then the accurate naming of culture is of first importance. What seems to be true of culture, even for many people with specialized education, is that they have a name for a vague reality but lack a way of thinking about it. Thus if one asked these persons to specify the various components that go to make up culture or the processes by which culture is produced or reproduced, they would be at a loss to do so.

135

In one place in his writings Williams offers three common meanings for culture: a developed state of mind, as in "a cultured person"; the processes that lead to this state of mind, by which a person is given a chance "to develop some culture"; and the whole way of life of a distinct people or other social group.[2] He finds these meanings too limited or too static.

Williams points out that in all its early uses in English, culture was a "noun of process," referring to the tending of something, such as crops, animals and so forth. For those wishing to think about culture, he recommends trying to retain this active sense of the word, as a way of alerting us to the fact that culture is not some inert abstract reality but is always in process, both in the sense that it is always affecting us but also in the sense that it is always being actively produced. As we shall see, his recommendation about giving special attention to the active side of culture has merit.

Williams' approach to culture is different from the approach of anthropologists who approach culture from an ethnographic angle. Ethnographers seek to chart culture as a system operating among some particular social group, by examining how a society works and how one part interacts with another.[3] Thus the ethnographer tends to be preoccupied with the system as a given and to ignore the origins of the particular practices in a society and how these origins are produced and re-produced. Often enough these origins are inaccessible to an ethnographer working in an oral culture without access to written records.

The ethnographer's concern is to chart the system as it functions. This concern shows up in the following description of culture, written by an anthropologist.

> We might also very usefully view culture—as many, if not most anthropologists do—as a socially shared design for living, as a tried and more or less successful system for coping with life, as the total set of norms learned from one's group for best dealing with the given physical, social, and ideational environment.[4]

The key phrases here, such as "shared design," "successful system," and "given . . . environment," suggest that the focus is on the functioning of the system rather than on the production of the system or on the shifts in the system from changes in production procedures.

Raymond Williams' approach to culture, however, seeks to chart, not simply the cultural system and its design but the precise ways the system of meanings and values is created. Notice how his description of culture recognizes the systemic aspect of culture while stressing its active, dynamic outcome. "Culture is the *signifying system* [italics his] through which . . . a social order is communicated, reproduced, experienced and explored."[5] If one judges, as I do, that the most pressing cultural question of our time is the rapid way that culture is produced and reproduced, Williams' concerns assume special importance. Indeed the kinds of questions I seek to raise in this chapter emerge from Williams' analyses in a way they do not emerge from more mainstream ethnographic writings. Because of the electronic amplification and reproduction of visuals and sounds, the key cultural problem in our day is not one of charting stable cultural systems but of de-mystifying how shifts take place in meaning systems and how such shifts are related to other societal factors, such as economics. For many religious persons these shifts tend to be ignored or simply accepted as givens unable to be questioned or contested.

The task set forth by Williams in writings dating from the end of the 1950s has been taken up by others concerned for rapid shifts in meaning systems characteristic of cultures tied to electronic communications. One such person is George Gerbner of the Annenberg School of Communications at the University of Pennsylvania. Gerbner, like Williams is concerned not only with the system of culture but the patterns of cultural production. Notice how in the following description of culture, Gerbner acknowledges the system of culture, but at the end shows his concern is with how that system is created, produced.

> All animals react to things but humans act in a world of towering symbolic construction, called culture, including art, science, religion, statecraft, and all other story-telling. Culture is that system of messages and images which regulates social relations, introduces us into roles of gender, age, class, vocation; gives us models of conformity and targets for rebellion; provides the range of personalities, temperaments, mentalities said to be our "characteristics"; helps us rise to selfless acts of courage and sacrifice; and makes us accept (or even perpetrate) repression and slaughter of countless unknown people assigned to the appropriate categories of barbarians and other

enemies. In other words, culture is that symbolic organization which socializes us and cultivates our fantasies about a world we do not experience directly. It is a system of stories and other artifacts *increasingly mass produced that mediates between existence and our consciousness of existence and thereby helps shape both* [Italics mine].[6]

Both Williams and Gerbner highlight the symbolic or signifying functions of culture, and thus the relationship of culture to communications. Their stress is on the active, almost volatile, way signs can be manipulated and can shift in the process of communication. Religiously sensitive persons and those concerned with education need to pay special attention to how these shifts affect religious sensibilities and the task of education.

The Problem of Culture

The above paragraphs allude to the problem of culture in our time. A recent video seen on TV in the U.S. may provide a useful means of setting forth the scope of the problem. *The Rebellious Gardener*, produced for French television by Maurice Failevic, provides an extended metaphor for understanding the problem of culture in modern societies, and especially the problem confronted by catechesis in the face of popular culture. In the imaginary land of this visual tale, the people are not allowed to grow their own food. The citizenry have all they want to eat—far more than they need—but all of it is official government food. All food must be both grown by the government and distributed by the government, and at prices nobody objects to. Growing one's own food is illegal and a sizable police force works exclusively to monitor the non-production of food by private individuals or groups acting outside of government control. So successful has the government strategy become that at the time the story takes place, almost all persons have forgotten even the possibility of doing their own cultivation of crops. As a real possibility, cultivation of the soil is not even imaginable, except of course, by the rebellious gardener of the story's title, who, it turns out, has subversive, criminal tendencies.

The gardener in question runs a free, private Museum of Ancient Agriculture in what was once a grain mill, where he has on display some of the obsolete instruments used in those ignorant days when people thought to produce food for themselves. Occasionally antiquarians and school children doing history projects visit the museum, wander among the exhibits and listen incredulously as the curator lectures on the harebrained habits of yore. Not surprisingly the most frequent visitors to the museum are the police nervous about the possibility the gardener could be a troublemaker.

Indeed, the police have good reason to be concerned, since the museum curator is in fact a secret gardener, whose very act of putting hoe to earth is one of rebelliousness. In the mill he had discovered ancient packs of vegetable seeds and has been encouraging neighbors to use these seeds to grow their own food. He has also been guilty of demonstrating methods of cultivation in his own garden. His subversive claim, verified by the neighbors, is that locally grown food has a taste exquisite in comparison with the wooden flavors of the government produce. His contribution to his neighbors goes beyond giving them food. By being cut off from understanding the processes by which they were fed, they had lost their understanding of a basic human process, now restored to them. Alas for our gardener, his conspiracy is discovered and his rebellion quashed through decisive police action. He is arrested, his gardens defoliated, and all produce and seeds confiscated.

I take Failevic's visual story to be a brilliant metaphor of a key problem of culture in our society with special ramifications for catechesis: the problem of the production of meaning. More and more in modern society, persons do not till their own meanings but rather tend to consume the signification produced for their consumption almost entirely by others.[7] Our situation, however, has an important difference from the one Failevic presents. In our case, the government does not control the production of culture. Instead cultural production has been left in the hands of commercial interests, whose concerns are not primarily to inform or entertain but rather to make a profit. The end result is much the same as when government has total control of the production of meaning: persons are not producers of culture; they are relegated to being consumers.[8] The separation of production from consumption can easily lead to a situation of dependency on the part of those who have been enabled to consume but not to produce, or even further, to be unaware of the processes of production.

Failevic's use of agriculture as the social problem in his story is an apt way of showing us the analogous social problem of culture. Both words, agriculture, and culture come from the same root, meaning to grow and produce.[9] Culture is about the meanings and values produced to nourish a particular group of people. Just as no living creature can survive without nourishment, human beings cannot live without feeding off a system of meaning. The quest for meaning has about it an urgency analogous to the urgency of food. You cannot live without food; neither can you survive without human signification. To continue the analogy, if there is a kind of inevitability to food, which even where not planted springs naturally from the earth's vegetation, there is a similar inevitability to meaning. Persons will unfailingly find or produce a world of meaning. Part of this search for meaning includes the quest for the totally encompassing kind of meaning that persons find in religion.

In our time, there has been proliferation of signification that would have been unimagined a century ago. Visual images of all sorts, most of them produced with some kind of electronic assistance, surround us on all sides and at almost all times, as do aural amplifications. Clearly the fact of the proliferation of signification is not something to be deplored. The problem I attempt to lay out in this chapter is not the fact, but the difficulty many persons have of being able to think about the consequences of the fact, and if necessary, to contest these consequences. Much of the meaning communicated to us electronically is tied to narratives that feed us a version of the world concocted by persons we never see and rarely even consider, but a version we tend to "swallow" even when we do not consciously intend to do so. When these versions contradict and then threaten to overwhelm the world-version of religious groups, then these groups will rightly take close notice.

At this point readers may wish to ask two questions. How does this situation differ from earlier times when most people received their versions of the world in a way very similar to the way we do, from other agencies, such as schools, churches, unwritten customs and proverbs, and governmental agencies? What is the catechetical problem this situation causes?

The New Situation

In response to the first question, one would have to admit that we all take our versions of the world from agencies outside ourselves. Nobody makes up the world of meaning for oneself—except possibly an insane person. We all dwell within the artificial world of our second nature—the world of culture. So it has always been, even though our awareness of that fact is fairly recent.[10] However, I am claiming that what is new in our situation today is that we live, not just in a culture the way every other human being did, but in an electronic culture giving most persons a new kind of accessibility to versions of reality.

There was a time—and I do not care to grieve nostalgically for it—when versions of the world did not come into one's home unless one went out and brought them in. A book, which would always present a version of reality (and also one "concocted" by a person the reader might never meet), had to be purchased and then brought across the threshold of the home by some person. The same would be true of a song, which also offers a version of reality: it could only enter the home through some person. Today, however, once the TV or radio has been brought into the home and plugged in, its versions of reality enter the home, not across the threshold but in a quite different way, offering a new kind of accessibility to multiple versions of reality.

Since the point may seem like a belabored one, perhaps an example may help disclose its dramatic implications. I once went into a home to share a cup of tea with the parents of a large family. As I moved through to the kitchen, where the parents were, I passed several of the children intently watching a daytime soap opera at the front of the house. It suddenly occurred to me that if I entered the kitchen and announced that the children were watching someone doing a vile act outside the living room window, the parents would have rushed out in a rage to do something about it. But there they were, these children sprawled across the living room, at very different ages, all watching the same TV program. Their viewing went unquestioned, perhaps assumed to be innocent. However, they were viewing someone's version of some of the most important human concerns: affection, friendship, and marital love, and their opposites: manipulation, betrayal, and lust; commitment and self-sacrifice and their opposites: greed and the abuse of power. If the program they were watching was like most weekday afternoon dramas, it did not simply depict some of the most despicable of human vices; it tended to celebrate them. Thus it offered viewers a version of the world, and to these children, a version fully counter to that proposed by their parents. The subtle celebrative aspect of the narrative tends, I claim, to underline the acceptability of the conduct being portrayed.

The TV screen was at that moment was functioning as a picture window through which someone was exposing to those children matters *that might have been* obscene or at least inappropriate for them at their ages. The TV however seemed to be taken for granted, almost like another piece of furniture.

My point here is that there is a difference between the way persons now receive their accounts of the world and the way they did, say, before the production and marketing of electronically amplified signals. True, the children in my example still go to school, are active in a church, receive the same unwritten folkways of other U.S. eastern city dwellers, and so forth. What is new is that the accessibility of the electronically amplified versions of reality, especially via radio and television, puts these children under the influence of these versions in a dramatic way. Today, when some educators are alarmed at the limited influence of schooling in the face of these electronic influences, my own concern is about the catechetical dimensions of the situation.[11]

The Catechetical Problem

The catechetical problem disclosed by the above example is one of conflicting claims about the nature of reality and about the goals of life. Although the problem it poses may not be new, the scale of the problem is quite new. We know that among early Christian groups there was great concern that those accepted into their circle understood and lived according to their special vision of reality. Those in the circle did not merely consume someone else's special vision of reality; they also created or produced it too. That vision, actually the vision of Jesus, now made their own, conflicted with the vision common to the cultures of the Middle East at that time. Catechesis, both in the catechumenate and in on-going catechesis was a kind of "vision therapy" meant to correct the distortions of the larger society.[12] In later periods of the church, the first stage of the spiritual life was seen as the purgative stage, a stage during which there was concern for a therapy of the affections aimed at changing the habits of the heart. Thus it would be true to say that catechesis was a counter-cultural activity, just as it would be to say that the community's own life ran counter to the accepted mores of the day.

Possibly an effective way of suggesting the scope of the catechetical problem in the face electronically enhanced signification is the following quote from George Gerbner's reflections on the challenge of television. He writes:

> We have moved away from the historic experience of human-
> kind. Children used to grow up in a home where parents told
> most of the stories. Today television tells most of the stories to
> most of the people most of the time.[13]

In appreciating the importance of Gerbner's point here, we have to
remember two key matters about the stories told children—while
retaining his point that today's TV stories are not told to children
only.

First, stories are told with certain interests in mind. When parents tell children stories, it is because they want the children to
understand certain matters they consider important or to entertain
them by calling to their attention the fun or beauty or mystery of
certain persons or events. The question to be kept foremost when
the story tellers and the stories change is: What are the interests of
the new story tellers and what lessons do their stories have? The
second matter has to do with the stories of a religious tradition.
Every tradition embodies many stories, and the stories that make
up that tradition must be told and known if persons are to be part of
that tradition. When the stories die, the tradition is dead.

The agenda of the new story tellers and of their new stories are
obvious to anyone who cares to watch television at the times
children are expected to be watching. Many, though of course not
all, of the messages run counter to religious traditions, and if one
reflected at any depth, counter to many stated family values. Gerbner
puts it this way:

> By the time they can speak, let alone read, they [children] have
> absorbed hundreds of thousands of stories—programs, news
> commercials—produced on the television assembly-line to the
> specifications of adult tastes and industrial needs. The perva-
> sive mass ritual blurs, when it does not short circuit, social
> distinctions rooted in subcultural and class membership, blends
> community consciousness into its mainstream, and bends that
> in the direction of its own institutional interests.[14]

From a catechetical perspective the situation Gerbner describes
here calls for careful scrutiny. The word scrutiny is selected with
some care to suggest the sort of attention, study, and analysis
needed if the catechetical dimensions of the modern production of
culture is to be dealt with effectively. To make this suggestion is not
at all to imply that everything electronically communicated is de-
praved or even distorted but very definitely to imply that all mes-

sages must be open to evaluation from particular standpoints. If one agrees that the task of the theologian of culture is to identify "the pretensions to ultimate meaning embodied in its [culture's] social, political, economic, intellectual and aesthetic expressions,"[15] and to bring them under the critique of a truly transcendent norm, then that task is also at least partly the task of a catechist.

Although most of my examples here have been about children, the problem posed by electronically amplified and communicated versions of the world is far from limited to children. Vivid versions of human existence encounter all persons plugged into the electronic culture, and while these versions claim the kind of ultimacy alluded to in the previous paragraph, they also possess a more stubborn ultimacy, which they do not actively claim but merely assume. In its character as "second nature," already alluded to, culture's stubborn ultimacy is so taken for granted that it cannot be questioned; it simply is.

Persons of intelligence, good will, and religious sensibility can claim that electronically amplified renditions of the world have no effect and are thus no problem. Such a claim denies the problem that when those who have been soaking up TV fare cross the threshold into the sacred space where the community gathers, they cross with that fare as part of their lives, if not in their actual mindset then at least in their memories. This claim also shortcircuits attempts to deal with the problem I have been trying to describe here.

Perhaps the tragic meltdown at the Chernobyl nuclear reactor in Kiev in 1986 can provide an analogy that might help dispel the stubborn illusion of invulnerability some have in the face of the effects of popular culture. This illusion is analogous to the illusion many people had about the true destructive potential of nuclear power. Theirs was the illusion that the pollution generated by human decisions is somehow "out there," that is, related to us in some unspecified way but basically outside of us. What Chernobyl showed was that the true danger of various kinds of pollution is that it comes to reside within the earth and its chain of plant and animal life, and as part of that chain, within humans themselves.

This danger is not always immediately evident, since the infection may operate silently, not becoming evident for weeks, months, or even years. The illusion is that what cannot be seen does not exist, an illusion demonstrated by U.S. tourists in Kiev, who resented having their tour cancelled because they "felt fine" and found everything going quite normally.

If we define pollution as that which infects and eventually causes deterioration in life-fostering processes, we might be able to see an analogy between ecological pollution and cultural pollution. Cultural pollution involves the despoiling of the chain, not of bio-generative processes, but of the processes of human signification, of human meaning. Like ecological pollution, cultural pollution is silent and difficult to detect, but surely proceeds to cause a breakdown of the processes of human valuing and understanding. Though it is not unusual for critics to complain of noise pollution or even of visual pollution of the countryside through the proliferation of roadside signs, very few have noted that cultural pollution,[16] like biological pollution, comes to reside within us. Distorted or false images of life, of value, or of wants and desires do not pollute our environment of meaning in some way outside us. They come to reside within us—unless of course we work vigorously to contain them or to counter them. We become hosts to these distorted messages.

From a religious point of view, the question of cultural pollution becomes all the more alarming.[17] After all, religious consciousness claims to offer a world of meaning that enriches human understanding. The Christian understanding, for example, sees human persons as tabernacles of the Living God. However, what cultural pollution with its distortions of human valuing does is to make persons "tabernacles of the living idols," hosts of value systems and understandings fundamentally at odds with their religious convictions. In other words, cultural pollution finally comes to reside, not in some vague world apart from us, but within our very selves, and it does so far more quickly and with a greater finality than does any biological pollution.

Of course the matter of religious convictions is not so simple as it might first appear. When any religious group resists, it does so from a particular stance, which is always a committed stance. However not all the stances are committed to the same matters. Compare, for example, the range of committed stances among Christians in the U.S. who could be grouped under "evangelical." The position of the groups led by Jerry Falwell and Pat Robertson are quite different from the stance of the Sojourners Community in Washington, D.C., with their radical commitment to justice. One kind of group stance would be particularly concerned about distorted sexual messages of electronic media, while the other, though not ignoring the problem of these messages, is more concerned about the bald legitimation of violence and the more subtle justification of the oppression of the underclasses found in some media.[18]

Finding Solutions

The catechetical scrutiny I am advocating here will never become a reality until electronic imagery has been "problematized," that is, until the challenge it poses to religious commitments is exposed. The church also has a story and represents a zone of meaning, with a particular imagination of the world centered on the way Jesus imagined life's possibilities. Often enough there are not only conflicting claims but also a lack of fit between the version of the world ingested from TV at home of a Saturday evening and that offered worshipers of a Sunday morning around the altar. The precise problem lies not in the lack of fit but in not recognizing the lack of fit. TV's imagination of the world, like all imagination, affects not the mind only but comes to inhabit the heart and what an earlier spirituality called "the affections." The reorientation of those affections, as I have pointed out so many times throughout this book, poses an acute problem for religious groups of our day.

Since this chapter has been written as a kind of first step in suggesting the problem of electronically communicated versions of reality,[19] I wish to conclude with some suggestions about possible ways to proceed in attending to the problem. Already a fair amount has been written for parents, in encouraging them to counter electronic imagery counter to family values. This literature alerts parents to the problem and then shows them how to monitor what children see and hear, with special stress on what children see on television.[20] Prescriptions range from turning off the TV set to sitting down with children to watch with them and expose false or unacceptable versions of reality. These prescriptions say: pay attention to what children see and hear, and then pay attention with children so as to assist children to see through what they watch.[21] This seemingly simple strategy has behind it much wisdom. It recognizes that a dialogue is being carried on with children by the media marketeers, and it is a dialogue from which parents tend to be excluded. Someone other than parents is creating the agenda for children. This strategy invites parents back into the dialogue with their own children. Another set of prescriptions for parents involves public action to question the structures that provide children access to so much distorted reality.

In an important statement about the power of television, George Gerbner explained to a group of church leaders the importance of the proper kind of action. He said:

> Trying to be heard over the din of rival schools of public relations (rather than public philosophies), alternative voices can be so shrill and provocative as to justify their own isolation and repression. Our defense can be the determined effort to come to grips rather than to terms with the sweeping currents of our culture. Our power can come from a disciplined attempt to understand and expose the dynamics myth-making in society and discover what happens when that process touches the lives of millions of people.[22]

Gerbner's suggestions are insightful and helpful, but not simple or easily implemented. The "disciplined attempt to understand and expose the dynamics of myth-making in society" will require both study and a re-oriented way of thinking about and looking at visuals.

These strategies for parents appear to be also appropriate for catechetical leaders. Alerting persons to the problem is a first step, which can be followed by monitoring with persons what they watch in films or on TV for lack of fit. However, even these strategies may prove useless without a connection to a faith community that has staked its life on an alternative version to life, decisively different from that offered in popular media. As I have already pointed out, this question is one of spirituality. The most radical strategy, then, would be the *standpoint* offered by such a community.[23] Just as feminists have a standpoint from which to judge sexist imagery, so too a committed standpoint is one of the surest means of recognizing images or versions of reality not acceptable to one's religious stance.

A standpoint is not a static position but an engaged one. Standpoints that go against the dominant culture are engaged in the special sense of being actively produced and embraced. The most successful strategy open to catechesis is to be actively involved in the production of the alternate religious vision, that is, the alternate culture.[24] Stances of commitment to non-violence and of solidarity with victims, when active in the sense just noted, hold special power to question and counter much imagery in "popular" culture. To name such radical standpoints as the solution is actually to attend to the scope of the problem.

Catechists may need to find vibrant metaphors to guide their work of resistance to unacceptable versions of life. A good one was offered by Peruvian theologian, Gustavo Gutierrez in the title of his fine book on spirituality. The title, *We Drink from Our Own Wells*, suggests a people who have found their own source of sustenance, their own source of life. In this fine book, that source of life is a gospel spirituality suited to a particular condition of life in a particular place, at a particular time in history. Gutierrez is clearly concerned to stave off "cultural death," by which "those in power seek to do away with everything that gives unity and strength to the dispossessed of the world."[25] His metaphor has an interesting connection with Failevic's agricultural metaphor, though Gutierrez' is perhaps more powerful. He is suggesting his people avoid the wells that are poisoned with cultural pollution and stay close to the waters of life.

Perhaps those in so-called first-world countries could adopt Gutierrez' powerful metaphor as a way of resisting culturally obscene messages and images. My own sense, which should be obvious at this point in this book, is that adopting his metaphor is not enough; that step must be tied the kind of life-stance he describes in this book, a stance that moves away from the message of death and toward the waters of life.

Notes

1. Raymond Williams, *Keywords: A Vocabulary of Culture and Society* (New York: Oxford University Press, 1976) 76.

2. Raymond Williams, *The Sociology of Culture* (New York: Schocken Books, 1982) 10-12.

3. In making this point, I am aware that a cultural anthropologist might well reject as oversimplistic my position here. I realize that concern with culture must at some point deal with the systemic dimensions of culture. However, for lack of space here I choose not to lay out the various theories operative in social and cultural anthropology. My point is rather to contrast Raymond Williams' special concern for current forms of cultural production with that of more mainstream ethnology to chart the functioning of a system. A brief overview of the varied currents in this mainstream is the first chapter of Edmund Leach, *Culture and Communication* (New York: Cambridge University Press, 1976) 3-7.

4. Cited in Louis J. Luzbetak, "The Beneficiaries of Evangelization," in Kenneth Boyak, *Catholic Evangelization Today* (Mahwah, NJ: Paulist, 1987) 4.

5. *Sociology of Culture* 13.

6. George Gerbner, "The Challenge of Television," Unpublished Paper, 1982, 1-2.

7. Of course, all culture as a meaning system comes to us from outside ourselves, but my claim is that we are in a different situation today because of the electronically transmitted meanings and the problems they cause. A current thinker who has written most prolifically and insightfully about this shift is Walter Ong. For a good single source see Walter Ong, "Literacy and Orality in Our Times," *Journal of Communications* (Winter 1980) 197-204.

8. Here I am applying to cultural production an aspect of the church's teaching about economic justice, namely, that persons have not only a right to income and consumption; they also have a right to engage in the processes of production. This point, actually a principle about the place of participation in social structures, needs to be applied to participation in the production of culture, even among the very young. For more on this point from an economic angle, tied to church social teaching, see Gregory Baum, "Capital, Bishops, and Unemployment," *New Catholic World* (July-August 1983) 158-162; also National Conference of Catholic Bishops, "Economic Justice for All: Catholic Social Teaching and the U.S. Economy," (Third Draft) *Origins* 16:3 (5 June 1986) pars. 68-77 and 133-140.

9. See John Kavanagh, "Capitalist Culture as a Religious and Educational Formation System," *Religious Education* 78:1 (1983) 50-60. In this essay, Kavanagh offers an astute analysis of a nine-year-old girl, who has been manipulated by the consumerist culture, but also points out the relation between culture and agriculture. Another excellent examination of this relation, though from a somewhat different angle, is Wendell Berry, "The Agricultural Crisis as a Crisis of Culture," in *The Unsettling of America: Culture and Agriculture* (New York: Avon Books, 1978) 39-48.

10. Darrell J. Fasching, "Theologian of Culture," *Cross Currents* 35:1 (1985) 9-10; see also Gregory Baum, "Faith and Culture," *The Ecumenist* (November-December 1985) 9-13.

11. Perhaps educator Neil Postman of New York University has written most often about the problem from the point of view of a secular educator. Some useful titles are: "Engaging Students in the Great Conversation," *Phi Delta Kappan* (January 1983) 310-316; *Teaching as a Conserving Activity* (New York: Delta, 1979) esp. 3-86; *Amusing Ourselves to Death: Public Discourse in the Age of Show Business* (New York: Viking, 1985).

12. I will return to this point in greater detail below. See Note 15.

13. Gerbner, "The Challenge" 8.

14. Ibid.

15. Fasching, "Theologian of Culture" 9.

16. Raymond Williams uses the expression "cultural poverty" in his long essay, "Britain in the Sixties: The `Long Revolution' Analysis," and in many of his writings seems to be getting at cultural pollution without using the exact expression. For the above essay and another useful one on this question, entitled "Culture and Technology," see *The Year 2000* (New York: Pantheon Books, 1983). In a recent book, Gustavo Gutierrez uses a term related to but more powerful than "cultural poverty." His term is "cultural death," by which he means those processes that kill the sources of spiritual hope of a people; see below, note 22.

17 . In this connection I find very helpful the following description of how the act of seeing was understood in the fourth century.

> Medieval men and women's experience of religious images is far closer to a modern experience of media images than to a modern person's visit to a museum. Both contemporary media images and historical religious images were experienced daily. Moreover, three major differences between the visual experience of modern people and that of historical people must be taken into account when we try imaginatively to reconstruct the role of religious images in the life and worship of historical people.
>
> *First, modern understanding of physical vision in its popular version differs significantly from the understanding of medieval people.* In the theory of vision described by Augustine . . . is a fire within the body—the same fire that animates and warms the body—is collected with unique intensity behind the eyes; for an object to be seen by a viewer, this first must be projected in the form of a ray that is focused on the object, thereby establishing a two-way street along which the attention and energy of the viewer passes to touch its object. A representation of the object, in turn, returns to the eye and is bonded to the soul and retained in the memory.
>
> This strong visual experience was formulated negatively as the fear of contamination by a dangerous or "unsightly" visual object or positively as belief in the miraculous power of an icon, when assiduously gazed upon, to heal one's disease. Popular beliefs and practices support the conclusion that medieval people considered visual experience particularly powerful for one's good or ill. The persistence of belief in the "evil eye" from classical times to the sixteenth century and beyond is a good example. The evil eye was thought of as a maleficent visual ray of lethal strength. A person who had the evil eye reportedly could touch and poison the soul or body of an enemy. The only protections against the evil eye were making the

sign of the cross, keeping one's body thoroughly covered against the baleful touch, and, especially, never meeting the eye of such a person; to do so would be to connect the two visual rays and allow the evil ray direct access to one's soul.

This heightened, even exaggerated, respect for the power, for good or evil, of visual experience is very far from modern understandings of what occurs in vision. Modern theories of vision concentrate on the mechanics of vision without attention to the psychological, moral, or spiritual of visual experience . . .

Margaret Miles, *Image as Insight: Visual Understanding in Western Christianity and Secular Culture* (Boston: Beacon Press, 1985) 7-8.

It is worth noting that medieval people apparently had a similar respect for the power of words, especially in blessings and curses. A good example might be Verdi's Rigoletto, who after being cursed by Monterone, is convinced that the evil that haunts him is not so much the consequence of his own deeds as of the curse itself. Rigoletto's attitude is in sharp contrast to our attitude of understating and effectively overlooking the power of the spoken or heard word. The typical response of young people to the pernicious lyrics of certain songs is: "I don't listen to the words."

18. See for example Gregory Baum's analysis of various critiques of technology, including the reductionistic tendency to blame the dehumanizing trends in modern society on the power of bureaucracy and technology. Baum warns against such an either/or analysis. G. Baum, "Three Theses on Contextual Theology," *The Ecumenist* 24:4 (May-June 1986) 49-59.

19. For a more detailed account see Michael Warren, *Communications and Cultural Analysis: A Religious View* (Bergin and Garvey, 1992).

20. A popular example and one I recommend is Marie Winn, *The Plug-in Drug* (New York: Bantam Books, 1977); also Mary Lou Schropp, *Platform for Action: The Electronic Media, Popular Culture, and Family Values. A Report of the Proceedings of an Institute Sponsored by the Catholic Communications Campaign Project.* (Washington, D.C.: United States Catholic Conference, 1985).

21. The following suggestion, though for those beyond childhood, has considerable merit:

One version of control that I would find attractive would be the dissemination of technological capacity through the educational system, the de-mythologizing of technique, the establishment of a creative chaos which would develop a disdain for the bland and the packaged. Access in the end of the day is not about the drawing room recitation learned from one's elders; it is about the right to tell one's story, to hear the story of every other man and woman, to respond to one's environment, and put one's imprint with respect on it. To live in the whole world.

Michael D. Higgins, "The Tyranny of Images: Aspects of Hidden Control—Literature, Ethnography and Political Commentary on the West of Ireland," *The Crane Bag* 8:2 (1984) 132-142, at 142.

22. George Gerbner [Annenberg School of Communications, University of Pennsylvania], "The Challenge of Television," Unpublished paper given at the Trinity Church Conference on Communications, 1983, 2-3.

23. I have found the first and last two chapters of Margaret Miles' already cited book on imagery to be helpful in getting at aspects of the problem of images. However, at the end of the book she offers three "main steps" in training oneself to choose and use images (pp. 147-149), which seem quite out of context with her own account of how religious images in the early church functioned largely within a community of interpretation and within a context of worship (pp. 7-8). I would think that a prior requirement to the steps she notes is to live within just such a community with its "subversive" images of reality. See Miles, *Image as Insight*.

24. Two accounts that touch on the community's production of culture through a living catechesis are: (1) Oscar Beozzo, "Catechetical Problems in a Changing Society: Brazil," in Greinacher and Elizondo, eds., *The Transmission of the Faith to the Next Generation Concilium* 174 (Edinburgh: T & T Clarke, 1984) 11-20; (2) Robert Schreiter, "Local Theologies in the Local Church: Issues and Methods," CTSA *Proceedings* (1981) 96-112. Beozzo notes the use of songs and other means to allow illiterates to produce their own culture. For a more theoretical essay on this same matter of the community's embodiment of its own meanings see Stanley Hauerwas, "The Gesture of a Truthful Story," *Theology Today* (July 1985) 181-189.

25. Gustavo Gutierrez, *We Drink from Our Own Wells* (New York: Orbis, 1984) 10.

10

Relationship and Cultural Bias in the Eucharistic Assembly

Catechesis serves the life of the community in both corrective and directive ways. It seeks to point out what is deficient in communal discipleship and to remind the community of the full implications of what all are called to. The eucharist, on the other hand, does not serve the life of the community in quite the same way. Functioning out of the community's life rather than into it, the eucharist celebrates that life in a ritual act expressing the core of communal faith. Catechesis is at the service of the eucharist in the sense that it nourishes a deeper, more mature faith. Where that common faith becomes deficient or seriously flawed, the eucharistic celebration itself becomes deficient. This process of becoming flawed is a gradual one, as Aloysius Pieris hints in describing the fading of ancient religious forms.

> A religion fades out of history when its symbols and institutions lose their capacity to evoke among its followers the distinctive salvific experience that defines its essence. Did not this happen to the great religions of Ancient Egypt, Rome, Greece, and Mesopotamia?[1]

Sadly, in consumerist societies the presentation of that "salvific core" can too easily be presented, not in its own distinctive terms but in the terms of the consumerist ethos. Here religiousness, sometimes subtly, becomes enhancement, emotional uplift, security—any of the constellation of values around "having." Such a shift undercuts the religion's "distinctive salvific experience that defines its essence." Speaking more directly about the eucharist, David Power points out how easy it is for religious ritual to lose its center and come to express something other than a group's commitment to a distinctive religious vision—for Christians, the Gospel.

> The natural ritual tendency may be to sacramentalize one's own family or kin, one's own ethnic group, one's own social class where one feels at home, one's peers in age and profession, since such are the groups in which one is most secure, and indeed instinctively most aware of the sacred powers that govern life, and most protected against the chaos that could intrude.[2]

Pieris and Power warn those serving the faith of communities of the potential false paths that lie open. Since the task of catechesis is to help the community know and embrace the faith it is called to, in this chapter I seek to explore just how cultural biases in the eucharistic assembly can distort the way the eucharist is approached and understood and how this distortion can be corrected.

Christianity is a faith based on what I will call a radical relatedness. As Jesus' disciples, our connectedness to one another is so central and seminal that if we should forget it, we have seriously distorted our faith, replacing it with some sort of idol. Perhaps the clearest evidence of the unitive core of the Christian way can be found in the prayers of the Mass, which are actually a great hymn of unity. In the eucharist, the Father of Jesus is always addressed by a We, who are a people gathered in God. "From age to age you gather a people to yourself." And this people is clearly a people whose identity and unity is not founded on that of any single nation or race. And so the prayer continues, "From age to age, you gather a people to yourself, so that from East to West a perfect offering may be made to the glory of your name." The perfect offering obviously is made by the people gathered in unity, and yet, in contrast to the effort they correctly put into their gathering, they see themselves gathered, not by themselves but by God. It is worth noticing how the preface of the eucharistic prayer usually ends in a great vision of unity, bonding those on earth with those in heaven. "Countless hosts of angels stand before you to do your will; they look upon your splendor and praise you, night and day. United with them, and *in the name of every creature under heaven*, we too praise your glory as we sing." What we have here is a vision of global unity centered in God.

So central is this point to who we are as Christians that its nuances must be carefully understood. If the eucharistic prayer tells us that God gathers us as one people, it is very explicit that the bond of our unity is the Holy Spirit. We do not just name that unity; we ritually eat from the common table of our unity and drink from the cup of our bond.[3] The very same Spirit of Jesus is the one we all inhabit and, once entered, joins us together as a Holy People. "Grant that we, who are nourished by his body and blood, may be filled with his Holy Spirit, and become one body, one spirit in Christ." We are so used to hearing these words that they do not jolt us with their outrageous imagery. Look at these metaphors: "One Body" like the indissoluble unity of the human body; one spirit; one family. We are children of the same God, and thus in a common family. We ask, "Father . . . in mercy and love unite all your children wherever they may be." Sisters and brothers all. The last great word of praise of the eucharist, the doxology, makes clear that it is our unity in the Spirit that gives praise to God. "Through him, with him, in him, in the unity of the Holy Spirit, all glory and honor is yours, almighty Father, for ever and ever." Amen. So be it.

Such is the language we use in the eucharist. From a linguistic point of view, the eucharist is a hymn of global unity, because speech about unity is deeply embedded there. A problem arises when concern about unity and about the religious foundations of unity, though embedded in the prayer, is not embedded in the consciousness of those reciting or participating in the eucharistic prayer. When this language loses its *intention* of unity but continues to be spoken as rote speech, little reflected upon, then it has lost its character as true ritual language. As rite, it has ceased expressing the religious vision and hopes of a people. Religious language can be inert, possessing no power to move us. Whereas even the artifact disinterred from some distant field and now encased behind museum glass has the power to move us with its crafted beauty, inert religious language is like the artifact still interred beneath our feet, its beauty undiscovered and unable to stir us.

All who verbally announce unity can, with the easy overlooking of the obvious, forget that our unity in God is a central feature of our faith. It can easily cease to be a compelling reality for us. The words about our oneness do not seep into the ground of our lives to water their depths and bring forth fruit. Instead they hit a kind of cultural umbrella and flow off without effect, without touching us. When spoken from our own lips with little inner meaning for us, such words cannot direct the choices in our lives. Functioning this way, they can never test, as religious language must, our actual living over against what is most essential to it.[4]

Sometimes, however, an incident occurs that brings the seriousness of Jesus' message back to us. For me such an incident occurred when a nun who had spent the previous eleven years in Guatemala working among the Indians told me the following story.

> One of the best-loved men in our town was Luis. He was a catechist with ten children and somehow never lost his sense of joy in the struggle to earn a livelihood for them. He was loved because of his gentleness and his sense of fun. In the summer of 1986, in the middle of the night, as such things happen, the soldiers came to the home of his sister and brother-in-law and tortured the two of them to death in front of their two-year-old son. Everybody knew because they heard the screams, though nobody dared approach the house until many hours later, after dawn, when they found the child covered with blood, tugging at the dead bodies of his parents.
>
> It was a horror for all and especially for Luis. Nobody knew what his brother-in-law and his sister were supposed to have done. Inquiries in such cases can be fatal. People asked Luis if he himself was frightened. He said he was but that it was an irrational fear since he had done nothing wrong. A few weeks later about 2:00 A.M., people in the tight band of houses where Luis' house stood heard the army jeeps coming again and stop in the middle of town. Then they heard the boots of the soldiers coming into this small cluster of houses. A soldier called out for Luis to come out. The family locked the door and tried to hide Luis, but when the rifle butts pounded on the door, Luis himself declared it useless. He himself opened the door, and saw that the soldiers were led by a young boy, a close friend of his own son. As soon as the door opened, the boy started shouting that he hadn't wanted to help them, but that they had forced them to show where the family lived. At that moment a soldier blew the boy's head open with a burst of machine gun fire and he fell dead into the house.
>
> Luis himself was taken out the little patio area outside the door, made to kneel, and with his family forced to form a semi-circle in the same patio and watch, he was tortured for a period of time and finally killed with another burst from a machine gun.

> None of those who participated in this horror was known to
> the family—except one, a man of the town who was recog-
> nized by Luis' eldest son.

I asked my friend if the man continued to live in the town, and
she answered yes. She went on, "Yes, at the eucharist on Sunday he
is there in the same church as Luis' widow and her nine children."
There are but nine children present because her eldest son has now
been sent into hiding in order to save his life.

What does the eucharist mean to this man who participated in
such a horror? Do the prayers of unity addressed, partly in his
name, to the Father of us all cause him any shock or even any
reflection or any doubt about Luis' murder—or others that he may
have participated in? Does he know that Luis was his brother,
joined in the same spiritual body by the living breath of the Spirit of
Jesus? The same human womb did not produce Luis and this man
become his murderer, but both came forth from the one womb of
God. Possibly the killer understands none of this but participates
week after week in a ritual that is for him a little like sleepwalking.

Such questions could be asked about any in our assemblies,
including ourselves. When we hear the true story of Luis and his
murder that took place only months ago, how do we react? Luis
was not from the U.S., though the U.S. had more to do with his
murder than some of us might care to admit.[5] He did not speak our
language. His skin was dark. He was an Indian. He had no title
before or after his name. Neither was he what we sometimes call "a
name." He was poor. Most of us have never been to the place were
he lived and probably never will. So what of us? Do we grieve for
Luis, our brother in Jesus murdered so cruelly and unjustly? These
questions are rightly asked in the face of the eucharistic prayer we
recite so often. They are not asked to foster guilt but rather to
prompt reflection on where we stand, not theoretically but behaviorally, on the Gospel's good news of our human unity in the
Spirit of Jesus. Does the vision of unity at the core of our faith have
any compelling hold on our hearts?

> Lord Jesus Christ, you said to your apostles: "I leave you
> peace, my peace I give to you." Look not on our sins but on the
> faith of your Church, and grant us the peace and unity of your
> kingdom where you live for ever and ever.

Does the death of one like Luis stir us up in the face of this prayer?

I am fully aware that psychologically, it is impossible to be
moved by every unjust death we hear about. If we were, we would

not be able to get on with our ordinary duties of every day. My question is about what happens when we have time to pause and consider the death of one like Luis. Is it even possible for us to consider him as our brother in God, as having a part of our human connectedness? Christianity is a religion of radical relatedness. In a world so disrupted by national loyalties and national rivalries, so willing to contemplate the murder, not only of individuals like Luis, but of millions who live in the "wrong" country or under the "wrong" political system or who have the "wrong" religion, if anything is needed, it is the global unitive vision that Jesus announced. We are of one another. We are sisters and brothers in Jesus. If someone tortured a dog, a squirrel or a cat as cruelly as the soldiers did Luis and his sister and brother-in-law, there would be an uproar in most parts of our country. Yet somehow the torture and death of the poor ones can be somehow calmly heard and forgotten. It is as if these oppressed have the handcuffs on their wrists, and others have them on their hearts.

Ironically, the local church's pastoral ministry, so solidly centered on relationships both in its theoretical foundations and in its practice, can be immune to the wider significance of the relatedness that Jesus announces. Is it possible to have a local church bound by tight relationships mutually enriching to one another but still quite unaware of, and therefore unconcerned for, the true global significance of our human sisterhood and brotherhood? As David Power reminded us at the beginning of this chapter, it is all too possible for a community's concerns to be shaped not so much by their religious commitments as by their social status and economic privilege. Part of the problem lies in not understanding community deeply enough.

The Issue of Community

Bernard Lonergan has helped us understand community as more than a number of persons within some geographical boundary; it is rather an achievement of common meaning. Common meaning is not achieved automatically, since it involves common experiences, common understandings, common judgments, and common choices and decisions. In Lonergan's own words, "community coheres or divides, begins or ends, just where the common field of experience, common understanding, common judgment, common commitments begin and end."[6] The problem of achieving such a "commonality" is that it demands substantial shifts in perspective on the part of each person who would be part of it. These shifts are conversions, which, because they are both conscious and life-orienting, do not occur easily.

Lonergan describes three conversions: intellectual, moral, and religious. Intellectual conversion involves the elimination of a stubborn illusion: that the world of immediacy and of personal "experience" is the total world of meaning. Yet this world is but a tiny part of reality and knowledge. There is a much wider and potentially enriching world of knowledge that has been checked and evaluated and adjusted and correlated with other kinds of knowledge. Intellectual conversion is a shift to that wider world of commonly held knowledge. Moral conversion involves the elimination of another illusion, that it is appropriate for the goal of one's decisions to be one's own satisfaction. "Moral conversion consists in opting for the truly good, for value against satisfaction, even when value and satisfaction conflict."[7] Religious conversion is a conversion to "ultimate concern," not as some external idea but as a reality, a presence, that grasps one's entire being. Lonergan sees religious conversion as a dynamic state of surrender influencing all subsequent acts.[8]

What is important here is how careful Lonergan's insistence is that *all three conversions are toward community*. Although conversion happens to a person, its dynamic is towards shared meaning, shared commitments and shared action. The achievement of conversion is in its ability to forge common meaning, without which conversion lapses into a mere moment of insight that in the last analysis was more illusory than life-directing. The deepest dilemma of conversion lies in maintaining it as a transforming direction to one's life. Among Christians, one of the chief roles of catechesis is that of conversion maintenance. In the gathering of disciples, catechesis is watchful for distortions of its very attitude towards community. Are such distortions possible?

At some point in religious conversion, one enjoys the ecstasy of a newly recognized group unity in God. It is as if each person shimmers with the Spirit of God and the group itself is aglow in that light. Here we have a religious insight into the humanity of each person present, now recognized as being much more than appearances had indicated. These moments of epiphany offer insight into the human condition and human possibilities, and they

have *the potential* for being life transforming, adding another dimension to the original conversion. However, that potential will
never be realized unless the insight is reflected on, its implications
explored, and its consequences acted on. That potential can be
short-circuited by a tendency to remain locked into the comforts of
the group experience itself. We see this tendency in the gospel
epiphany called the transfiguration. The disciples want to camp out
there on Tabor, permanently it seems, but Jesus tells them not to be
afraid and moves on with them from the mountain ecstasy to the
work of the kingdom. In Matthew's Gospel, the first situation they
meet is a messy one indeed, a hard case of a boy possessed by a
demon able to be cast out only through prayer and fasting (see Mt
17:1-21).

Extending Our Relatedness

It is quite possible for religiously ecstatic moments of human
unity to be subverted by the kind of attitude described so well by
Richard Sennett.

> The reigning belief today is that closeness between persons is a
> moral good. The reigning aspiration today is to develop indi-
> vidual personality through experiences of closeness and warmth
> with others. The reigning myth today is that the evils of society
> can all be understood as the evils of impersonality, alienation, and
> coldness. The sum of these three is an ideology of intimacy: social
> relationships of all kinds are real, believable and authentic the
> closer they approach the inner psychological concerns of each
> person. This ideology transmutes political categories into psycho-
> logical categories. This ideology of intimacy defines the humani-
> tarian spirit of a society without gods; warmth is our god.[9]

Sennett reminds us that intimacy and warmth are not the whole
of human relatedness. The friendship relationship is a necessary
one for human beings but not sufficient to express the full scope of
relationships. Not all personal relationships are intimate ones like
friendship; some important personal relationships are public, social, or relationships around work or craft.[10] Political relationships
and economic relationships are also part of the human connectedness that Jesus' followers must take seriously if they are to be true
to his message, because these relationships have such effects in
people's lives. Though Jesus used intimate imagery, such as that of
the meal, to speak of the kingdom he announced, he clearly pointed

to the social systems of his time, especially the economic system, that fostered injustice and disrupted human relationships. The kingdom Jesus proclaimed was a social order in which all relationships, intimate ones included, would follow the norms of justice.

Parker Palmer has shed light on the problem of community in religious groups. He shows that the grounding metaphor for the use of community in many churches is *family*, that is, the zone of intimate relationships. In itself the metaphor of family is appropriate, since it is found in scripture as well as in the text of the eucharistic prayer. Yet, the question remains whether our own understanding of family is the same as that intended in sacred texts. We live in a time when the most common image of family—in contrast to the biblical concept of family—is that of the nuclear family, whereas in Jesus' culture, for example, family seems to have meant a far wider network of relationships. To expect the church to yield the kind of intimate relationships envisaged in a small family household of four or five persons is a serious error. Judged against this expectation, the church can only fail. According to Palmer, "the problem arises when closeness and warmth become the criteria of all meaningful relations, when we reject and even fear relationships which do not yield to these standards."[11] Though Palmer does not wish to excise friendship from the *ekklesia*, he situates the church in the public sphere rather than the private or family sphere. The church stands publicly for the agenda of the kingdom.

> The problem arises when we impose the norm of intimacy (which applies primarily to private life) upon the public sphere. For within the public realm, where most relations are necessarily distant and impersonal, the demand for closeness and warmth distorts and eventually destroys the potential of public experience.[12]

The origins of such misplaced expectations of a family-type intimacy in the church lie in the wider culture in which we live. The meaning of "community" for us tends to have a particular connotation, even for church leaders.

> Today when clergy and lay people say they want "Christian community," they often mean they want the converse of mass society in every respect. Instead of conflict, the church should offer comfort; instead of distance between persons, intimacy; instead of criticism, affirmation and good will . . .[13]

Palmer's concern here is two-fold: on the one hand, defining the church in such terms of intimacy that creative conflict, heterogeneity, and freedom are curtailed; on the other, making the church a private place when it should be a public working-together for the realization of the kingdom of justice.[14] The title of his book, *The Company of Strangers*, contains a metaphor for the church: those non-intimates who gather with bread, sharing bread (com-panis) as a sign of their commitment to the kingdom.

Daniel Maguire puts the matter this way.

> In the social order . . . talk of love and friendship can be a prescription for disaster. There [in the social order] justice is the closest one can get to friendship. Justice is incipient love, and in the political order it is the only form that love takes. Privatistic talk of love is at that level unavailing, naive, and ultra-conservative in effect. Ironically, love talk in the social-political sphere provides an ideological veil for injustice and inures one to the needs of the poor for whom justice is life blood.[15]

Would all members of the local church immediately understand Maguire's point or for that matter, Sennett's or Palmer's, if they were able to hear them? I doubt it. Like so many other aspects of the Gospel, the wider implications of our relatedness are not so obvious and become even unacceptable when they challenge the privileges we enjoy. The work of catechesis is to assist the community in seeing the implications of the Gospel for their lives.

The sometimes exhilarating unity of our churches can indeed open out to the not-so-easy, even painful unity with those of other nations, races, and classes, who are children of the same God, no matter how that God is named, but that opening out will not happen by chance. The unity of our churches tends to be among those of similar race, similar socio-economic status, similar sexual orientation, similar religious affiliation, similar locality. It can be a unity based on feelings of comradeship and on face-to-face familiarity. The appropriate gesture to express that unity may be the hug.

The wider unity I have been getting at here is not based on face-to-face familiarity but on understanding and insight. Friendship is not the issue, because it is only one level of relatedness. Hugs are not appropriate or even possible expressions of this wider unity, which, once understood, helps us recognize the face of Jesus in the countenance of someone like Luis. There are some whom we will never be able to encircle with our arms, but whom we still are called to encircle with our attention and with various forms of political and social action. Sad to say, Jesus' global vision of oneness is not so popular everywhere, not even in the churches. Its absence can function not just as a silence but a structured silence in our assemblies. Catechesis can aid in disrupting that silence.

Relationships and Identifications

Several years ago, a Jesuit magazine edited by Daniel Berrigan ran a cover comprised of two questions in huge bold letters: Who in the world is He? Where in the world is He? These are serious questions for a follower of Jesus. The real problem of relatedness is that it does not mean much without identifications. Who actually are these people we are joined to in Jesus? How do we name them and identify them? The problem is one of learning to identify properly who is our brother, who is our sister, who is our neighbor. "Who is my neighbor" is one of questions put to Jesus that has echoed down through the ages. So has Jesus' answer. That answer shocked his listeners because he identified as the neighbor two most unlikely candidates: a Jew lying wounded and helpless along the roadside and a person of the wrong religion, the wrong ethnicity, the wrong locality: a Samaritan.

The task of re-identifying those whom we are related to as sisters and brothers is not easy. It is hard enough to widen the circle of those we name as connected to us; coming to identify *with* these people is a process I would expect to be much slower. Still, we are aided in this effort by enormous religious resources in our Scriptures, in our worship, in the person of the one we name Lord. Catechesis can make available to the local church the scriptural bases for our wider relatedness. It can assist in bringing back to life the inert language used in our assemblies, especially when catechesis is linked to other strategies. The way we pray our eucharist, the concerns we petition for during it, the homilies we prepare for it, and the sort of communal action planned by the assembly all can assist the work of re-identifying. So can the issues that come before our youth groups, our programs of adult catechesis, our weekends of Christian living, or that can be found in the material available for reading in our church entrances. All aspects of the life of a local church can contribute to a possibility of enlarging the circle with whom we identify. If a local church ever decides to identify with the oppressed and to espouse solidarity with victims, part of its work will be to document their injustices, meaning, to care enough about them that we will not allow the world to forget what happened to them.[16]

More and more, I have come to see that "identifying with" is in large part a work of imagination. The shock of Jesus' parable of the loving Samaritan must have been that his hearers had never imagined Samaritans that way. They were, well, you know, *Samaritans*. They're not us. They're *them*. The early Christian community carried this work of imagination a step further. They had the wit to realize that the Samaritan is Jesus himself. In Matthew 25, the "Son of Man come in glory" clearly announces this extended imagination of who is our neighbor. What you did to one of these least ones you did to me. The Lord is saying: I am to be identified with these. When you see them, have the imagination to see me in them. And this New Testament passage suggests further that even if you do not happen to name them properly but if you treat them as neighbor, you are still doing good as to God himself. The important thing is to live your life this way.

The Problem of the Social Horizon

In the United States the social horizon of many in our congregations is shaped not so much by the church as by the wider society. That social horizon encourages us to think this way: Love your own: if they live at the same address as you, if they have the same last name, if they are the same color, if they speak the same language, if they are of the same religious affiliation, especially if they have similar amounts of money in their pockets as you. Notice how similar to this attitude is that of the Rich Man in the parable of Lazarus (Lk 16:19-31), where the Rich Man's only concern at the end is his own family, his five brothers, so they would not end up in the same place of torment as he. There is no indication in the parable that the Rich Man ever actually came to recognize Lazarus as his brother.

It is all too possible for Jesus' gospel mandate to be swallowed up by our own social horizon, the culture we live in, which says, "Grab all the gusto you can get." I am not against gusto, but I am against grabbing. Grabbing is always for oneself, and the consumerist culture encourages those who "have" to set their hearts against those who "have not." Our social horizon as followers of Jesus is different from this. It is the horizon of the altar around which we gather and proclaim our unity in his Spirit. For the church to be faithful to Jesus, the social horizon of selfish grabbing must be resisted: actively, strongly, programmatically.

Catechesis Again

As I have repeated so often here, catechesis serves the common meanings that join the community together and works to keep that meaning faithful to the Gospel. The catechetical leader in a local church has the task of listening to the word that is spoken, from the pulpit as well as in more informal conversation. That leader must have an ear for dissonance, not in the sense of dissent or disagreement, for these are important features of any true human coming together, but the kind of dissonances that are out of harmony with Jesus' message. If it is true that conversion, like friendship, can never be taken for granted—that it is an achievement and must be maintained—then catechesis seeks to maintain and deepen conversion.

In deepening conversion to the human family gathered by one God, catechesis cannot shy away from a series of issues that must be faced today if we are to be true to our human family and to our inter-relatedness as imagined for us by Jesus.[17] Ironically, few of these issues can be faced by groups without their going through some conflict over them. Such issues are disarmament, but understood in relation to the ancient Christian tradition of non-violence; economic justice,[18] including what lifestyle shifts an economics of greater sharing and equity might demand from us; hunger and oppression in other lands, sometimes, with the collusion of our own political and business leaders; and the question of human rights worldwide. All these issues are about relationships.

As human beings our primal relationship is to the earth. The earth is the great sacrament of God's presence; it is also the great father/mother of us all. We tend to forget our relationship to nature: to the air, the waters, the land, but probably today it is the relationship most in need of being understood and reclaimed. Facing that relationship and our responsibility for it may be as troubling as facing economic issues, but it could also be a "redemptive troubling" that moves us to more study and more concern and more action to preserve the delicate balance of life. This issue brings us back to the eucharistic table where, considering the pollution of the earth, it becomes more and more difficult to sing words like these:

> Sing to the Lord a new song all the earth! Raise your hymn of
> gladness . . . Raise up a joyful noise and sing to God. Let the
> earth and its fullness join in gladsome praise.[19]

Obviously not all these issues can be faced at one time or in a single year. Progress in coming to understand these issues from a gospel perspective will probably be slow and painstaking. However they can be avoided only at the risk of reducing Jesus' message to one affecting only our individual choices but not our public policies and not our brothers and sisters in other parts of the world. It could very well be that the reason we cannot imagine our human connectedness when we stand around the altar is that we have been unable to imagine it in economic terms or in terms that connect it to disarmament and to the re-distribution of wealth. The work of catechesis is to make just such connections, to enable followers of Jesus to approach the Eucharist aware of the fullness of their relationships, which must always include victims such as Luis of Guatemala.

Notes

1. Aloysius Pieris, "Christianity and Buddhism in Core-to-Core Dialogue," *Cross Currents* 37:1 (Spring 1987) 57.

2. David N. Power, "Households of Faith in the Coming Church," *Worship* 57:3 (May 1983) 237-254, at 249.

3. In John Paul II's encyclical on social concerns, *Sollicitudo Rei Socialis*, the underlying theme is this one of human unity. In his concluding section, the pope moves to the eucharist as the sign par excellence of that unity; see *Origins* 17:38 (3 March 1988).

4. I have found helpful the first section of Craig Dykstra, "Youth and the Language of Faith," *Religious Education* 81:2 (Spring 1986) 163-174.

5. But the military system behind his murder are supported by the U.S., which is "virtually the sole foreign source of military goods and services," which include "cash, credit, grants or aid." In 1981 Guatemala's security forces were 18,000 and their purchases from the U.S. were $4,000; in 1986, the security forces numbered 43,600 and purchases, 5.1 million. James LeMoyne, "Central America's Arms Buildup," NY *Times* (19 April 1987) A 1, 16.

6. Bernard Lonergan, *Method in Theology* (New York: Herder and Herder, 1972) 79.

7. Ibid. 240.

8. Ibid. 240-241. For some other key statements on conversion see B. Lonergan, *A Second Collection*, Wm. Ryan and Bernard Tyrrell, eds., (Philadelphia: Westminster Press, 1974) 65-66, 153, 166-172.

9. Richard Sennett, *The Fall of the Public Man* (New York: Alfred A. Knopf, 1977) 259.

10. "Personal" and "intimate" are not synonymous. I presume this distinction lies behind what Thomas Merton meant in his "Letter to a Young Activist" when he wrote: "Do not depend on the hope of results . . . In the end, it is the reality of personal relationships that saves everything." Basically, all human relationships are meant to foster the dignity of the human person, but they do not all foster intimacy.

11. Parker Palmer, *The Company of Strangers* (New York: Crossroad, 1983) 49.

12. Ibid.

13. Ibid. 50.

14. See Ibid. 119-120, 124-125.

15. Daniel Maguire, "The Primacy of Justice in Moral Theology," *Horizons* 10:1 (Spring 1983) 74.

16. A vivid example of care in documenting injustice is the work done by the Archdiocese of Sao Paolo in bringing to light the hidden social horrors committed during almost twenty-five years of dictatorship; see Lawrence Weschler, "Brasil: Nunca Mas—Parts I and II, *The New Yorker* (25 May and 1 June 1987); also in Weschler, *A Miracle, A Universe: Settling Accounts with Torturers* (New York: Penguin Books, 1991) 7-79.

17. It must be clear, even if I do not deal with the matter here, that another catechetical challenge is to affirm also the importance of the particularlity of the local church at the same time we affirm our global unity. I am reminded of this "other" challenge by a remark of Giancarlo Collet: "The `glory' of the Western Church is its universality in world history; its `sorrow,' however, lied in misunderstanding particularity." Giancarlo Collet, "Liberation for Freedom: Reflections on the Task of the Church," in Mary Motte and Joseph R. Lang, eds., *Mission in Dialogue* (New York: Orbis, 1982) 570-578, at 571.

18. On this matter alone specific details are needed to disclose the connection between economic policies and the concrete lives of people. For example, between 1963-73, about 44 percent of the new jobs created in the U.S. were in the high-wage category, more than $29,600 per year and about 15 percent were in the low wage category, less than $7,400 a year. Between 1979-85, only ten percent of new jobs were in the high wage category and 44 percent in the low wage category. Since 1979, middle wage jobs [7,400--29,600] declined 30 percent. These facts are not abstract or subtle, and they spell out the shape of the future for many families; see Barry Bluestone and Bennett Harrison, "The Grim Truth about the Job `Miracle'," NY *Times* (1 February 1987) F 3.

Another example is that in the 1987 tax law, the tax rate of those making $200,000 and over fell from 50% to 28%. Taxpayers making over $500,000 per year [0.3% of the total number of taxpayers] will in 1988 save

19.7 billion dollars in taxes, which is 32% of the bill's benefits to all individuals in that year. See Henning Gutmann, "The Bad News Tax Law," NY *Review* (12 February, 1987) 26.

19. Roc O'Connor, "Sing All the Earth," (Phoenix: NALR, 1985).

11

The Local Church and Its Practice of the Gospel: The Materiality of Discipleship in a Catechesis of Liberation

In an essay on Christian initiation in the Episcopal Church, William Adams explores the place of baptism by examining the use of space and the use of ritual in a sampling of Episcopal parishes.[1] Adams probes whether the symbolic ritual enactments, both in their use of space and in the ritual unfolding itself, back up the church's stated convictions about the key place of baptism. Officially, the baptismal pool or font, in keeping with its importance in the community's total life, is to have a significant place in the space where the community assembles. Thus there are to be three key areas in the space where the community assembles for worship: the altar, the pulpit from which the word is announced, and the place of baptism. Adams' study sought to determine whether the place of baptism was in fact spatially significant. The study also scrutinized the ritual of baptism as practiced, contrasting the ritual of ordination with that of baptism to see the assumptions embedded in each and whether the practice of these rituals squares with stated teaching that baptism is to have greater significance. In the way the rituals are actually carried out, he found, the "physical observable evidence" shows ordination has much greater significance, at least when examined as ritual action. Thus, he is examining what the church does in its ritual and its use of space to see if it is coherent with its teachings. What he is after is *actual practice* rather than stated theoretical positions.

My essay here seeks to lay out for educators the significance of the material conditions of church practice. I begin with attention to Adams' study because of its interesting way of examining whether what we practice is what we proclaim in our official teachings and its determination to focus on *the teaching represented by the practice.* The teaching embedded in patterns of behavior lived but not reflected on must be an issue for Christian educators or catechists, especially if we accept that what a community lives is at least as formative as what it teaches about itself.

Here I wish to lay a groundwork for considering what might be called "the symbolics of practice" at the level, not of liturgical symbolics, but on that of life structure symbolics. This entire book has been about these "symbolics"; what follows is an attempt to suggest not only further theoretical work to be done but some lines for analyzing the life structure of a local church. What people say and do in the liturgical assembly, including the arrangement of space in which they say and do it, provides clues to what these people are all about. However—and this is a central point in my argument—what they say and do in the non-liturgical spaces of their individual and corporate lives has a more decisive effect on them than does liturgical speech and action. The material structures of their lives have already formed them—their consciousness, their mentalities, their biases and priorities, their spirits—before they cross the threshold of liturgical space.

Though attention to this matter is growing, I find insufficient attention to it in the literature of religious education under its various sub-headings of Christian education or catechesis. Even those who purport to deal with shaping the practice of particular ecclesial groups do not deal with either liturgical symbolics in Adams' sense or life-practice symbolics in my sense. Story-telling as a technique of formation or of reformation of the assembly is not sufficient for coping with the kind of life practice I seek to get at here. One of the few Christian education theorists who has gotten at the issue of the life practice of local churches is C. Ellis Nelson in his *Where Faith Begins.* Though it was written twenty-five years ago, I know of no other religious/Christian education book that raises the communal practice issue the way his does. Edward Farley's writings consistently raise the issue at an abstract level not yet accessible to many.

Though the matter of practice surfaces consistently in Roman Catholic catechetical documents, and I presume, in those of all the denominations, the matter has still not been brought forward in a cohesive way that highlights its key place in Christian education/ catechesis. Here, in seeking to lay out the importance of the issue and some reasons why it has been so long neglected, I begin with one of the few places where the matter of practice is raised consistently and forcefully: the literature of liberation theology. I hope to suggest some lines of further work to be pursued for the material conditions of practice to receive the emphasis it deserves in Christian education.

Liberation theology begins with the concrete conditions of people's lives, what we call the "material conditions" of life, and engages communities in reflecting on these conditions, in judging them, and, where appropriate, in working to change them. Those material conditions are the earthy clay out of which skilled communal hands guided by a gospel vision seek to fashion a more useful and beautiful social vessel. While the process of working on the concrete conditions of living is widely known to be crucial to the liberationist approach, this process has yet to be recognized as a key task for the renewal of first and second world churches. Is it possible for this task to assume among Christians of privilege the centrality in pastoral reflection and activity it has in the churches of the oppressed?

Concrete Conditions of Life

In the very first paragraph of his now-classic work, *A Theology of Liberation*, Gustavo Gutierrez maintains that built into the way of life of every ecclesial community is a theological understanding in rough outline. The "life, action, and concrete attitude" found in the community provide the soil into which theological reflection "sinks its roots and from which it derives its strength."[2] Though never stressing the negative side of this principle, Gutierrez implies that the material conditions of the community's life can be for good or ill. The title of *A Theology of Liberation*'s first chapter, "Theology: A Critical Reflection," means not so much *Gutierrez*' critical reflection on theology but rather that theology itself is done as a critical reflection on the concrete circumstances of the local church's life. ". . . [T]he very life of the Church [emphasis his] . . . [is] a locus theologicus" (p. 8), that is, a zone for doing theological reflection. Throughout this chapter he stresses the importance "of concrete behavior, of deeds, of action, of praxis in the Christian life" (p. 10).

The goal of such reflection on the material conditions of life is to fashion a concrete practice of the Gospel worked out in the face of a probing examination of the specific economic and socio-cultural circumstances in which a community finds itself. Far from downplaying "truths" and wisdom, this approach employs them in fashioning a concrete practice of discipleship that itself rescues truth and wisdom from becoming static and sterile. This specific practice is sacrament and verification of both a community's faith in God and of the system of "truths" that elaborates that faith.

Understood in this way, liberation theology seeks the local church as both an accessible sign of the presence of God's promised Christ and a habitable sign. Neither feature is easily attained. An accessible sign is different from a simply "claimed" or purported sign, because one can see what the accessible sign stands for; the way the sign functions makes its meaning tangible and sense-able. A habitable sign is a sign inviting one to live its meanings in communion, as others do. In the early 1960s when I tried for several years to teach ecclesiology to skeptical teens, I found the unavoidable stumbling block for the young to be, not the claims of the church but the lack of coherence between those claims and actual concrete life-practice of the local parish. The young found the embodiments of my ecclesial theory to be neither accessible nor habitable. In so finding, they verified Joseph Komonchak's description of ecclesiology as "a theory about a practice";[3] the ecclesiology I was presenting was a theory about a theory, not about a practice. I came to see the most convincing way of presenting the theory of the church was to ground it in a convincing practice—which at that time was an alternative practice.[4]

Fewer than four years after Gutierrez' book appeared in its first, Spanish edition, an important papal statement backed up his basic position. In December 1975 *Evangelii Nuntiandi* appeared over the signature of Paul VI, as a papal response to the issues raised at the 1974 Synod of Bishops on the issue of evangelization. Opening with several anguished questions about the possibilities of proclaiming the Gospel in our day, the exhortation returns again and again to the matter of the church as an accessible and credible sign. The very first step of evangelization involves the church itself being evangelized and converted to God, becoming a community of believers making real their hope through loving kindness to others.[5] Evangelized itself, the church finds its foundational way of evangelizing others to be by means of witness: the sign of an *ecclesia* embracing the humanizing vision of the Gospel and living not only in communion with its own members but in solidarity with all seeking what is "noble and good." Such witness is basically "wordless," but deeply provocative, i.e., raising questions about the vision and intent of those living this way. This witness renders God's presence accessible to others in tangible signs.[6] Though never stating the centrality of the material conditions of the local church as concretely as does Gutierrez, the document clearly implies their importance in many places, particularly near the end using language of self-confrontation:

> Either tacitly or aloud—but always forcefully—we are being asked: Do you really believe what you are proclaiming? Do you live what you believe? Do you really preach what you live? The witness of life has become more than ever an essential condition for real effectiveness in preaching (par. 76).

Here *Evangelii Nuntiandi* echoes the description of belief set forth by a nineteenth-century U.S. philosopher, Charles Sanders Peirce: "Belief consists mainly in being deliberately prepared to adopt the formula believed in as the guide to action; the essence of belief is the establishment of a habit; and different beliefs are distinguished by the different modes of action to which they give rise."[7]

Implied, however, in *Evangelii Nuntiandi*'s description of a believable ecclesial community is a process of struggle whereby a group seeks to embrace specific patterns of practice by which a gospel perspective can be lived out in its concrete circumstances. The conversion of the community sparked by its encounter with the message of Jesus is not a one-time ecstatic event based on euphoric insight into "truth." Translating conversion into patterns of practice that go beyond ritual enactments of the tradition and become embedded in specific ways of living is no euphoric matter. In fact it is the opposite. Ecstasy means standing outside the self, being lifted out of the self. Establishing gospel living in a specific set of circumstances involves standing not outside the self but squarely within one's materiality, one's embodiedness within networks of particularities. Ultimately, as we shall see, it involves judgments and decisions about a range of life practices.

Resistance to the Issue of Life Structure

Middle- and upper-class ecclesial communities have for the most part not faced the challenge of specific life practice. One way to support this claim is simply to note the lack of pastoral literature on the matter. In all fields of human endeavor can be found intense interest in standards of practice, with practitioners ready to submit themselves to the best standard so far achieved. This interest in practice and readiness to examine and learn from virtuoso performance can be found in sports, in the arts, in the crafts, even in management theory. Among those who work to hone a particular kind of human skill, any field of practice demands this kind of relatedness among practitioners, involving mutual examination and evaluation—and consequent appreciation or criticism. Basically, "we cannot be initiated into a practice without accepting the authority of the best standards realized so far."[8] This is as true for the playing of the French horn as it is for the practice of virtue.

Quite simply, in pastoral theology the literature showing this interest in practice hardly exists. There is ample literature, called pastoral or practical theology, about the theory of practice but with little to say about the wider patterns of action that make up a specific structure of life for any person or community. There is also a literature of case studies, valuable in themselves, but which tend to focus on the pastoral skills of a practitioner but with little critical reflection or even attention to the concrete social conditions of living within which the pastoral skills function. When the problematic of practice surfaces in these studies, it is not the problem of the specific kinds of life patterns embedded in the local community, say, patterns of rampant consumerism—what one could term "operational greed"—being lived out by the majority in the community.

Though patterns of behavior can pass into repetitive, embedded practice without ever going through discourse, they cannot, as Pierre Bourdieu warns us, be contested and changed apart from the intentionality that goes with discourse.[9] In many churches persons have been empowered to speak knowledgeably about their sacred texts and about those texts' meaning for their inner life. Many, however, do not have a language by which to apply the texts to the patterns of exteriority in their lives, to the way they spend time, money, attention, and energies. These patterns, both among individuals and in the church's own corporate life, are outside of discourse. When practices, for example those of consumerist greed, are ignored they tend to generate their own false theory of Christian living, a theory that supposes gospel fidelity to be unconnected with the use of money. Jacques Ellul reminds us that false practice can generate false theory but in a particularly subtle and stubborn way:[10] we continue to maintain our stated "theory," when in fact it has been replaced by an unacknowledged operational theory derived from false practice. With the ease of the child in "The Emperor's New Clothes," my secondary school students of yesteryear objected that the actual ecclesiology in force in their parishes was quite different from the stated "theoretical" ecclesiology. Practice of any kind encodes in our lives values and attitudes we may never wish consciously to admit to ourselves. We are unwilling to see or decode what we ourselves have written into our own lives.

If it is true that one is what one does, then patterns of action determine the sort of person one becomes. Some of these patterns are consciously chosen, but many are simply fallen into, adopted through unspoken social permission or initiated in choices made but not examined, choices that bypass discourse. Often initiated without thought or even innocently, these patterns are not maintained without our own complicity. Whatever their origin in choice, all patterns shape the human spirit and a way of being an embodied spirit, that is, a spirituality.[11] At some point in its activity, religiousness must reflect on, not just its system of meanings but on the conditions under which these meanings can be realized in concrete behavior. The word "conditions" here is important because it suggests behavior is not simply individual but also contextual and social. One could ask, Under what conditions do persons claiming discipleship with Jesus come to overlook the consequences for that discipleship of deeds—if not all deeds, then at least whole categories of deeds. These conditions for overlooking or attending to deeds are my concern here.

Why has the liberationist concern with concrete patterns of behavior not been taken up by the churches of privilege? Historical or tradition-laden reasons present themselves, as well as more immediate ones. Paulo Freire suggests to me one of the more immediate ones in a recent brief comment. He notes one of the conclusions of a 1975 UNESCO-sponsored international meeting on adult literacy: that programs of adult literacy "have been efficient in societies in which suffering and change created a special motivation in the people for reading and writing."[12] In other words, social conditions of suffering created among some a need for literacy not felt by those illiterates who were more comfortable. In a similar way, the positions of privilege occupied by those in the churches of the well-off and very well-off do not spark the need for change. Among the classes of privilege, the conditions of prosperity hinder their probing the religious implications of these same conditions of prosperity.

To be sure, all patterns of practice tend to be taken-for-granted and invisible until the pattern is somehow disrupted. To return to the previous example, patterns of spending money become sharply visible when for some reason the money dries up; patterns of using transportation, when one's means of transportation breaks down; patterns of eating, when medical imperatives demand change. Built into the very nature of religious meaning is the possibility of calling into question patterns of practice. Religious meanings claim to be ultimate ones, worth suffering for, normative for living. Though this aspect of religiousness is not always called into play or can be muted in various ways, the claim of ultimacy remains embedded in religious traditions and its latent implications for living are always capable of being activated.

The fact remains that religions are not simply ways of thinking; they are also ways of living. Their religious understandings are to become lived realities. Practice remains the test of adherence to the religious system. In another of his writings, Gutierrez explains the prominence of practice for Christianity.

> Practice is the locus of verification of our faith in God, who liberates by establishing justice and right in favor of the poor. It is also the locus of verification of our faith in Christ . . . Easter life is the life of practice . . . The only faith-life is the one the Scriptures call "Witness." And witness is borne in works. To believe is to practice.
>
> Only from a point of departure at the level of practice, only from deed, can the proclamation by word be understood. In the deed our faith becomes truth, not only for others, but for ourselves as well. We become Christians by acting as Christians. Proclamation in word only means taking account of this fact and proclaiming it. Without the deed, proclamation of the word is something empty, something without substance.
>
> . . . [T]he relationship between deed and word is asymmetric. What basically counts is the deed. Of course it will not do to overemphasize this or push it to extremes; its only purpose is the better to express a complex reality. Jesus Christ, the heart of the gospel message, is the Word made flesh, the Word become deed. Only in this unity of deed and word is there any sense in the distinctions we make in the task of proclaiming liberation in Jesus Christ.[13]

Unfortunately, this relationship of word and deed, of understanding and practice has not always been maintained in Christianity, and residues of earlier misunderstandings remain in the tradition. How these misunderstandings emerged must now be examined.

Pieris' Analysis of the Displacement of Agape

The Jesuit theologian Aloysius Pieris reminds us that any religion must combine both loving action (*agape*) and the search for wisdom (*gnosis*). Along the roadsides of his own country, Sri Lanka, he finds two sets of statues that spell out for him the importance of the unification of loving action or agape and wisdom or *gnosis*. Each statue involves a tree, one symbolizing knowledge, the other, love-in-action:

> the tree beneath which Gotama, the Indian mystic, sits in a posture of contemplative calm, and the tree upon which Jesus the Hebrew prophet hangs in a gesture of painful protest—... the tree that bears the fruit of wisdom and the tree that bares the cost of love.[14]

For experiencing God and for expressing the fruits of our intimacy with God, each, *agape* and *gnosis*, is important. Together they represent "complementary idioms that need each other to mediate the self-transcending experience called salvation . . .; any valid spirituality, Buddhist or Christian . . . retains both poles of religious experience, the gnostic and the agapeic."[15] Pieris' analysis of the functioning of the agapeic and the gnostic poles brings to light an historical irony, that the religion using the gnostic symbol of the tree of wisdom, Buddhism, has been able to hold onto the actual practice of love and the one using the agapeic symbol, Christianity, has tended to emphasize a particular gnostic strain. Pieris explains how this occurred.

In its early formative centuries, Christianity found itself in a gnostic milieu tending to assert that knowing the liberating truth is or leads to salvation. From the first, Christianity was able to find a theological formula able to maintain the gnostic pole without compromising the agapeic. The theologies of John and Paul, according to Pieris, give concrete evidence of this formula. In John, the knowledge of the Father and the Son is given by the Spirit but leads to a discipleship which is a concrete way of loving one's neighbor. Here loving one's neighbor is a way of knowing God. One finds a similar bonding of knowledge and love in Paul's stress on brotherly love.

> Paul admits the possibility of knowing divine things but clearly considers such knowledge worthless without love. Paul puts a

greater distance than John between *ginoskein* and *agapan* as between two different modes of human experience. But one can infer that for both [i.e., John and Paul] the Sinai covenant of justice has received its final fulfillment in Jesus in whom mutual love among humans is the path to true gnosis—the knowledge of God through the Son in the Spirit.[16]

The wedding of these two elements was maintained in the carefully monitored catechumenal process of the early church, with its emphasis on helping neophytes re-structure their patterns of living. The catechumenate was a method of formation, not just in doctrinal purity, but even more basically in the re-imagined self, with a re-directed affectivity and re-structured life patterns. Willingness to shift primary commitments at odds with Jesus' way is a recurring theme in early Christian writings. So important were these re-oriented commitments as prior conditions for admission to full fellowship, the three-year length of the catechumenate was dictated by the usual length of time it took for the re-direction of one's life structure.

In the long run, however, the center did not always hold. Though he died three to five decades before either Origen or Tertullian, Irenaeus, Bishop of Lyon in Gaul, influenced the shape of theology for centuries. Irenaeus' apologetical treatment of Christianity directed at Greek *thought* had behind it a legitimate academic thrust common to intellectual adherents of all religions.[17] This apologetic thrust, which influenced the Cappadocian and Latin Fathers, eventually became an academic tradition centering on systems of thought, encountering pagan philosophy rather than pagan religious ways. These Fathers looked to non-Christian philosophy for the intellectual means of grasping revelation conceptually. In such a movement, Christianity as a way of living—experiencing concrete symbols and embodying specific practices—though never completely overlooked, tended to be pushed into the background and became, in its radical embodiments, reserved for the monastic tradition and later, for communities practicing the evangelical counsels of poverty, chastity, and obedience. When intellectual elites produced doctrinal statements as norms of the community's authenticity, the text of the community's own life-practice as a radical and indispensable means of interpreting the wider world received less focus. The double text meant to be bound together, the text of Scripture and the text of practice, came to drift apart.

In several places in his writings Edward Farley explores the more recent ways the disjunction of doctrine and practice has been carried into our own time.[18] Though the importance of living the Gospel has never been lost—i.e., the norms for acclaiming "heroic" holiness have always been centered in life practice—the emphasis on practice for more ordinary individuals and communities diminished. It is possible to conceive of religiousness as unconnected or only marginally connected with patterns of life practice, with the consequence that one's "religion" is a matter of the head, not of the hands and feet. Whole regions of human activity can become exempted from gospel norms, such as the way one holds property or uses money; one's employment, its kind and outcomes; or one's exercise of social or political power. A tendency to envisage doctrinal instruction as a sufficient means of incorporating the young into the life of the community might be another contemporary instance of this error. Bureaucratic preoccupation with doctrinal exactness while overlooking anti-gospel patterns of life might be another. To those who ask, "Who envisages doctrinal instruction this way?" I point out that we do not so envisage doctrinal instruction in our theory but rather in our expecting religious commitment to emerge from instruction cut off from the lived patterns of discipleship in communities of worship. My students of the early 1960s nimbly leaped to point out that error.

Pieris' analysis of this history is actually getting at Christianity in its character as a way of life, as agape, a way of living out a message of love in concrete practice.

> To say "Jesus is the Word" is not enough; the word must be heard and executed for one to be saved. To say "Jesus is the path" is not enough; one must walk the path to reach the end . . . What saves is not the name of Jesus in the hellenistic sense of the term, but the name of Jesus . . . in the Hebrew sense of "the reality" that was operative in Jesus . . . In fact, the knowledge of the name or title is not expected by the eschatological Judge, but the knowledge of the path is (Mat. 25:37-39 and 44-46).[19]

Consequently, the *kerygma* is not a theoretical, logical proposal but a "metalogical proclamation which cannot be demonstrated rationally." Its most convincing proof is witness, the lived-out agapeic behavior of some person or persons. In a passage that challenges all local churches in the way they embody the gospel message, Pieris claims:

> Saying that Jesus is the medium of salvation requires that the ones who say it display the fruits of liberation . . . A christology receives its authenticity from a transforming praxis which

> proves that in the story of Jesus, which continues in his follow-
> ers, the medium of salvation is operative . . .[20]

One can communicate the coherent vision of Christian faith to any person who will stay still long enough to hear it. However, the communication of *the way of being a Christian* and the embracing of that way for oneself is quite another matter. Usually the validation of the Christian way is through action, first the action of those who show it is possible to live it and that indeed it does save, and secondly, the action of the one who embraces it for oneself and finds that, yes, for me it is salvific. Of course Christianity claims more than this. It claims that its way is also socially salvific, as announced by Jesus in the Kingdom of God. That part of the Christian reality is verified in the social action of Christians for a just world. Multiple implications for pastoral action emerge from these ideas, as we shall see. An obvious one is that the church is a zone where all offer thanks to God, ponder God's message, and also, struggle with the problematic of practice.

The Material Conditions of Living

So far I have used various expressions to name the kind of life we live: the material conditions of life, life patterns, life structure. Some readers may have found this use of language unhelpful because inexact or vague. I sympathize because I myself have not found a literature laying out the material conditions of life with the specific-ity I would like. Marx' important works on the material bases of life were ground-breaking, but never worked out with highly specific examples. Possibly the specificity needed can best be attained by particular people struggling to name the patterns they themselves live, first in their own homes and then in their communities of worship and places of work. As already pointed out in Chapter 5, I have found help in this matter in a few pages of Daniel Levinson's ground-breaking study of sequential stages in the lives of men, *The Seasons of a Man's Life*. Readers may at this point want to review Levinson's descriptions of life structure, which I will be referring to below. In his approach to life structure, Levinson uses what I would call "descriptive analysis," which lays out patterns easily overlooked. This is a first analytic step. A second step would be a critical analysis, by which the life structure is not only described but judged from some other, "outside" vantage point. The only such vantage point Levinson uses is "psychological adjustment," i.e., whether the person remains tolerably happy in the particular life structure and if not, whether he can make adjustments. My own critical vantage points are different, and have to do with the person's contribution to the human good and with the life structure's coherence with religious commitments.

Unfortunately Levinson leaves us to work out any more specific descriptive details for ourselves. The task is not a simple one, as I found out in attempting to apply life structure to the brief period of the young adult transition. What many young people do not realize is that in one's late teens one is in a key phase of establishing one's *ways*. At that time one is developing behavioral patterns and life structure that will direct one's life for a long time to come: tastes in food; patterns in the use of time; preferences in and even styles of watching TV; ways of being with older people or of avoiding them; ways of behaving in groups; ways of studying, of reading, even of reading the newspaper—or a way of not reading it. It is not that every one of these ways is being newly formed, for indeed many of them go back to childhood. Still, freed from the countervailing childhood pulls from parents and home, these ways are being cemented into place. Being formed are ways of driving a car, ways of using alcohol, ways of relating to the opposite sex, ways of dealing with the truth, ways of getting one's own will, and far from the least important, ways of thinking about and using money. Behind the nexus of these patterns is a life structure that affects commitments.

Even these suggestions could be fleshed out in ever greater concreteness. Some research into rape by young men shows that a relatively high percentage of such rapists are members of athletic teams. Apparently there are ways of talking about women that become patterned in particular groups, such as fraternities or athletic teams, and these ways of talking can reinforce attitudes toward women that lead to rape.[21] On the other hand, there could also be groups of men who in their way of speaking of women exhibit and reinforce attitudes inimical to rape. What I am getting at here are patterns of interaction and of speech. A life structure is a pattern of choices and ways of living that become the accepted and eventually the established way for a person. Once it is established the pattern tends to perdure, in spite of shifts in location, career, or even marriage partner. For every age-group after childhood (though children inhabit life structures too, at first, chosen *for* them but eventually chosen *by* them), life structure then says a lot about what we pay attention to. Evidence of what matters are attended to in a particular life structure is found in specific documents of the sort that could be entered into court records:

> in one's check book;
> in a list of the things one has read over the past week or month;
> in what one watches on TV or how one watches TV or whether one watches;
> in the tickets one buys and for what;
> in one's phone bill;
> in the kinds of liquids one consumes and under what circumstances;
> in one's credit card bill;
> in one's ways of spending leisure time;
> in the patterns of eating;
> in the mileage of one's commute to work or school;
> in one's patterns of religious practice or lack of it.

These examples are set out here to provoke application to specific situations and ways of living. One could do a useful descriptive analysis of the material conditions of one's life by examining patterns of ingesting: food, drink, visual/aural information, visual/aural entertainment. What one ingests, where, at what times, with what others might provide the basis of a fruitful analysis. A similar one could be undertaken about residence, its size, cost, its demand for care; its proximity or distance from work; its proximity or distance from other family or friends, and so forth. For some people the costs and other consequences of buying a home set the overall framework for life structure: the income needed; disposable income available; the transportation needs; the possibilities for leisure, and so forth.

"Sacralizing" Life Structure by Refusing to Judge It

At this point, some readers will have realized this essay is exploratory, in the sense that the writer is seeking to lay out a problem largely ignored in literature of a pastoral nature. Church bureaucracies remain much more troubled by what they consider lapses of orthodoxy than by lapses of orthopraxis. Except for sexuality, entire areas of life are excluded from gospel norms. In one of his writings, the Renaissance humanist and reformer, Erasmus of

Rotterdam, offers a blistering but comic critique of such blindness to the more important aspects of Christian living in his own time.

> It may happen; it often does happen, that the abbot is a fool or a drunkard. He issues an order to the brotherhood in the name of holy obedience. And what will such an order be? An order to be sober? An order to tell no lies? No one of these things. It will be that a brother is not to learn Greek; he is not to seek to instruct himself. He may be a sot. He may go with prostitutes. He may be full of hatred and malice. He may never look inside the Scriptures. No matter. He has not broken any oath. He is an excellent member of the community. While if he disobeys such a command as this from an insolent superior there is stake or dungeon for him instantly.[22]

Again and again in the history of Christianity one finds re-surfacing the sort of question Erasmus raises here about lived discipleship. As a social movement affecting European Christians, the Reformation itself is an important instance of such re-surfacing.[23]

Once alerted to the dangerous shift in some patristic writings to right understanding as more crucial than right doing, the churches, we might expect, would have have greater sympathy for liberation theology's contemporary re-emphasis on practice. Yet, in the nations of economic privilege and in the churches of the middle and upper classes this re-emphasis on practice has not taken place. Why not? One could further ask how it might be possible to move this issue more to the forefront of the agenda of local worshiping assemblies. I seek to pursue these two questions before reflecting on some of the problems I myself see in moving toward greater attention to life structure.

Why then has not this shift toward practice assumed greater attention in the churches of privilege? There are many reasons, one of the chief being that in any society some groups are economically privileged by its social institutions. Those in the economically privileged strata find their privileges are right and just. Their sense of rightness is reinforced by the social order's meaning system—the society's culture. For what a good human life is like, culture presents a set of norms most easily met by the privileged classes. As products of persons of privilege, those meanings maintain the social order supporting their interests.

One should not be surprised if religious understandings are also enlisted to promote such a social order and the privileges it offers some. It could even happen that those trained to mediate religious meaning have themselves sprung from the privileged classes, accustomed from their earliest ages to interpret religion so as not to contradict social class. Unwittingly perhaps, these religious teachers can sacralize social class. If their sacred texts seem to privilege the poor, they may conclude that the true, deeper poverty is not economic misery, which does not afflict them, but emotional deprivation, which may.[24] It can happen that just as the lives of the privileged classes are dramatically different from those of the poor, so the religion of the privileged can be fundamentally re-oriented so as to suit their privileges. Thus, the very places where the privileged assemble to worship provide them with a chorus of other voices affirming their status of privilege, in much the same way as do their network of friends and family, their neighborhoods, schools, places of business, social services, and so forth.

The situation is not hopeless, for the possibilities of conversion away from a "God for me" to Jesus' "God for the dispossessed" are always latent in any Christian group, if only because of the ultimate and normative claims their meanings make on them. Such normative claims make religion a zone of judgment, evaluative of all reality. If some group's sacred texts in fact privilege the poor as a key *locus* of the manifestation of God and if they as a group ever embrace this feature as normative for their lives, they will soon find they have to live a religion different from the one described above. Such a shift will not happen automatically but only from approaching the interpretation of sacred texts from what I will call a hermeneutics of dislocation. Here the norms of fidelity are not found via self-interest but by crossing over to the needs of those trapped in situations of economic misery and other forms of oppression. Stances of dislocation point to the strangers, to those who first appear non-neighbors but come to be seen as the human face of God. Bonds with such neighbors are forged through actions of solidarity. Such actions dislocate the comfortable from their life structure, allowing it to be scrutinized.

And so, since Christianity does privilege the poor, it bears within itself radical possibilities of contesting the privileges of wealth. Here is the answer to my second question of how it is possible to move the question of practice more to the center of worshiping assemblies. This move will never happen easily but only as part of a struggling, step-by-step recovery of a seminal feature of Christianity's own religious understanding. Once any ecclesial group recog-

nizes and embraces the radical or culture-contesting features of its
faith, its search for religious coherence will involve a struggle with
life practice.

Reflecting on Life Practice: Further Problems ———————

Working on life practice is not without problems, three of which
I describe briefly here: the need to recognize multiple options
among valid choices; the temptation to avoid the work of discernment and to substitute moralizing; and the need to accept religion
as a zone of judgment.

I have used the term "struggle" here to speak of a local church's
effort to discern its religious faith's consequences for life practice.
The word struggle implies that the correction of life practice cannot
be done by formulaic cut-and-dried patterns that settle the matter
forever.[25] The struggle with life practice also suggests there are
multiple possibilities for answering the gospel call for discipleship.
Jesus' own way of living and his teaching provide the definitive
norms for those who would follow him. But since Jesus' preaching
shows wide boundaries of what is acceptable discipleship, even
here we have no blueprint done to exact scale. Though the norms
provide guidance, their nature is to offer general directions within
which persons and communities have leeway, depending on circumstances and insight. The process of discernment is an ongoing,
indeed endless, feature of discipleship and of discipleship's discourse about life practice. At the core of the problem of becoming
more preoccupied with specific patterns of behavior lies the question of how discernment comes to be located at the heart of a
community's life. Superficial communication on superficial issues
leads to a superficial church. Significant discourse on significant
issues of discipleship is the antidote. Discernment is not the task of
leaders only but of the whole local people seeking to make sense of
the gospel in particular circumstances. What may be acceptable in
one situation may be deplorable in another. The history of response
to any seminal feature of the Christian way reveals the variety of
choices that have in fact led to heroic fidelity.

Moralizing, a process by which one person seeks to prescribe
behavior for another but from outside the horizon of that other
person, is an inappropriate way of fostering the life practice I am
advocating here. Moralizing is a lazy way of dealing with the
dilemma of specific response to the call of Jesus. Basically non-

dialogical, from a position of assumed power it offers glib oughts and musts, when what is needed is a grappling with the dilemma of multiple acceptable choices in concrete circumstances. In the end the problem with moralizing is that its demands are so cheaply made anyone can walk away from them unaffected. Being invited to enter a community of ethical discourse based on normative sacred texts would seem the proper way of engaging people's religious consciousness. What I advocate here are reflection and analysis, not so much about particular acts as about the entire context of living and how particular acts relate to it. Reflection and analysis engage, in a way moralizing cannot, the problem of behavior from the point of view of particular persons and groups in particular circumstances. When a community engages its members in the problematic of behavior—in exploring Jesus' proposals for human living and their meaning for a particular time and place—those members will have entered a process they can inhabit as their own, not one pushed on them by religious bosses.[26]

Basically, the process I have in mind is one that embraces the role of judgment in religious traditions. By its nature, a religion is a zone of judgment. This same nature involves it in an endless process of interpretation of situations and events toward judgment and decision. Holding its meanings to be ultimate and salvific—normative—a religion uses those meanings as a yardstick for evaluating all of reality. It is not that persons of good will may not opt for other norms and arrive at different conclusions deserving respectful dialogue,[27] or that particular areas of life do not have their own norms, such as aesthetic criteria of beauty in the arts. Still, for religious persons ultimate norms are always there in the background able to be activated when claims conflict about what is truly or ultimately good or beautiful or just. As already noted, these norms can be subverted by being reduced, usually unwittingly, to legitimations for society's institutions and culture. In such a case religion undergirds, and in a sense verifies, society's unspoken claim that *its* meanings and institution are the ones that are truly ultimate. Religion can still sell its heritage for a bowl of pottage.

Searching Out a Method for Reflecting on Practice

I have here claimed an absence in pastoral literature—liberation theology excepted—of the question of living practice of discipleship. The absence is not now total, nor has it ever been, as shown in the long history of the veneration of those who proved themselves virtuosos in embodying gospel values in their own lives, the saints. There are contemporary authors who deal explicitly with the problem, while others are dealing with questions, such as inculturation, that if followed through to their logical end, will lead to the matter of life practice.[28] Are there methods for exposing the difficult to discern features of the life practice lived by the local church or by individual households? Put this way, the question itself must first be examined for its assumptions. Is the practice of discipleship a science or an art? If a science, then, it should be possible to find formulaic methods sure to lead to desired results. Skillful analysis discloses steps designed to produce predicted outcomes. However, the human dilemmas at the heart of finding appropriate responses to the gospel mandate in particular circumstances do not lend themselves to formulaic solutions. The very elements of such dilemmas: persons already embedded in patterns of action; consciousnesses already affected by culture; normative but open-ended texts calling for response; proposed ways of interpreting these texts; complex situations calling for response; ways of being together in community—such elements indicate what is needed is an art of practice, not a science of using tested procedures for predictable outcomes.

Though both science and art call for vision and skill, art makes greater use of flexible creativity in solving the problems of realizing vision. The visual arts alone show us the infinite ways of depicting some aspect of reality or artistic vision: there is no one correct way. Further, failure in art is not so easily named as in science, where, say, an experiment at its completion is either successful or not. However, artists scorned in their lifetimes can later be hailed as creative geniuses. If there is any method—apart from methods of developing skill—in art, it is best uncovered in an "after the fact" examination of what actually happened rather than in an a priori statement of theoretical outcomes.[29] Here the appropriate descriptive word may be "process" rather than method. In examining an actual process used in art, one may discover valuable methodological clues as to how vision and skill were melded at particular junctures in the actual doing of something.

Conclusion

Some will note that here I have often alluded to specific patterns of life-practice but in very few places have I actually named some of these patterns. What are some ways of exposing and naming the practices we actually live or of finding alternative practices? Are there any procedures that might be suggested as a way forward in the task I have sought to examine here? This chapter is already over-long, and the elaboration of such procedures is the further work I myself seek assistance with. The following are some suggestions for further work on the material conditions of the practice of discipleship.

Case studies of local churches as they have been able to transform concrete church practice toward a more radical gospel life would provide helpful clues about how such a transformation takes place. My hunch is that any such transformation comes from a kind of "cultural dislocation," a shift from the comfortable assumptions driving church life structure to a series of troubling, problem-filled matters that need attention and a new way of proceeding. These case studies cannot remain with shifts in the church's inner operations; they must get at how the church responded to gospel challenges in its own social context, especially in its responses to the victims of society, those proxies of Christ in our midst. One of the problems I have with the capsule case studies in Patrick Brennan's *Parishes That Excel*[30] survey is that so many of the excellent developments so carefully described remain at a managerial and programmatic level without sufficient attention to the wider social context in which the church exists. To describe "excellent youth evangelization" in a church ringed by military bases, without at the same time probing the church's stance toward the programs of death and domination embodied in those bases, does not help get at the sort of life structure conditions I have in mind here. Could a youth evangelization program be named excellent at the same time that it has removed from its good news Jesus' call for non-violence or a critique of militarization and weapons production? Could there have been parishes that excelled managerially in Nazi Germany but never offered significant resistance to evil?

Concrete procedures are called for, by which local groups might work toward the sort of cultural dislocation that could lead to transformed life practice at the communal but also in individual homes and lives. Edward Farley offers an outline of such a procedure in his abstruse essay, "Interpreting Situations."[31] This outline could be concretized and made accessible to many. A similar sort of procedure is offered in the 1984 statement of the Canadian Roman Catholic Bishops, *Ethical Choices and Political Challenges*.[32] What they call a pastoral methodology for helping the church make judgments about social conditions is as follows.

A. Being present with and listening to the experiences of the poor, the marginalized, the oppressed in our society;

B. Developing a critical analysis of the economic, political, and social structures that cause human suffering;

C. Making judgments in the light of Gospel principles and the social teachings of the Church concerning social values and priorities;

D. Stimulating creative thought and action regarding alternative visions and models for social and economic development; and

E. Acting in solidarity with popular groups in their struggles to transform economic, political and social structures that cause social and economic injustices.

In my view this process has built into it clear elements of cultural dislocation.

A third suggestion that might help take forward the project of greater attention to life structure would involve "cognitive mapping." Frederic Jameson suggests such a procedure in his response to the problem of helping people separate out for themselves a moment of truth from the many moments of illusion. He suggests the possibility that the material conditions of our lives, even when we become aware of them, may tend "to demobilize us and to surrender us to passivity and helplessness,"[33] because of their seeming historical inevitability. Indeed Jameson himself suggests that culture is no longer an area of social life that can be considered separate from economics or politics. In our time he finds "a prodigious expansion of culture throughout the social realm, to the point at which everything in our social life—from economic value and state power to practices and to the very structure of the psyche itself—can be said to have become "cultural" in some original and as yet untheorized sense."[34] All cultural "space" has been taken over and colonized by the logic of late capitalism.

Jameson believes the new situation can be countered only by means of a new kind of activity he calls "a radical cultural politics." His proposed new form of human agency is grounded in cognitive mapping, an activity analogous to the mapping of urban space. An alienated city is a space where people are unable to map in their own minds either their positions in the city or their relationship to the city as a whole. Such a city is lacking markers like monuments or boundaries like parks or road patterns, to allow people to see where they are. Urban mapping disalienates because it discloses the human construction of urban space hidden to the casual observer. Similarly, cognitive mapping disalienates because it shows persons their relationships to their wider social space: their cultural space.[35]

I find merit is Jameson's suggestion for cognitive mapping—vague as it is. He admits it is an idea that needs to be worked out in concrete strategies. In reading Jameson, I found myself thinking of another kind of space, the space inhabited by those gathered around an altar as a sacred space uniting them to all others as children of God. This space, and the imagery brought to bear there on all of life, offers those gathered a fundamental point of orientation in their perception of reality and in their relation to the world. Because of its claims to ultimacy, here is a "cognitive map" of *potentially* transformative power. Its potential becomes actual when the community embraces the poor, the marginal, the victims, and the despised. My question: will religious persons make use of this power to free themselves from the false imaginations of what human existence is meant to be?

The obvious way to finding new forms of practice in the church is to engage in new, more radical forms of action, since action will be both the heart of a struggle for these forms of practice and will provide a concrete basis for evaluating what the church does.[36] However we look at them, these forms of practice will continue to provide the context for the church's work of catechesis. The teaching taught by the practice is certain to remain more powerful than any kind of teaching that ignores practice.

Notes

1. William Seth Adams, "De-Coding the Obvious: Reflections on Baptismal Ministry in the Episcopal Church," *Worship* 66:4 (July 1992) 327-338.

2. Gustavo Gutierrez, *A Theology of Liberation*, trans. Caridad Inda and John Eagleson (New York: Orbis, 1973) 3.

3. Joseph Komonchak, "Ecclesiology and Social Theory," *The Thomist* 45 (1981) 283.

4. In this chapter I step away from the using the word *praxis*, at least in the sense used by Paulo Freire, with its necessary connection to theory.

Neither do I delve into the history of the idea of action/praxis so helpfully explicated by Hannah Arendt in *The Human Condition* (1958) 175-247, and *Between Past and Future* (1961) 91-141.

Sometimes practice and praxis are used interchangeably, as seems to be the case in Martin Jay's *The Dialectical Imagination* (1973). Here I have selected practice as my category, to call attention thereby to Alisdair MacIntyre's proposals on practice in *After Virtue*, cited below. His positive meaning for practice needs a complementary *pejorative* meaning to describe patterns of behavior that are in place but not reflected on. There seem to be elements of this pejorative sense in Pierre Bourdieu's meaning for practice in *Outline of a Theory of Practice* (New York and London: Cambridge University Press, 1977) and other writings of his, and its attempt to recover such patterns for reflection.

Thomas McCarthy's translation of Habermas' two volume *Theory of Communicative Action* consistently uses the work "action" for what some might prefer to call praxis.

5. Paul VI, *Apostolic Exhortation, "Evangelii Nuntiandi,"* ["On Evangelization in the Modern World"] (Washington, D.C.: United States Catholic Conference, 1976) par. 15.

6. Ibid. par. 21.

7. Cited in Thomas McCarthy, *The Critical Theory of Jurgen Habermas* (Cambridge, MA: MIT Press, 1978) 63. The source of the quote is Pierce's essay, "How to Make Our Ideas Clear," in *Writings of Charles Sanders Pierce: A Chronological Edition*, vol. 3 [1872-78] (Bloomington: Indiana University Press, 1986) 257-275, at 263-264.

8. Here I am following a description of practice and its conditions found in Alisdair MacIntyre, *After Virtue* (Notre Dame: University of Notre Dame Press, 1981) 175-178. The quote is on page 177. For an attempt to apply MacIntyre's ideas to specific practices of the church see Craig Dykstra, "Reconceiving Practice," in Edward Farley and Barbara Wheeler, eds., *Shifting Boundaries; Contextual Approaches to the Structure of Theological Education* (Richmond: John Knox Press, 1991).

9. Bourdieu, *Outline of a Theory of Practice* 87-88.

10. Jacques Ellul, *The Subversion of Christianity* (Grand Rapids, MI: Eerdmans, 1986) 4.

11. Here I am following the fine analysis of Roger Haight in "Critical Witness: The Question of Method," in Leo J. O'Donovan and T. Howland Sanks, eds., *Faithful Witness: Foundations of Theology for Today's Church* (New York: Crossroad, 1989) 185-204, esp. 202-204.

12. Brenda Bell and others, eds., *We Make the Road by Walking, Miles Horton and Paulo Freire: Conversations on Education and Social Change* (Philadelphia: Temple University Press, 1990) 77.

13. Gustavo Gutierrez, *The Power of the Poor in History* (New York: Orbis, 1983) 17.

14. Aloysius Pieris, "Christianity and Buddhism is Core-to-Core Dialogue," *Cross Currents* 37:1 (Spring 1987) 47-75, at 48. For a version of this essay see Aloysius Pieris, *Love Meets Wisdom: A Christian Experience of Buddhism* (New York: Orbis, 1988) Chapter 10.

15. Ibid.

16. Ibid. 52. In another essay Pieris explains the same phenomenon:

> In the formative centuries of Christian monasticism, the gnostic spirituality of the non-Christian gradually filtered into the agapeic religiosity of the monks. While this symbiosis was taking place in the silence of the monastic cells, the academic theologians of the church were busy experimenting with the legal language of the Latins and the philosophical thought of the Greeks to make "precision instruments" that would enable the human mind to fathom the Mystery of Christ, thus producing a vast corpus of theological literature that paved the way for Christological dogmas and, centuries later, *for an overgrowth of scholasticism* [Italics mine]. A. Pieris, "Western Models of Inculturation: How Far Are They Applicable in Non-Semitic Asia?" *An Asian Theology of Liberation* (New York: Orbis, 1988) 56; also in *Vidyajota* [Sri Lanka] (October 1985) 435-445, at 442.

17. Here I am following Pieris in *Love Meets Wisdom* 17-42, esp. 18-23. In *The Liberation of Dogma* (New York: Orbis, 1992), Juan Luis Segundo, while never making Pieris' precise point, obliquely but insistently deals with the underlying issue of how the inner life of the *ekklesia* is communicated; see pp. 117-158.

18. Some particular examples are: Edward Farley, "Theology and Practice Outside the Clerical Paradigm," in Don S. Browning, ed., *Practical Theology* (San Francisco: Harper and Row, 1983) 21-41; *Theologia: The Fragmentation and Unity of Theological Education* (Philadelphia: Fortress Press, 1983) esp. Chapter 4, "Schleiermacher and the Beginning of the Encyclopedia Movement," 73-94 but also 127-134; "Interpreting Situations: An Inquiry into the Nature of Practical Theology," in Lewis S. Mudge and James N. Poling, eds., *Formation and Reflection: The Promise of Practical Theology* (Philadelphia: Fortress, 1987) 1-35.

For Farley on the materiality of ecclesial life see *Ecclesial Reflection: An Anatomy of Theological Method* (Philadelphia: Fortress, 1982) esp. Chapters 9, 10, 11.

19. Pieris, "Core to Core Dialogue" 73.

20. Ibid.

21. Chris O'Sullivan, "Campus Rape Is Usually Fraternity-Related," Letters to the Editor, New York *Times* (5 December 1990) A 26; see also Gerald Eskenazi, "The Male Athlete and Sexual Assault," New York *Times* (3 June 1990) L 1, L 4.

22. Cited in Harry Emerson Fosdick, *Great Voices of the Reformation: An Anthology* (New York: The Modern Library, 1952) xx-xxi.

23. I realize the Reformation's complexity is such that it cannot be reduced to this single aspect.

24. See the description of this process in Gregory Baum, *Truth Beyond Relativism: Karl Mannheim's Sociology of Knowledge* (Milwaukee: Marquette University Press, 1977) 60-62.

25. Cut-and-dried formulas also tend to be reductionistic, even trivializing the open-endedness of the Gospel's demands. The lists of sins offered for preparation for the sacrament in Roman Catholic devotional books, even for years after Vatican II, though they do call attention to concrete behavior, reduce the behavior to negative acts easily numbered for the sake of accuracy. This kind of limiting has a long history, as can be seen in the following handbook for determining both sins and the penalties needing to be fulfilled before they could be pardoned. "Haltigar: Prescriptions for Sins," in Charles Jaeckle and William A.Clebsch, eds., *Pastoral Care in Historical Perspective* (New York: Jason Aronson, 1975) 148-164.

26. See the helpful comments on "discourse ethics" in Paul Lakeland, *Theology and Critical Theory* (Nashville: Abingdon, 1990) 174-207.

27. Here I do not emphasize the matter of dialogue, a basic issue in our world. I agree with Johannes Metz that religious people have to enter a "hermeneutical culture" marked by respectful dialogue ("encountering others in their otherness") toward coping with human problems. Johann Baptist Metz, "With the Eyes of a European Theologian," in L. Boff and V. Elizondo, eds., *The Voice of the Victims Concilium* (London: SCM Press, 1990) 113-119.

28. Among Roman Catholics, Francis Schüssler Fiorenza's *Foundational Theology* (New York: Crossroad, 1984) raises important issues related to practice, as does Edward Schillebeeckx in his more recent *Church: The Human Story of God* (New York: Crossroad, 1990); also *Faithful Witness*, already cited in note 12. In the writings of the most philosophical of modern Roman Catholic theologians, Karl Rahner, I find practice a seminal concern.

29. My point here is similar to Edith Wyschogrod's argument against moral theory as basically failing to achieve its predetermined goal of transforming moral conduct. Her examination of saints and saintliness chooses instead to examine life histories and recover from them their "exhortative force" and their patterns of practice; see *Saints and Postmodernism: Revisioning Moral Philosophy* (Chicago: University of Chicago Press, 1990) xiii-xxvii.

30. *Parishes That Excel: Models of Excellence in Education, Ministry, and Evangelization* (New York: Crossroad, 1992).

31. See Lewis S. Mudge and James N. Poling, eds., *Formation and Reflection: The Promise of Practical Theology* (Philadelphia: Fortress Press, 1987) 1-35.

32. Canadian Conference of Catholic Bishops, *Ethical Choices and Political Challenges: Ethical Reflections on the Future of Canada's Socio-Economic Order* (Ottawa, 1984) 2.

33. Frederic Jameson, "Postmodernism, or the Cultural Logic of Late Capitalism," *New Left Review* 146 (July-August 1984) 53-92, at 86.

34. Ibid. 88.

35. See ibid. 89-92.

36. Roger Haight writes: "Christian spirituality means living out . . . vision in action. When spirituality is thus conceived as human action, one has the basis for an objective consideration of the adequacy of the method of theology. Christian life and action unfold within the church in its mission to the world and within the world itself. "Critical Witness" 203.